JAPAN'S GREATER EAST ASIA CO-PROSPERITY SPHERE IN WORLD WAR II

JAPAN'S GREATER EAST ASIA CO-PROSPERITY SPHERE IN WORLD WAR II
SELECTED READINGS AND DOCUMENTS

edited and introduced by
JOYCE C. LEBRA
Professor of History
University of Colorado

KUALA LUMPUR
OXFORD UNIVERSITY PRESS
TOKYO   LONDON   NEW YORK
1975

Oxford University Press, Ely House, London W.1
GLASGOW NEW YORK TORONTO MELBOURNE WELLINGTON
CAPE TOWN IBADAN NAIROBI DAR ES SALAAM LUSAKA ADDIS ABABA
DELHI BOMBAY CALCUTTA MADRAS KARACHI LAHORE DACCA
KUALA LUMPUR SINGAPORE JAKARTA HONG KONG TOKYO
Bangunan Loke Yew, Kuala Lumpur
● *Oxford University Press 1975*

All rights reserved. No part of this publication may be reproduced, stored in a retrieval system, or transmitted, in any form or by any means, electronic, mechanical, photocopying, recording or otherwise, without the prior permission of Oxford University Press.

Printed in Malaysia by
CHARLES GRENIER SDN BHD KUALA LUMPUR,
and bound by
ART PRINTING WORKS, KUALA LUMPUR

Acknowledgements

I am indebted for support for the research for this volume to the American Philosophical Society for a fellowship during the summer of 1967 for travel to Japan, to the University of Colorado for a Council on Research Grant for the summer of 1968 in Japan, and during 1970–71 to the National Endowment for the Humanities, the Australian National University, and the American Philosophical Society for fellowship support.

It is impossible to adequately express my gratitude to the many individuals who generously gave their encouragement, assistance, and advice on the translation and editing of this volume. Among them I wish to mention my particular indebtedness to the following individuals in Japan and the U.S.: Professor Oka Yoshitake, Professor Hayashi Shigeru, Dr. Tsunoda Jun, the late Mr. Kishi Kōichi, the late Col. Nishiura Susumu and staff of the War History Library of the Defence Agency, Professor Mori Katsumi, Mr. Hashizume Shōzō, Mr. Nagaoka Shinjirō, Mr. Nakano Keiji, Mr. Katō Mikio, Mr. Fujino Yukio, Miss Hirano Midori, Dr. Andrew Kuroda, Mr. Kano Masamichi and Professor Yoji Akashi. I am grateful also to Professor Akashi for providing the Who's Who.

Grateful acknowledgement is made to the following publishers and agents for permission to quote from copyrighted works under their control:

R. P. Garcia Publishing Co., Quezon City, for excerpts from

ACKNOWLEDGEMENTS

The Fateful Years, Japan's Adventure in the Philippines, by Teodoro Agoncillo.

Pacific Affairs, University of British Columbia, for excerpts from *Pacific Affairs:* 'Japan's Co-Prosperity Sphere' by Andrew Grajdanzev, and 'Japan's New Order in the Pacific,' by William Magistretti; and for excerpts from *Asian Nationalism and the West*, edited by William Holland; and for excerpts from Willard H. Elsbree, *Japan's Role in South-East Asian Nationalist Movements, 1940–1945*.

University of California Press for excerpts from *The Politics of Korean Nationalism*, by Lee Chong-sik.

Oxford University Press for excerpts from *Japan's New Order in East Asia: Its Rise and Fall, 1937–1945*, by F. C. Jones.

Yale University Press, for excerpts from *Japanese Military Administration in Indonesia: Selected Documents*, edited by Harry J. Benda, James K. Irikura, and Kishi Kōichi.

University of Chicago Press, for excerpts from *Asia for the Asiatics? The Techniques of Japanese Occupation*, by Robert S. Ward.

University of Michigan Press, for excerpts from *Philippine Collaboration in World War II*, by David Joel Steinberg.

Iwanami Shoten, Publishers, for excerpts from *Taiheiyō Sensō*, by Iyenaga Saburō.

Professor Shinmei Masamichi, for excerpts from his book *Tōa Kyōdōtai no Risō*.

Misuzu Shobo, for excerpts from *Gendaishi Shiryō*, vol. 8.

Kaizō Shuppansha, for excerpts from *Tōa Remmeiron* by Miyazaki Masayoshi, and *Tōa to Sekai*, by Rōyama Masamichi.

Daitō Bunka Daigaku, for excerpts from *Tōyō Kenkyū* article, 'Southern Policy Decisions and the Shōwa Kenkyūkai,' by Kishi Kōichi.

Mrs. Theda Maw Sturtevant, for excerpts from the book by her father, Ba Maw, *Breakthrough in Burma, Memoirs of a Revolution, 1939–1946*.

Simon and Schuster, Inc., for excerpts from *The Cause of Japan*, by Shigenori Togo.

Contents

Page

Acknowledgements	v
Introduction	ix

PART I: THE IDEAL CONCEPTUALIZED 1

1. East Asian Federation, Miyazaki Masayoshi 3
2. East Asia Cooperative Body I, Ozaki Hotsumi 9
3. East Asia Cooperative Body II, Shinmei Masamichi 14
4. The New Order and Regionalism, Rōyama Masamichi 20
5. Japan's Monroe Doctrine, Kamikawa Hikomatsu 25
6. Greater East Asia Co-Existence Sphere, Yabe Teiji 31
7. The Spiritual Basis of Asian Revolution and Unity, Ōkawa Shūmei 36
8. Strategic Imperatives in the Pacific, William Magistretti 41
9. Japan as Economic Leader of Asia 48

PART II: GOVERNMENT PLANS 55

1. Army and Navy Position Papers 57
2. Konoye on the New Order in East Asia 68
3. Proclamation of the Greater East Asia Co-Prosperity Sphere, Matsuoka Yōsuke 71
4. The Greater East Asian Sphere of Common Prosperity, Arita Hachirō 73
5. Tōjō on the Greater East Asia Co-Prosperity Sphere 78

		Page
6.	Foreign Minister Togo Opposes the Greater East Asia Ministry	82
7.	Tōjō Greets the Greater East Asia Conference	88
8.	The Co-Prosperity Sphere Viewed from the West, Andrew Grajdanzev	94
9.	Southern Policy Decisions and the *Shōwa Kenkyūkai*, Kishi Kōichi	99

PART III: POLICY IMPLEMENTATION IN THE FIELD: THE REALITY — 105

1. The Case of Korea, Lee Chong-sik — 107
2. Principles for Administration of Southern Areas, Adopted by the Liaison Conference of 20 November, 1941 — 113
3. Plan for Leadership of Nationalities, General Staff Headquarters — 118
4. Military Idealism in the Field, Fujiwara Iwaichi — 122
5. Occupation in Burma, Dr. Ba Maw — 126
6. Occupation in the Philippines, Dr. Teodoro Agoncillo — 132
7. Occupation in Indonesia, Waseda University Social Science Research Institute — 136
8. Occupation in Malaya, Professors Silcock and Aziz — 141
9. Goals and Methods in the Sphere, Andrew Grajdanzev — 146

PART IV: EVALUATION AND RETROSPECT — 151

1. Post-War Implications of the Sphere, Robert S. Ward — 153
2. Inversion of Japanese Goals, Dr. Ba Maw — 157
3. Inadvertent Stimulus to Nationalism, Willard H. Elsbree — 159
4. Critique of the Greater East Asia War, Iyenaga Saburō — 164
5. A New Asian Approach to Asia, Maruyama Shizuo — 171

Glossary — 175
Who's Who — 178
Bibliographical Note and Suggested Readings — 187
Index — 204

Introduction

JAPAN'S Greater East Asia Co-Prosperity Sphere during World War II has been generally viewed in the West as an example of aggressive Japanese imperialism directed toward China and South-East Asia. In the West, and even more in Japan, scholars until very recently have avoided examining the ideology and rationale on which wartime policies were predicated. Although American and Japanese scholarly attention is being drawn now to the prodigious task of reassessing Japan's wartime goals and programmes in Asia, many problems still demand careful scrutiny. Controversy on the war, whether by apologists or Marxists in Japan, has centred on the role of capitalism and imperialism in the origins and causes of World War II rather than on specific goals and means in Asia.[1] On the American side studies have dealt with Japanese military occupation in individual nations in South-East Asia, China and Korea.[2] There has been no more recent attempt at a comprehensive analysis of Japan's role in wartime Asia than F. C. Jones', writing in 1954.[3]

The plethora of Japanese writings on the ideological foundations of Japan's policy in Asia during the 1930s contrasts sharply with the paucity of Japanese scholarly attempts to evaluate the Greater East Asia Co-Prosperity Sphere after the fact. This difference stems from several factors. There is still a reluctance to deal with what is felt to be an embarrassing phase in Japanese history, embarrassing both because of military defeat and also because of the failure of the civilian sector to prevent military control over Japan's domestic and foreign policy. There is also hesitation to discuss even in scholarly terms Japan's military and economic control over South-East Asia at a time when Japan's relations with South-East Asia are delicate, and at least in the economic sector are reminiscent of the wartime Sphere. Japanese reluctance in turn reflects in part the hesitance of some South-East Asian leaders to discuss openly Japan's contributions to South-East Asian independence.

Though military men played a prominent part in formulating foreign policy in the 1930s, and though World War II was preceded ideologically by the enunciation of several Pan-Asian constructs, it is not demonstrable that the military operated as a monolithic decision-making force or that the war followed ineluctably the articulation of Pan-Asianism. On the contrary, disagreements between Army and Navy, and disjunction between Imperial General Headquarters and armies in the field at all levels of command, at times nearly paralysed decision-making, even in the midst of war.[4]

Inchoate goals toward South-East Asia meant that the structure of the Greater East Asia Co-Prosperity Sphere was highly divergent from one country to the next. Lack of coordination between agencies and offices within the military establishment regarding a given country was the rule.

Nor was there any consensus on the geographic limitations of the Greater East Asia Co-Prosperity Sphere. There were many versions and they differed in geographic compass. For some, by early 1941, the 'Greater Sphere', or sphere of influence, would sweep across Asia to embrace India, even Australia and New Zealand. In actuality, military strategy was never devised to push the western perimeter of the sphere beyond Burma, and how much of Burma Japan should embrace was in dispute within the Army chain of command even as late as January 1942. Though India was included in the vision of the sphere of influence, Imphal inside the Indian border was the westward limit of strategic operations, and that campaign was a disaster for Japan.

Military and civilian concern with China and the continent had a long and sanctioned tradition in Japan. Objective events — the Taiwan expedition, the Sino-Japanese War, the Russo-Japanese War, the annexation of Korea, and the Manchurian Incident — were all predicated on the priority of Japan's relations with the

INTRODUCTION   xi

continent of Asia. Japan, China, and Manchukuo were conceived of as the pivotal area of Japan's concern. This view was military orthodoxy until 1941, even later for some. The image of Korea as a 'Russian dagger pointed at the heart of Japan' provided the rationale if not the right of expansion in China and Korea to ward off the thrust of the dagger. Japanese influence in this 'core' continental area was seen as the key to Japan's national security and economic viability.

Apart from ideological and security considerations, China and particularly North China, Manchukuo and Korea were vital to Japan for economic reasons. China's 'independence' had to be safeguarded against continued Western encroachment because China was essential to Japan. Japan's insularity made her vulnerable to disruption of access to essential natural resources and overseas markets. Railway investments and developmental industrial enterprises in Manchuria were crucial to the maintenance of Japan's industrial establishment at home.

These economic and strategic considerations were invoked to justify Japan's posture in Manchuria in 1931–2. These pragmatic concerns also generated the ideology and vocabulary of Asian co-existence and co-prosperity. Constant reiteration of the themes of co-existence and co-prosperity was designed to gain Japan friends in Asia who would cooperate rather than resist. Recalcitrance in China was viewed as nationalistic backsliding from the consciousness of common Asian brotherhood.

To this ideology of co-existence with China in the 1930s was added the earlier Pan-Asian ideology dating from the turn of the century. Meiji Pan-Asianism had another significant ingredient: romantic idealism. The idealism of Meiji Pan-Asianists stemmed in part from consciousness of a common cultural heritage. Asian spirituality was celebrated by Japanese and other Asians alike. Rabindranath Tagore and his Japanese confrères Noguchi Yonejirō and Okakura Tenshin saw in Asia's spiritual heritage a bond which made Asia superior to the materialistic West.

This early Pan-Asianism was spawned at least by the turn of the century and in some cases somewhat earlier. Okakura Tenshin put the argument in the context of Asian spiritual unity and the legacy of India, the home of Buddhism. Ōkuma Shigenobu saw as Japan's duty the repayment of an ancient cultural debt to China. This debt could be redeemed through Japan's mediation between the intuitive East and the scientific West. For the patriotic societies — the *Kokuryūkai** and *Gen'yōsha** and others — Pan-Asianism meant encouragement and protection of political exiles and revolutionaries from other Asian nations. Sun Yat-sen, Kim Ok-siun, Aguinaldo, U Ottama, and Rash Bihari Bose were beneficiaries of this Japanese insistence on Asian brotherhood. Those who were frustrated at not being able to achieve their political goals at home in Japan saw in China and other parts of Asia a fertile ground for fostering political change and achieving their visions of utopia. The *Shina rōnin** were an example of this vicarious revolutionary idealism. Fukuzawa Yukichi's *datsua* (Depart from Asia) argument that Japan should look outside backward Asia for friends did not lead to abandonment of the critical concern with Asia. Ethnic, geographic and cultural ties made Japan irrevocably a part of Asia.

This early idealism, then, combined in the 1930s with the more pragmatic and realistic considerations of strategic and economic necessity. In the fusion some of the Meiji idealism was reflected in the resulting ideological constructs of the 1930s. But part of the Meiji idealism was also eroded away by more realistic concerns of the immediate pre-war and wartime years.

At the outbreak of war in the Pacific, General Staff Headquarters of the Army and to a lesser degree the Navy had practically ignored South-East Asia, by contrast with China. During nearly five long years of military involvement in China, the military requisites for prosecuting the war had pre-empted the attention of the strategists. The preoccupation with China was re-enforced by the military orthodoxy of concern with China and Russia as the priority areas for Japan's national security.

With the abrogation of the naval treaties, however, one of the early official portents of concern with South-East Asia came in an August 1936 statement of 'Fundamentals of National Policy', in which advance into and development of the South were seen as essential to defence of the Empire on the Asiatic continent and to the economic development of Japan. But two years later, in 1938, when the cabinet proclaimed the New Order in East Asia, it embraced only Japan, China and Manchukuo.

Those who urged greater attention to the South were still in a

---

*For asterisked items *vide* the Glossary.

much less vocal minority. Beginning in 1936, the Navy, through its network of research groups, took the initiative in studying problems relating to South-East Asia. There has been as yet almost no scholarly treatmen. of the plethora of research organizations operating under Army and Navy sub-contract during the late 1930s and into the war years. These research groups were staffed by scholars, persons with experience in the countries under scrutiny, professional military men, businessmen, and bureaucrats. The position papers resulting from their studies often formed the basis of governmental policy decisions.

Among the many research groups sub-contracted by the Navy, for example, were the *Kokusaku Kenkyūkai** (National Policy Research Group) and the *Sōgō Kenkyūkai** (General Affairs Research Group) besides the regularly constituted Navy Ministry *Chōsaka* (Research Section) and its predecessor the *Rinji Chōsaka* (Provisional Research Section). Many other research organizations and institutes also operated with Army and Navy backing, with or outside official connexion. The *Mantetsu Chōsakyoku** (South Manchurian Railway Company Research Office) was one of the largest of these. Under the umbrella of the South Manchuria Railway Company empire, the *Chōsakyoku* was organized in 1907 and was funded from a number of sources within the government, including the Army. It in turn had a number of sub-organizations, the largest and most significant being the *Tōa Kenkyūjo**. Other research groups such as the *Biruma Kenkyūkai** and Nan'yō Kyōkai* were supported by secret funds from the Army or Navy Ministries.

One 1939 position paper is included here from the Kokusaku Kenkyūkai. Titled 'Outline Draft for a Southern Policy', it deals with economic, political and cultural considerations. A second selection related to the research groups is an article by the late Kishi Kōichi in which he discusses the impact of the *Shōwa Kenkyūkai**, Premier Konoye's influential brain trust, on Japan's policy decisions regarding South-East Asia.[5]

Official disregard of South-East Asia came to an end with the proclamation of the Greater East Asia Co-Prosperity Sphere in August 1940. Foreign Minister Matsuoka and Premier Konoye called on all Asia to break the shackles of Western imperialist control. Japan would help to liberate the rest of Asia from oppressive Western control in a new 'Asia for the Asiatics'. The powerful allure of this concept served Japan well in South-East Asia, particularly in Burma and Indonesia. South-East Asian nationalists still remembered Japan's startling victory over Russia in 1905.

The enunciation of the Greater East Asia Co-Prosperity Sphere, however, was followed by many months of vacillation before practical measures to implement the goals were devised. It was not until the policy of 'Japanization' of occupied South-East Asia was well under way that South-East Asian nationalist movements turned against Japan, seeing Japan as merely a substitute for Western imperialist power.

The reason for the hesitation in formulation and implementation of policy toward the South was that at the end of 1941 Japan was still ill prepared to deal with South-East Asia. The Foreign Ministry, the Cabinet Planning Board, the China Affairs Board, Asia Development Board and Army and Navy Headquarters had all suddenly and belatedly become involved in policy planning for South-East Asia. This served only to compound the confusion and overlapping jurisdiction and did not immediately allay the earlier neglect of South-East Asia. Plans were devised in 1942 to create a Greater East Asia Ministry which would co-ordinate administrative matters in areas under military occupation. Now for the first time jurisdiction in civil matters in areas under military occupation came under centralized control. Policies were hurriedly conceived on an *ad hoc* basis without much ideological foundation or basis in experience. In actuality, fundamental policy with regard to the degree of local autonomy to be allowed in various South-East Asian nations in the Sphere was still determined in practice by Imperial General Headquarters or by staff officers in the field rather than by the new ministry. The reason was that no problem was without military significance in wartime.

Realization of the Sphere took substance through a diversity of activities under jurisdiction of the Greater East Asia Ministry, under Japanese armies of occupation locally, and particularly under Military Administration Headquarters in each country. Educational and cultural programmes, writers' conferences in Tokyo, encouragement of Islam and Buddhism, fostering political and youth groups, training volunteer and independence armies, diffusion of the Japanese language, sending South-East Asian students to Tokyo for study, mobilization of labour and requisitioning of raw materials and agricultural products were all enterprises designed to promote Japanese goals in Asia. Some of these activities are referred to in selections in Sections II and III.

In selections included in Part I from writings of scholars and military men in the 1930s and early 1940s, some of the above-mentioned ingredients can be identified, singly and in combination. The vocabulary of Japanese imperialism in the first half of the twentieth century reflected the primary concern with China, Manchukuo and Korea, and slight awareness of South-East Asia. As early as 1931–2, the Manchurian Incident precipitated both military and scholarly arguments for a closer relationship between Japan and her continental neighbour. Colonel Ishiwara Kanji and his associate Miyazaki Masayoshi argued for an East Asian Federation *(Tōa Renmei)*.* Based on the traditional Army fear of Russia, Ishiwara and Miyazaki hoped for closer ties with China in the form of a federation partnership. Through an East Asia Federation Western imperialism in East Asia would be expunged and East Asians liberated. Thus would the aims of the Shōwa Restoration* and the ideal of *'hakkō ichiū'** be achieved. Japan, China, and Manchukuo would form the nucleus of the federation.

Another construct which presaged the ideology of the Greater East Asia Co-Prosperity Sphere was the concept of the East Asia Co-operative Body *(Tōa Kyōdōtai)*.* Several of the selections included in Part I discuss various bases for the idea of an Asian cooperative structure. Shinmei Masamichi surveys some of the literature, emphasizing variously the bonds of ethnic affinity, geographic proximity and cultural similarity as possible bases for cooperation. He also alludes to problems of delimiting the sphere of the Kyōdōtai in East Asia. For Ozaki Hotsumi the construct had the multiple advantages of a moral ideal and a practical means of dealing with Chinese nationalism and with Japan's defensive and economic needs on the continent.

Yabe Teiji invokes a somewhat different phrase, 'The Greater East Asia Co-Existence Sphere' *(Dai Tōa Kyōzonken)*.* Yabe's primary concern is to delineate an autonomous sphere for defensive and economic reasons. For Yabe, writing in 1940, this sphere would necessarily extend to the Kuriles in the North, the Netherlands Indies in the South, and Hawaii in the East. Anything less would not ensure Japan's minimum security requirements.

Kamikawa Hikomatsu, writing in 1939, compares the imperatives and impact of the American and Japanese Monroe Doctrines, as two similar expressions of regionalism. To many Japanese in 1932 and later the analogy seemed well taken and justified Japan's Asiatic enterprises to the same extent that the Monroe Doctrine could be justified.

Ōkawa Shūmei, writing of the establishment of the New Order in Greater East Asia, draws on his background as a Pan-Asian philosopher. He quotes Rabindranath Tagore and other exponents of Asian spiritual unity in support of his claim for the depth and intensity of the Asian cultural and spiritual nexus.

Rōyama Masamichi lends his influence as Japan's leading contemporary political scientist to the argument for a New Order in East Asia. For Professor Rōyama the rationale for a New Order in East Asia rests primarily on the concept of regionalism. In his definition of regionalism he has joined many dimensions of the argument.

A selection from economist Takahashi Kamekichi emphasizes the idealism of Japan's endeavours as a peacekeeping force, while admitting that the Co-Prosperity Sphere is economically imperative for Japan. Though critical of Western capitalism and imperialism, he sees Japan's expansion in another light.

In a western contemporary selection, William Magistretti discusses Japan's strategic objectives in the Pacific, quoting widely from Japanese sources.

Section II deals with official policy. The government made several policy declarations on the Greater East Asia Co-Prosperity Sphere and its predecessor, the New Order in East Asia. Selections from Army and Navy Headquarters documents head this section. The first official indiction of Navy concern with South-East Asia in 1936 influences both the Army and the Five Ministers' Conference draft of 'Fundamentals of National Policy' in the same year. In a 1939 selection from the Kokusaku Kenkyūkai the Navy's interest in critical resources in the South is apparent.

First official mention of the Greater East Asia Co-Prosperity Sphere came in a speech by Foreign Minister Matsuoka on August 2, 1940, and in a radio broadcast by Premier Konoye a few days earlier. Matsuoka defined the Sphere to include, besides China and Manchukuo, the Netherlands Indies and French Indo-China.

A selection from a 1941 article by Arita Hachirō, Foreign Minister in four cabinets between 1936 and 1940, pleads Japan's case for the same type of economic bloc on which the American and British industrial establishments depend for their viability.

Following the outbreak of war in the Pacific, Prime Minister Tōjō on 21 January 1942 addressed the Diet on the Greater East Asia Co-Prosperity Sphere. By this time Tōjō also includes Malaya, Burma, and the Philippines in the Sphere. He enumerates Japan's strategic and economic desiderata in the South and the goal of expelling Britain and America from Asia and liberating all Asia from colonial oppression.

Of some importance for Japan's South-East Asia programme was the creation of the Greater East Asia Ministry in November 1942. For many months the need to co-ordinate policy decisions and military administration had become increasingly apparent because of overlapping functions and jurisdiction of several cabinet-level agencies. Once plans for the new ministry began to take shape, hovever, they were opposed by Foreign Minister Togo Shigenori, who made public his opposition in the House of Peers on 20 January 1942, whereupon he resigned. Togo saw the new ministry as a move to circumvent the power and functioning of the Foreign Ministry and was fearful of unchecked military control. It was several months before the new ministry actually came into being in November 1942, and even then its function remained ancillary to the basic military policy-making process.

Other official documents included in Part II relate to the Greater East Asia Conference of early November 1943, when the Greater East Asia Ministry invited to Tokyo delegates from most South-East Asian nations under Japanese military occupation. Tōjō twice addressed the conference in idealistic terms, and leading Asian delegates also spoke to the assemblage. The Joint Declaration of the Conference, drafted by Japanese officials and unanimously adopted by the delegates, is also included here.

One Western contemporary selection in this section, by Dr. Grajdanzev, indicates a Western view of the significance of the Sphere, referring to some Japanese sources.

A post-war article by Kishi Kōichi analyses the influence of views of members of the Shōwa Kenkyūkai, Premier Konoye's 'brain trust', on government policy decisions toward the 'Southern Area'.

Section III is concerned with policy formulation and implementation in the field. A post-war selection from a study by a Korean-American political scientist, Professor Lee Chong-sik, provides a critical, generally negative view of Japan's presence in Korea, tracing Japan's occupation policies back to the early years of this century.

Shortly after the August 1940 proclamation of the creation of the Greater East Asia Co-Prosperity Sphere and its goals, a Liaison Conference* of Imperial General Headquarters and the Cabinet announced the 'Principles Governing the Administration of the Occupied Southern Area'. The 20 November decision anticipated integration of military governments in all occupied areas into 'new administrative machinery to be established by the Government'. The utilization of local natural resources and facilities was mentioned in six of ten principles enumerated to govern occupied areas. Though the tone of the document was clearly less idealistic than the proclamation of the Sphere, military administrators were enjoined to observe 'due respect for past organizational structure and native practices'. Aims and methods in exploiting local natural resources were further detailed in a document adopted at a conference of ministers on 12 December and sent the same day to a session of Liaison Conference. Another official statement of policy from Army General Staff Headquarters, 14th section, in the 'Plan for Leadership of Nationalities in Greater East Asia', clearly outlines the primary place of the Japanese among the peoples of Asia.

Also included here is the wartime view of Japanese policy in occupied Asia by an American, Dr. Grajdanzev again. He discusses political mechanisms and religious and educational policy in countries in the Sphere.

A different order of evidence appears in the selection from Fujiwara Iwaiichi, *Memo of the Chief of the 'F Agency'*. Fujiwara, then a young major in intelligence, was sent to South-East Asia by Imperial General Headquarters to establish liaison with overseas Indians, Chinese, and Malay sultans. His words reflect at their most idealistic the military sympathy and commitment to South-East Asian independence aspirations. During Fujiwara's brief career as chief of the *F Kikan**, he assisted at the birth of the Indian National Army and mediated between the Japanese Army and the Indians in the independence movement.

A local reaction to Japanese military administration is provided in the excerpt from Ba Maw's memoirs. As Premier of wartime Burma Ba Maw's responses were ambivalent. He recognized the idealism of Colonel Suzuki Keiji, a counterpart in his sympathetic support of Burmese independence to Fujiwara. Suzuki's role in the Burma Independence Army paralleled Fujiwara's role in the Indian National Army, yet Burmese suspicions of Japanese motives ultimately turned the B.I.A. against the Japanese.

Another South-East Asian response to Japanese military rule is found in the excerpt from Dr. Teodoro Agoncillo's two-volume study. He emphasizes the subtleties and intricacies of Filipino attempts at survival and national integrity amidst thorough-going Japanese thought control.

In the final section Japanese, Burmese, British and Americans evaluate the Greater East Asia Co-Prosperity Sphere in historical perspective. Robert S. Ward views the propaganda goals of the Sphere as part of a broader long-range political struggle in Asia. Mr. Ward implies Japan contemplated projection of these aims long after the end of the Pacific War. Willard Elsbree, in his classic study, *Japan's Role in Southeast Asian Nationalist Movements*, concludes that, despite Japan's tremendous initial propaganda advantage, Japan failed, through underestimating the strength of nationalism, to identify the interests of South-East Asians with her own.

Ba Maw is again invoked in his analysis of the Japanese role in retrospect. Ba Maw discusses the anomaly that the Japanese as Asian liberators from white domination were nevertheless misunderstood by the Asians they helped to liberate. This was because, despite the idealistic commitment of men like Suzuki and Fujiwara, the Japanese military in general displayed a high-handed incapacity for understanding other Asians.

Japanese reluctance to this date to discuss the Greater East Asia Co-Prosperity Sphere is reflected in the scarcity of scholarly attention to the problem. Professor Iyenaga Saburō is quoted from his study *Taiheiyō sensō* (The Greater East Asia War), in which he attacks Hayashi Fusao's defense of the war and analysis of it as a hundred-year war against Western imperialism. Japan's thrust on the continent, argues Iyenaga, represents a fifteen-year war beginning in Manchuria. It was a brutalizing and inhumane endeavour, and Japan's role can be described as liberating only inadvertently and indirectly.

Maruyama Shizuo, wartime correspondent in Burma and presently editorial writer for the *Asahi Shimbun*, suggests that Japan could learn some lessons for the present and future from the wartime experience. Mr. Maruyama feels that final judgement must await a definitive study of the whole Pacific War. He observes that Japanese policy regarding South-East Asian independence suffered from a 'campaign first' stance which of necessity gave priority to tactical requirements. Nevertheless, he feels Japan displayed a sense of sympathy, equality and encouragement toward Asian nationalism which was never demonstrated by European colonial powers. This was reflected in the unprecedented experience South-East Asians acquired in governing themselves under Japanese military administration, experience which contributed positively to independent, postwar South-East Asia.

[1] See discussion by Hata, Ikuhiko in 'Japanese Historical Writing on the Origins and Progress of the Pacific War', pp. 79–90 in D. Sissons, ed., *Papers on Modern Japan*, Canberra, Australian National University, 1968.

[2] These studies include: Akashi, Yoji, 'The Japanization Program in Malaya With Particular Reference to the Malays', Paper Presented to the Annual Meeting of the American Political Science Association, 1971; Boyle, John Hunter, *China and Japan at War, 1937–1945, The Politics of Collaboration* (Stanford, 1972); Benda, Harry J., *The Crescent and the Rising Sun, Indonesian Islam under Japanese Occupation, 1942–1945* (The Hague, 1958); Benda, H., K. Kishi and J. Irikura, *Japanese Military Administration in Indonesia, Selected Documents* (New Haven, 1965); Guyot, Dorothy, 'The Political Impact of the Japanese Occupation of Burma' (Yale Ph.D. dissertation, 1966) Kanahele, George, 'The Japanese Occupation of Indonesia, Prelude to Independence' (Cornell Ph.D. dissertation, 1967); and Steinberg, Joel David, *Philippine Collaboration in World War II* (Ann Arbor, 1967).

[3] Jones, Francis C., *Japan's New Order in East Asia; its rise and fall* (London, 1954). Mr. Jones' sources are primarily documents of the International Military Tribunal in the Far East. There has been some more recent scholarly attention in, for example: Iriye, Akira, 'The Failure of Military Expansionism', in James W. Morley, ed., *Dilemmas of Growth in Prewar Japan* (Princeton, 1971); and in Silverstein, Josef, ed., *Southeast Asia in World War II; Four Essays* (Yale University Southeast Asia Monograph Series No.7, 1966). This generalization does not apply to general military histories of the war, of which John Toland's *The Rising Sun* (Random House, 1970) is a fine example.

[4] For a discussion on the disjunctions in military decision-making in Japan during the war, see for example, the author's discussion of this point in Lebra, Joyce, 'Japan and the Genesis of the Burma Independence Army', in *Papers on Far Eastern History*, No.5, 1972, Canberra, Australian National University. See on the same point Nakamura, Mitsuo, 'General Imamura and the Early

Period of the Occupation of Indonesia', in *Indonesia*, No.10, 1970, Cornell University Modern Indonesia Project.

[5]For the most authoritative account of the Shōwa Kenkyūkai in English see Crowley, James B., 'Intellectuals as Visionaries of Japan's New Asian Order', pp. 319–73 in James B. Morley, *Dilemmas of Growth in Prewar Japan* (Princeton, 1971).

PART I
The Ideal Conceptualized

1
East Asian Federation

ONE of the earliest constructs which defined Japan's relationship with the continent of Asia in the 1930s was the idealistic notion of East Asian Federation, or *Tōa Renmei*. Col. Ishiwara Kanji and Miyazaki Masayoshi were the two leading exponents of this view. The rationale for Federation was that Japan would ultimately have to deal with one or more of the Western imperialist powers, including the Soviet Union. Japan should therefore avoid protracted war with China but rather form a federation with China and Manchukuo. This was the only way Western imperialism could be expunged from East Asia. An East Asia Federation Society was organized in 1939 by Col. Ishiwara to advance the ideals of Federation on an equal basis. The organization survived after World War II. Premier Konoye was attracted by the idea, but Tōjō and the Army Ministry leadership frowned on the suggestion.

Miyazaki Masayoshi argues here for East Asian Federation in an excerpt from his volume *Theory of East Asian Federation* (1936), *Tōa Renmei ron*. Miyazaki was a graduate of Moscow University and influential in the South Manchuria Railway Company.

EAST Asian Federation is to my way of thinking a 'good' and moral action, but I don't advocate it simply as social good and international righteousness. I do advance it because in

THE IDEAL CONCEPTUALIZED

the present stage of the history of the Orient, centering around Japan, and of the world, it is inevitable that it will be realized soon. I affirm that the East Asian Federation will be the essence of the Shōwa Restoration.* I will explain the theory and outline of the plan for creating the East Asian Federation in the following chapters and sections. In brief it will be the achievement of the great mission of 'hakkō ichiū'* and the denouement of the Shōwa Restoration.* It seeks the liberation of East Asia through destruction of the Western imperialistic structure in the Orient. The first stage of the plan is to create a New East Asia Structure combining Japan, Manchukuo and China, and also to create a new order in our own country which will be closely related. It also includes as primary aims the fundamental solution of the Sino-Japanese Incident and preparation for mobilization for total war.

In my view East Asian Federation is a program for tomorrow which will be achieved on the basis of the progress of today. I believe it is the only revolutionary movement, both abroad and internally, whose realization is inevitable. Why do we call East Asian Federation the essence of the Shōwa Restoration as the only revolution both abroad and at home? I propose to clarify the essence of the Shōwa Restoration by arguing from the standpoint of our world policy, national defence policy, and also the domestic revolution.

How can we make China give up protesting against Japan and liberate her from dependency on Europe and America? To what purpose should [the Chinese people] achieve unity after discarding anti-Japanese propaganda? What should be substituted after they lose their dependency on Europe and America? The answer will be apparent from what I have already said. The purpose of unity should be joining the East Asian Federation, and Japan should be its practical support for the time being. Many tasks are incumbent on Japan to achieve this great transformation. The first is to completely liquidate the vestiges of the idea of imperialistic aggression and return to Mahayana* and the rule of righteousness which is distinctive to the Orient, and to make the Chinese people understand the real significance of the East Asian Federation. But first the Japanese people themselves should appreciate this thoroughly.

For Japan to completely accomplish these tasks, however, she must have the requisite ability and the military power necessary to displace the support of Europe and America and to achieve pure protection without any selfish motives in place of the support of Europe and America. Behind China's recent dependence on Europe and America and the anti-Japanese sentiment is the fact that Japan has not had the power to expel Europe and America from Asia. She did not even have the power to defend herself against oppression by Europe and America, but was continually forced to concede. Since the Versailles Treaty, although we gained our right of autonomous action in East Asia, military preparations have been markedly delayed, as I have related. In contrast to the remarkable progress of defensive power of Germany, Italy, the Soviet Union, etc., in recent years our country has been extremely slow. This is because in these nations dictatorial authority was able to attain defensive power, while in our country pressure by the military was not sufficient to suppress liberal parties. Not only that, but the military has often been counter-attacked by the liberal parties, and time has passed with national opinion divided. With the outbreak of the Incident the death knell of outdated liberalism has tolled. Now defensive strength must be achieved commensurate with fulfilling our responsibility as leader of East Asia. Only when Japan achieves the rule of righteousness and achieves a genuine 'Asia for Asiatics' with sufficient power behind it will a revived China surely begin its strides toward the same great goal.

Following the creation of Manchukuo we discarded such special rights as administrative authority and extraterritoriality on the assumption that Japan and Manchukuo were one. This policy must be reaffirmed again in relation to all China, and revolution in our continental policy must be achieved. It is clearly impossible to correct the relationship of conflict between Japan and China through a single treaty of both governments on the basis of military occupation. Therefore, a cooperative peoples' movement is necessary. The mission of the Manchuria Imperial Harmony Society *(Manshū Teikoku Kyōwakai)* and New Peoples' Society *(Shinminkai)* is particularly important in this respect. It is no exaggeration to say that the key to success of East Asian Federation depends on a peoples' cooperative movement.

Secondly, the policy of East Asian Federation means a shift from following Western imperialistic colonial policy to rejecting it. In other words, East Asian Federation will abandon imperialistic policies, destroy the Western establishment governing East Asia, liberate East Asia, and develop into the formation of the new structure of East Asia. This will change our continental policy fundamentally. I must insist that we not prevaricate in relinquishing our imperialistic policy. Today the motive of rationalizing all our claims has a strong hold on Japan. But our great people should not maintain the attitude of insisting on all our past policies. Although our continental policy effected such things as the peace and welfare of Korea and achieved a harmonious union of the Japanese and Korean peoples on the one hand, we should not overlook the fact that we are losing support of our policy even in the Orient. Japan must return to her own position. We should return to the position of leader in the Orient. To do this it is necessary to discard entirely the remnants of imperialistic ideas still apparent officially and unofficially. Unless this attitude is pre-supposed on the part of Japan it will be difficult for the goal of East Asian Federation to be understood even among Oriental people, and the policy will not have moral force behind it.

In this regard Japan, chief advocate of Federation, must perceive the psychology of the suppressed people in every stage of the Federation program and should refrain from replacing Western-style exploitation by Japanese-style suppression in organizing the Federation. [Japan] should adopt a cautious attitude so as not to create such an impression. Since East Asian Federation aims at the liberation of East Asian peoples, the right of political independence of the liberated peoples must be completely assured. While Japan and friendly nations work for the liberation movement of Oriental peoples, they must have free choice as to whether they will join the Federation or remain completely independent nations, and the right to withdraw after joining must be recognized.

East Asian Federation is an alliance which should be established firmly on an autonomous basis through the bond of political and economic mutual dependence between Japan and allied powers. It is not a compulsory body. Therefore the ultimate aspirations of the liberated nations must not be fettered. I believe that if Japan and friendly nations adopt such an attitude it would be extremely unlikely for those people to withdraw from the Federation, and such a centrifugal effect would gradually be eliminated.

Most of the Orient is either a complete colony or a semi-colony of the West. Even within the districts occupied militarily by Japan there exist British and French settlements in Shanghai and Tientsin which govern anti-Japanese China within the Western imperialistic system. We feel Western imperialism is trying in every way to take revenge. The Western establishment in East Asia which is the adversary of our Federation movement is a policy for world domination by the white races built up through the past century. Formally we are fighting Chiang Kai-shek's army in China but substantively we are fighting against British and French imperialism and Soviet Red Imperialism which are taking clever advantage of the peoples' unity movement in China. Therefore the final goal of the Incident must be the destruction of the Western establishment in China. But destruction of the Western establishment shouldn't be achieved through reckless attitudes. In the process of achieving the goal a flexible policy must naturally be adopted. Compromise with Britain and America can be considered. The destruction must be gradual in the process of creating the new order, the East Asian Federation, which will be composed of a free union of liberated East Asian nations. But to complete it we must radically root out the source of evil.

The New Order in East Asia which we are about to establish must be a substitute for aggressive invasion of East Asia. On the one hand it will have the negative aspect of self-defence of the Orient, but on the other hand it will have the positive aspect of establishing a strong world-wide political and economic bloc and preparing for international political eventualities. It will also aim at creating a great Oriental society of world-wide universality based on the new Oriental culture (a culture of the rule of righteousness). The Western establishment in the Orient will be destroyed, and as time goes on its remnants will be absorbed into the new Oriental order. The theory of culture supporting the Western structure will be replaced by the rule of righteousness which is the basic theory of our structure.... What is most important is that the New Structure in East Asia will replace the Western concept of freedom underlying the Western establishment with the Eastern concept of morality. We Orientals know that such Western ideas as freedom, equality, democracy, etc. are based on the concept of racial and class differences. For example, the free societies of the British and French white peoples are built on the foundation of the slavery of billions of colored people living in vast colonies and semi-colonies. It is like the democracy among the nobility of ancient Rome which was conjoined with use of slaves of many different races.

2
East Asia Cooperative Body I

OZAKI Hotsumi was a scholar and spy who gained notoriety in the Sorge Spy Case as a Soviet agent. As one of the most important theorists of the Shōwa Kenkyūkai*, Ozaki felt that Japan, through the East Asia Cooperative Body, should expel European colonial oppression from Asia and promote Communist revolution throughout Asia. At home Ozaki helped draft plans for the New Structure Movement (*Shin Taisei**) which sought to create a mass totalitarian party as a bulwark against the Army. For Ozaki the East Asia Cooperative Body had multiple advantages. It was a moral ideal and a practical method of dealing with Chinese nationalism and with Japan's defence and economic requisites. He argues his case here in an article from *Chūō Kōron*, 'The Concept of the *Tōa Kyōdōtai* and the Objective Bases for its Establishment,' Vol. 16, January 1939. Ozaki feared that when the ideal became government policy there would be a confrontation with capitalists at home.

THERE is a great diversity in the concept of this 'New Order in East Asia,' for example, the 'East Asia Cooperative Body' theory and the 'East Asian Federation' theory.... The desire to control the realities and the new situation between

THE IDEAL CONCEPTUALIZED

Japan and China, produced through the progress of the war, by means of this 'New Order' is an attitude which will generate the New Order. Also, we find this spirit in the radio broadcast of Premier Konoye who formulated the government's proclamation of November 3,

To wit: 'To cooperate with China without subjugating China.'

'To carry out the mission of a united Asia leading a regenerated China.'

'The Chinese people will share in the great undertaking of the New Asia.'

'We will establish a new peaceful order in Asia.'

Through phrases such as 'Joining with the countries of East Asia we will build a new autonomous joint organization based on a genuinely moral foundation,' the distinctive parameters which the 'New Order' would take on have already been demonstrated in top-level political declarations. These certainly demonstrate '*Tōa Kyōdōtai*'-like features.

Thus what we should note particularly and consider primarily is the 'Greater East Asia Cooperative Body' ideal as the basic Japanese policy for coping with the [China] Incident. In the final analysis the 'East Asia Cooperative Body,' has become a *sine qua non* for policy to resolve the Incident.... How will the East Asia Cooperative Body ideal be developed? And further, how will the concrete structure be constituted? Another interesting point is what is the relative importance and position of this 'Cooperative Body' in the overall policy for handling this Incident? There is the matter of coordinating other important considerations and conditions in overall policy for dealing with it.

...I think in the '*hakkō ichiū*'* spirit there are some similarities to the 'Cooperative Body' ideal. It has no doubt merged in the Pan-Asian stream of thought, together with views on the 'East Asian Federation.' But the 'East Asia Cooperative Body' which has emerged as a realistic measure for the 'New Order' in the present situation was surely an historical result of the development of the Japan-China Incident.

...Proposals and explanations of the 'East Asia Cooperative Body' theory have recently appeared in several places, but we find it remarkable that almost no criticism of it has appeared. Originally, there was no reason to expect that the 'East Asia Cooperative Body' ideal would be supported by the capitalistic status quo faction. From the first it was anticipated it would arouse some severe criticism. The reasons for it [lack of criticism], or Japan's most distinctive reason, is probably one of the following: lack of a critical spirit, or insufficient understanding of the problem, or underestimating the actual weakness at present of the 'East Asia Cooperative Body' theory, or some ulterior motive of taking advantage of this view. Writers looking at the inevitability of the 'East Asia Cooperative Body' believe in the possibility of its development in the future. Nevertheless, realistically, the problem of the 'East Asia Cooperative Body,' has some weak points and some problems from the practical standpoint. At present, because we believe it is absolutely necessary to clarify this aspect of the problem, I propose to take an actively critical view of the problem. Considering the 'New Order in East Asia' and the 'East Asia Cooperative Body,' as a new ideal, we see that there are many people who cannot understand it as a real phenomenon. For those who think only of the changes in our wartime Chinese opponent, through recent great historical events, and who think there is absolutely no change in their own pace, there can be absolutely no understanding of this 'Cooperative Body' ideal. Some people think of the 'Cooperative Body' ideal as a step toward establishing the domination of the battle victor, Japan, on the East Asiatic continent, or of it only as a front for this domination. There is no denying that the China mainland has been regarded as a market for developing the Japanese economy and also as a source of supply of raw materials. And doubtless certain districts on the continent have been regarded from the viewpoint of defence. After the Manchurian Incident when the economic bloc of Japan, China and Manchuria was often discussed, this economic bloc system was directed mainly at supplementary mobilization of Manchuria and China, particularly North China, for the sake of developing the Japanese economy. When in the early period of the development of this Incident it was thought to limit the problem only to the sphere of North China, it was based precisely on this system. Even now Japanese capitalists and many ordinary people will probably put their chief hopes in this system. It was from this viewpoint that the establishment of the company to develop North and Central China was expedited. The problem of the enterprise on the mainland was first concerned with matters of control and exploitation. Iron and coal were thus the focus of interest.

One of the premises for establishing the 'East Asia Cooperative Body' theory resulted from the impossibility of organizing East Asian nations economically in accordance with Japan's unilateral system, as I have said. In this sense the birth of the 'East Asia Cooperative Body' theory was generated by reevaluation of the problem of nationalism in China, it seems to me. Everyone will agree that the nationalism problem in China is the largest problem in modern China. But, just as something too close and too overwhelming often tends to be neglected, so the nationalism problem in China often tends to be overlooked in considering problems regarding China. When we say 'problem of nationalism' we of course mean that the Chinese people live in a vast area populated by four hundred millions. This is of course important, but what we think especially significant is not a static view but the nationalism problem seen dynamically....

Most Japanese fought without hating the Chinese people but fought against the Nationalist Government for adhering to its mistaken policies.... But on the Chinese side they thought this was a racial war with their nation at stake and acted accordingly. We can divide China by force into two spheres, foe and friend. But even then this nationalism problem will remain in both these areas ....

We must stop and reconsider the meaning of 'sacred war.' There are some who believe that our warriors shedding honorable blood will not rest in peace and soldiers in the midst of hardship will not be at peace unless Japan attains her demands from the mainland concretely and clearly. But this is a completely mistaken notion.... We are certain that those who sacrificed their lives for the sake of the country never shed their blood in expectation of compensation. They surely wanted to become pillars of the 'New Order in East Asia' which would bring ultimate peace in East Asia.... It will not be until the Chinese themselves cooperate in the building of the East Asia Cooperative Body as their own concern that this aim will be fulfilled....

There is a complete contradiction in theory and application of the East Asia Cooperative Body in practical policy. This is due to the change in objective conditions from the time when the theory was generated and developed. This is not a great problem yet because the East Asia Cooperative Body is not more than a private plan. The time has not yet come when there will be negotiations with China based on it, though it has appeared vaguely in government statements. But when the pure and leading principles of the East Asia Cooperative Body are gradually developed, and when it is applied to practical policy, it will cause great conflicts with the capitalist sphere at home.

3
East Asia Cooperative Body II

SHINMEI Masamichi here discusses the basis for the East Asia Cooperative Body as advanced by several authors. He deals with origins of the concept and the vocabulary of the East Asia Cooperative Body: regionalism, 'cooperationism' ethnic affinity, cultural ties. He is concerned with the theoretical implications of these concepts, for example with relation to individualism and totalitarianism. Mr. Shinmei develops his arguments in the volume *Ideals of the East Asia Cooperative Body* (*Tōa kyōdōtai no risō*, 1939). Professor Shinmei is a graduate of Tokyo Imperial University and Professor Emeritus of Tohoku University where he taught political science. He was associated with the Patriotic Press Association. He is somewhat critical of the East Asia Cooperative Body concept as advanced by scholars.

RECENTLY there have been proponents of the idea of cooperation in the world of ideas. Mr. Funayama Shin'ichi is the most cogent advocate of the view of cooperation, and the term '*kyōdōshugi*' (cooperationism) comes from him. But there are many others who do not call themselves cooperationists who advocate the principles of national or Asiatic social reconstruction in harmony with this. Mr. Miki Kiyoshi takes about the same stand. Actually Mr. Miki was a pioneer and leader in this line of thought. And it seems this idea has other protagonists than these two. This idea began to emerge last year. It coincided with the rise of the idea of *Tōa Kyōdōtai*, and as the name itself implies the idea is directly related to the latter. It was developed as a theoretical framework for the *Kyōdōtai*. Of course the idea of *Tōa Kyōdōtai* didn't claim as its theory *kyōdōshugi*. But as the *kyōdōtai* idea becomes more influential, *kyōdōshugi* is discussed more. So it can't be said that there is no relationship between the idea of *Tōa Kyōdōtai* and *kyōdōshugi*. Already there is some criticism of the idea of *Tōa Kyōdōtai* for trying to identify the two. This is because the formal principles of the idea of *Tōa Kyōdōtai* haven't been established... But this is not to say that all *Kyōdōtai* advocates recognize *kyōdōshugi* as the basis. The principles of *kyōdōshugi* have only recently been advanced, just as the idea of Asian unity has been. So the principle is only a rough outline, and there are some differences among theorists belonging to this school. We don't think these ideas have been well developed yet. But judging from the opinions published so far, the general trend is clear.... Though I do not hesitate to support the idea of *Tōa Kyōdōtai*, practically I find some aspects I don't entirely agree with. Needless to say, we can say that *kyōdōshugi* is an idea independent of *kyōdōtai*. But since this idea has been presented as the basis of the idea of *Tōa Kyōdōtai* we must be particularly concerned with the relation between this and the *kyōdōtai* theory. However, from what I see, *kyōdōshugi* as it is has a structure which can't be adapted as the principle behind the idea of *Tōa Kyōdōtai*. *Tōa Kyōdōtai* needs a basic principle but *kyōdōshugi* cannot qualify. At least looked at from the standpoint of contemporary human society we must say it lacks logical components as the basis of *Tōa Kyōdōtai*.

The idea of *kyōdōshugi* is a name only; no one can clarify its ideological content. *Kyōdōshugi* has connotations which can't be clarified simply by defining the word 'cooperation.' Generally *kyōdō* means a phase of activity in which many people do some necessary or useful work in cooperation. This factor of course is included in *kyōdōshugi*, but this is not all of it nor most characteristic of it. *Kyōdōshugi* has a more distinctive character. To clarify the essence of *kyōdōshugi* we need to understand the essential characteristics, ... apart from the meaning of the word

16 THE IDEAL CONCEPTUALIZED

kyōdō. The central problem of *kyōdōshugi* concerns the relationship between the individual and the whole. Needless to add, in relation to this there arises the confrontation of individualism and totalitarianism, but *kyōdōshugi* does not affirm either of the two; rather it subsumes both comprehensively and advances this *kyōdōshugi* as a principle beyond both.

Kyōdōshugi can be considered to be individualistic by association with cooperatives *(kyōdō kumiai).* It is wrong of course to view the idea of a cooperative as individualistic. But through a vague association it can be considered individualistic because it is based on benefits. Therefore it is possible to think of *kyōdōshugi* as individualistic also. But the sense of the word *kyōdōshugi* conveys a meaning closer to totalitarianism. It can be said that the most typical ideas of totalitarianism in the world emphasize cooperative ideas.

But although there is some common fundamental viewpoint there has been some dispute regarding several problems. The main disputes are: the problem of area and ethnic character in the structure of the *Tōa Kyōdōtai.* There are of course more important problems for the development of the idea of *kyōdōtai*.... Through his articles Mr. Rōyama acted as a pioneer in the idea of *Tōa Kyōdōtai.* He advanced the idea of a predestined *kyōdōtai* as a basis for the *Tōa Kyōdōtai.* He didn't originate this idea, but it was used by the *Dai Ajiya Kyōkai*.... But in his case [Rōyama's] the idea is given theoretical content leading to the *Tōa Kyōdōtai* theory. What he particularly emphasized is regionalism. He regards the predestined *Tōa Kyōdōtai* as a regionally determined, total society. Japan, Manchuria and China which form the *Tōa Kyōdōtai* are regionally adjacent societies, so we can call this syncretic society regional. But there is some question as to why we should define it as distinctively regional. Regional society means one limited to a region and with it as the object of vital concern. A national society is also a regional society in a sense. Therefore it seems natural to view the new united society as regional. But he advances his theoretical regionalism from another viewpoint too. He describes as the future theoretical structure of the world a skeletal international organization and a regional three-dimensional cooperative organization. The former appears in the form of continental or foreign development tried by Europeans in past world history and is intrinsically imperialistic. On the other hand the latter is aimed at indirect development through gradual development of adjacent territory. He regards the second theory as the theory of the *kyōdōtai* and affirms that the intrinsic theory of Japan's continental development was carried out with the object of establishing a defence zone and development and administration of adjacent territory. It is quite different from the imperialism advanced by capitalism as seen in European imperialism. There is a regional predestined *kyōdōtai* formed by a race in a certain region.... He attempted to construct a regional predestined *kyōdōtai* in Asia through this basic theory. These are the grounds on which he advanced regionalism....

Dr. Takada opposed his theory. Dr. Takada insisted that the idea of one great people based on the several peoples of Japan, Manchuria, and China should be the basis for the unity of the *Tōa Kyōdōtai*, and that this is what creates unity, and that the regional idea is not a possible basis for unity. His criticism wasn't limited to regionalism. He was also against the concept of 'predestined cooperation,' as predestined cooperation exists only through destiny, an historical common ground. 'What predestined cooperation has there been between Japan and China, which have been primarily in a situation of separation and confrontation?... What we seek is unity in East Asia. We don't unite because we are a predestined *kyōdōtai*. Because we are united we have predestined cooperation, and through this cooperation our unity is renewed'.... He thinks predestined *kyōdōtai* is not something already given but something to be realized in the future. But the essence of his objection consists of course in the idea of a regional *kyōdōtai*. He insists: 'To regard the unity of East Asia as a regional predestined *kyōdōtai* misses the important point.... If it is a regional *kyōdōtai* why not include the Russians of East Siberia? It is not that I don't recognize the significance of region in the unity of East Asia. I have often referred to this. But I don't consider it the most representative tie. If you believe this why not consider other important bonds of similar character and kind? By 'same character' I don't necessarily mean identity of character. As I have already said I mean the commonality of culture, such as commonality of customs, manners, beliefs, learning, etc. To represent the unity of East Asia as a regional predestined *kyōdōtai* is to slight a most fundamental ethnic bond (European scholars sometimes call Japan the cousin of China)

THE IDEAL CONCEPTUALIZED

and to neglect a very significant instance of cultural similarity'.... He considered the bonds of culture and of ethnic affinity as more important than regional factors as bonds of the new East Asian society. He especially emphasized the blood or race bond, and called this viewpoint *Tōa Minzoku-shugi* (East Asian nationalism).

Contrasting Mr. Rōyama's viewpoint of regionalism with Dr. Takada's of ethnicity points to a big difference between them in fundamental grasp of the *Tōa Kyōdōtai*. But practically their views don't have a very different meaning, for they admit each other's viewpoints. Mr. Rōyama, who is thought to be for regionalism, does not exclude race, and Dr. Takada, advocating ethnicity, doesn't neglect regional factors. Mr. Rōyama uses the phrase 'regional racial *kyōdōtai*', meaning the same as regional predestined *kyōdōtai*, and says that the idea of *Tōa Kyōdōtai* has come from race and territory.... It is clear that his regionalism is not solely regionalism; racial factors are also included in it.

On the other hand, Dr. Takada doesn't neglect the significance of regional factors. He says there are three bonds uniting East Asia fundamentally, including cultural and regional factors in addition to race.... It is understood that common regional factors make the bond of social community closer. So the difference of their views lies in which points are emphasized in forming the *Tōa Kyōdōtai*. They aren't discrete and separate opinions. The problem is how to evaluate the different emphases....

Ethnic ties are permanent. But this does not automatically mean the formation of a syncretic society. Why is it that even if the nations in East Asia have had blood ties in the past they weren't able to form a united society? It is because the nations of East Asia had blood ties but they did not form a really influential sphere in social content. We think it is a fact that through social development communications between nations have been expanded and mutual dependence in social life has been increased, and the commonality of destiny and benefit in international status has been established, and that we have come to find a new meaning in ethnic ties.

It is obvious that if this dynamic sociological factor hadn't operated there would not have been any opportunity for the significance of blood ties to manifest itself. Therefore, it is not proper to see this as the final and decisive factor, even if blood relationship plays a limited role as a basis for the *Tōa Kyōdōtai*. We must conclude that the development of sociological commonality of action creates a tendency toward formation of the *Tōa Kyōdōtai*. Therefore sole emphasis on race or blood alone cannot be the influential factor in regionalism.

Mr. Miki, who represents the cultural viewpoint, thinks that the basis for the structure of the *Tōa Kyōdōtai* must be sought in the cultural arena. He says, 'It is impossible that the principle of unity of the *Kyōdōtai* is as irrational as racist totalitarianism. Of course, it can't be thought of as a *gesellschaft* rationalist approach. The basis of unity of the *Tōa Kyōdōtai* must not be something irrational like blood but the tradition of Oriental culture as a whole beyond racism.'.... I don't object to accepting the cultural viewpoint if culture is considered to include the reality and results of social action. But according to him culture means a narrower spiritual culture. This makes this standpoint too narrow and insufficient as the basis for the *Tōa Kyōdōtai*, especially when this is thought of as an East Asian cultural tradition.

When they form a new *kyōdōtai*, East Asian nations may find support in the cultural similarity they have had in the past, but this cultural similarity, as I have said elsewhere, is not so syncretic as to be the basis for a new Asian synthesis. It is clear that in reality this is not a decisive motive force dictating the formation of a *Tōa Kyōdōtai* at present.

4
The New Order and Regionalism

RŌYAMA Masamichi was one of Japan's first political scientists and is still a leader in the field. He graduated from Tokyo Imperial University in 1920, was professor at that institution from 1922 to 1928. He helped organize the *Shinjinkai** and published the magazine *Shakai Shisō* in which he wrote articles about British socialism from an anti-Marxist standpoint. In 1934 he accompanied Prince Konoye to the U.S. and lectured on East Asia in Hawaii. During World War II he resigned from Tokyo Imperial University when Professor Kawai Eijirō was expelled. As a member of Premier Konoye's brain trust he advised Konoye's wartime administration. After the war he was purged from public office for having been a member of the Imperial Rule Assistance Association. He was depurged in 1950. In 1954 he became president of Ochanomizu Women's University. Here he advances the concept of regionalism as the rationale for a New Order in East Asia in an excerpt from his book *East Asia and the World* (*Tōa to sekai*, 1941). This regionalism he felt held the hope for reconciling the demands of Japan and China and bringing peace between them and the rest of the world.

AT present, anxieties and uncertainties prevail everywhere as to how the New Order in East Asia will effect a readjustment in relations between Japan, China and other powers having interests in China, how the recently established Nationalist Government of China under Wang Ching-wei will progress, and how it will adjust their relations with the Kuomintang Government, and finally how they will reach any understanding with the interested powers, especially Great Britain and the United States.

...This Japanese policy of a New Order in East Asia has not been a policy suddenly or accidentally conceived, but has been nationally formulated after long and serious deliberation and with a view to settling not only the present conflict but rather the age-long instability of the Far East. For the first time since the 'opening' of the country in the Meiji era, Japan now possesses a national policy really her own, Japan is truly 'supported by her own feet.' The success or failure of the policy will not, of course, depend solely upon Japan's will, but it must equally be admitted that the Japan of today with such a policy of her own is vastly different from the Japan of yesterday which, without any such policy was simply accommodating herself as best as she could to general world trends.

In what way, then, does this policy bear upon peace in the world, and what international organization does it envisage? What will be the formula or process by which it can be attained? In regard to these questions, public opinion in Japan is yet to be formulated. At present the government does not seem to be sufficiently experienced to give any ready answer; nor have the people been given a strong enough intellectual incentive.

What follows is only a tentative conclusion which the author has reached after studying, as objectively as possible, the historical facts of the past as well as the internal and external situations prevailing today.

First, it is one form of regional international organization. The new relationship of mutual reliance which Japan is inviting China to build jointly is neither the ordinary treaty relationship between one sovereign power and another, nor a simple 'planetary' organization like the League of Nations, comprehending all the countries of the world. Its geographical boundaries may be somewhat ambiguous, but it is an organization which covers only a region inhabited by the nations or races possessing given qualifications at a given time. The 'East Asia' envisaged by Japan comprises, for the present at least, Japan, Manchukuo, and

THE IDEAL CONCEPTUALIZED

China. This is so, because there exist common to these three countries political, economic, and cultural conditions and because any other contiguous regions lack some of them, though geographically there is no reason why they should be excluded.

Secondly, the New Order in East Asia is an organization in which nationality, independence and freedom are to be respected in the fullest sense of the terms. That the conflict between Japan and China in recent years has been characterized by a clash between Japan's territorial and economic imperialism and China's demand for national unity and independence is clear. That the present armed strife, whatever its immediate occasion, was fundamentally caused by this issue is also clear.

This strife might be settled temporarily if Japan either forcefully assumed the position of a conqueror or were beaten back. But Japan never either intended to conquer China or believed that she could. On the other hand, it is inconceivable that China might be able by herself to beat back Japan. If such is the case, clearly there will be no other way of bringing about a Far Eastern stability of any duration, except by discovering some common basis for readjustment between the demands of both countries. The New Order in East Asia is one attempt to do this and, in this attempt at least, it can claim its *raison d'être*.

Thirdly, the New Order in East Asia is a form of cooperation or co-existence of states which ensures international intercourse and world peace. The relationship within the new order is closer than the ordinary relationship between states, but it is not an alliance inimical to international peace; nor is it such a bloc as would interfere with intercourse with the outside world. In fact, to have safeguarding provisions in this connection will be a necessary requisite for the New Order in East Asia. It has come to be recognized increasingly of late that the international organization of the future should consist of a few such regional organizations established for regions where they are possible and desirable. For it would then reconcile the conflicting forces of modern times, *viz*, nationalism which tends to contract, and industrialism which seeks to expand, and thus promote a sound development of international organization as a whole. It would also ensure equitable distribution of economic forces. This is, in fact, what Japan has in mind when she claims, as she often does, that international justice should be realized in the Far East.

THE NEW ORDER AND REGIONALISM 23

The New Order in East Asia cannot possibly be realized by any arbitrary method. It can be realized only by that of diplomatic negotiation and the common consent of all parties concerned. However, this is a most difficult method; indeed, it looks so difficult to some people in Japan that they think it would be futile to attempt it. In their opinion, the only method of realizing the new order is to make it a *fait accompli*. In other countries, too, especially in England and America, there are perhaps not a few people who expect Japan to succeed in such diplomatic negotiations. Leaving it to the historians of the future to judge, we are of the opinion that the only and proper method of realizing the new order will be diplomatic negotiation.

The first thing to remember in such negotiations is that all the facts and arrangements which have been and will be brought about during the course of the present conflict are not necessarily facts and arrangements of the new order. It has been pointed out in the preceding chapter that there has been a confusion in this connection in the negotiations with Great Britain and the United States. The New Order can be claimed to be established only when the *de jure* recognition by all parties has been conferred. This will necessitate a revision of the actual situations created as well as of the existing treaties in the Far East, and for this purpose international conferences will have to be convened. But as a matter of policy, it will be advantageous for all parties concerned to let any two countries reach an agreement prior to any multilateral conferences.

Secondly, it is clear that the international principles pertaining to China, especially those of the Open Door and equal opportunity, will at a number of points conflict with the principles of the New Order. But in this connection a distinction must be drawn between the trading rights of other countries in China and their trading practices or processes. The New Order in East Asia does not propose to disregard or impair in any way the trading rights of other countries in China, although it would result in restricting or modifying at some points the practices or processes of that trade. Such restrictions or modifications of trading practices should not be viewed as a disregard or impairment of trading rights. There seems, however, to have been both a lack of understanding and a difference of opinion on this point between Japan and other countries. This should be remedied and given the consideration of all parties, and it will not then be difficult to close the gap now existing.

Thirdly, the New Order in East Asia will not depend for its success solely upon its technical perfection or the benefits it confers upon this region. Above all else, it will depend upon whether it will promote peace in the Pacific and the world at large. Therefore, as the United States has frequently pointed out, any agreement concerning the New Order would necessarily involve readjustment of other matters directly or indirectly affected. Any revision of the Nine-Power Treaty would thus involve a new understanding by all parties concerned of the general questions common to Pacific countries as well as those questions affecting particular countries. It does not necessarily follow, however, that negotiations for these purposes should be conducted either simultaneously or at the same place. Each of them may be undertaken separately or at different times. In view of her past experiences in 'conference diplomacy,' Japan will probably object to the method of dealing with all questions at the same time and place. However, she will not fail to realize that all of them are essentially interdependent and mutually conditional.... And it will not be at all impossible to discover a compromise between the diplomatic process preferred by Japan and that desired by the advocates of collective security.

5
Japan's Monroe Doctrine

PROFESSOR Kamikawa Hikomatsu graduated from Tokyo Imperial University and taught there for many years. An authority on diplomatic history, he was awarded the Japan Academy Prize for his three-volume study, *Current History of Diplomacy* (1952). He here traces the origins and development of America's Monroe Doctrine and Japan's counterpart in Asia, which he sees as basically analogous. Since the U.S. developed regionalism as a policy with the Monroe Doctrine, he expected the U.S. to sympathize with Japan's adaptation of regionalism in East Asia. This selection comes from *Contemporary Japan*, vol. VIII, no. 6, Aug. 1939, titled 'The American and Japanese Monroe Doctrines'.

The analogy between Japan's Pan-Asianism and the Monroe Doctrine of the U.S. was also noted by other scholars. Professor Emeritus Takagi Yasaka, for example, while he viewed the two expressions of regionalism as fundamentally similar, was critical of both in that he saw them as acquisitive threats to peace.

During the war Professor Kamikawa carried his argument in favour of Japanese regionalism further (*The Japan Times*, 5 November, 1943) when he declared, 'Greater East Asianism which we are advocating and carrying into practice is different, superior and more progressive in comparison with the types of continentalism and Grossraum-ism as advocated and advanced already by Europeans and Americans'.

THE IDEAL CONCEPTUALIZED

IN modern world politics East Asia and the American continents have similarities in regard to their position and characteristics. It is strange, therefore, that there should be so few among the intelligentsia of Western countries, especially the United States, who appreciate this fact. If thinking people on the other side of the Pacific understand that East Asia and the American continents have similar interests and a common purpose in world politics, there is no doubt that American opinion regarding events in East Asia would undergo a radical change.

In conceiving the idea of regionalism in international politics the United States was the leader among the nations of the world. Early in the days of her emergence as an independent nation, the United States held that idea. George Washington, the father of his country, clearly indicated the nature of such regionalism in his famous farewell address. Emphasizing the importance of America's political detachment from Europe by taking advantage of the geographically isolated position of the American continents, he urged the nation to maintain a policy of political isolation ....

This isolationism — a policy to keep the United States as well as the American continents, her sphere of influence, detached from the rest of the world and to avoid all kinds of permanent political association with the Old World — became the guiding principle of the American foreign policy and has since been maintained consistently .... As for the foreign policy of the United States it consists of three basic doctrines, namely, the Monroe Doctrine, Pan-Americanism and Imperialism. The first two doctrines are clearly the outgrowth of the policy formulated within the range of isolationism.

The Monroe Doctrine is unquestionably the one that expresses most precisely the conception of regionalism which is the cardinal point of the American foreign policy .... The doctrine originally embraced three principles. The first is the so-called principle of non-colonization .... The second principle of the Monroe Doctrine is what is known as the principle of non-intervention .... The third principle of the Monroe Doctrine is the principle of isolation ....

During the century after its proclamation the Monroe Doctrine has passed various stages in the course of its evolutionary development. It has developed with the growth of the national strength and the increasing requirements for the territorial, political and economic expansion of the United States. In its original form the doctrine was well adapted, as has already been explained, to meet the national and international requirements of the country and was successful in checking further territorial expansion and political intervention of the European powers in the American continents. This is attested by the fact that not a square inch of land has been acquired by the European countries on the American continents since the doctrine was proclaimed by President Monroe. On the other hand, the United States has in the same period acquired a vast new territory on the continents. This was due to the fact that while the Monroe Doctrine imposed restrictions and prohibitions on the European powers, it did by no means prohibit the United States herself from making territorial acquisitions. On the contrary, it facilitated territorial acquisition by the United States and, moreover, made American intervention in various regions of the American continents inevitable and easy.

Now, turning to East Asia it is found that the relation between Japan and the continent of East Asia closely resembles that between the United States and the American continents. In fact the continental policy of Japan since the Manchurian Incident has been frequently called the Japanese 'Monroe Doctrine' or the East Asiatic 'Monroe Doctrine.' But not a few Western writers find faults with the Japanese 'Monroe Doctrine' while they justify the American doctrine by stressing unduly the negligible differences they discover between the two. It should be pointed out, however, that these doctrines are essentially similar, the only difference being that the Japanese 'Monroe Doctrine' has East Asia for its field of operation and the original Monroe Doctrine the American continents. The essential characters of the two as international policies are the same, though the processes of their development have differed.

Like its prototype in America, the Japanese 'Monroe Doctrine' is Japan's policy toward East Asia with reference to her relations with the Western powers. It has no concern with the relations between Japan and other countries of East Asia. The present condition of East Asia greatly resembles that which existed in the Western Hemisphere in the early part of the 19th century in that, with the only exception of Japan, all the regions of East

THE IDEAL CONCEPTUALIZED

Asia are in status the colonies or semi-colonies of European and American powers. Naturally the Japanese 'Monroe Doctrine', now in its first stage of development, bears a close resemblance to the original Monroe Doctrine of the United States. Japan's 'Monroe Doctrine' must of necessity contain the principles of non-colonization, non-territorial acquisition and non-intervention. It cannot but be operated, therefore, as a principle of defence and preservation of East Asia, since the acquisition of territory in this region by any one of the European or American powers is a violation of the territorial integrity of this part of the globe and is a menace to its security; and Japan, as the defender of East Asia, must determinedly oppose such an encroachment. And if the Western powers intervene and extend their political influence over this region, such action must be construed as disturbing the peace and order of East Asia which Japan, as the guardian of peace in this region, must vigorously oppose. These principles of non-colonization, non-intervention and non-territorial acquisition are the minimum claim of Japan under her 'Monroe Doctrine.'

As to the principle of isolation contained in the American doctrine, Japan also observes a similar principle in her 'Monroe Doctrine' as strictly as circumstances permit. She has not only withdrawn herself from the League of Nations but participated in no political affairs of Europe. Moreover, she has never had anything to do with political affairs in the American continents. Unlike the United States, which has abandoned the principle of isolation in the Pacific area and East Asia where she has intervened unrestrainedly, Japan has been acting strictly within the confines of East Asia making no positive attempt to interfere with European or American political affairs.

That the American Monroe Doctrine is fundamentally an economic principle despite its apparent political feature and that it served effectively to facilitate the United States policy of territorial expansion to meet the demand of her internal economy in the last century are as explained above. It cannot be denied that the principle of Japan's 'Monroe Doctrine' is primarily a political one, but at the same time it contains an economic principle as a secondary attribute. However, it is never invoked for the purpose of territorial expansion as in the case of the American doctrine. Manchukuo, though established with the help of Japan, is clearly an independent country and is not in any respect the territory of Japan. In brief, Japan has not the slightest territorial ambition. This attitude has been clarified beyond any doubt by various public statements of the Japanese Government since the outset of the current Sino-Japanese hostilities.

In the economic sphere the Japanese 'Monroe Doctrine' envisages what may be termed East Asia continentalism, which is none other than a movement, based upon the geographical, racial, cultural and economic solidarity of the countries of East Asia, with the object of bringing about the closest possible intercourse among them. This is not at all an activity of an imperialistic character; it is a joint movement of the East Asiatic peoples. The countries of East Asia are already a single community viewed from geographical and historical standpoints, and they are now in the process of forming an economic community. Japan is at present undergoing a rapid industrial development while the other countries of the region are still in the stage of agrarian economy. But, because of this they complement one another, maintaining the relationship of mutual aid. Thus Japan's requirements arising from her capitalistic system and the needs of her neighbours arising from their agrarian economy are mutually harmonious and accommodating. It is utterly erroneous, therefore, to regard Japan's 'Monroe Doctrine' as a doctrine of imperialism.

There are some American writers who criticize Japan, asserting that while the United States does not close the door of the American continents under the pretext of the Monroe Doctrine, Japan closes the door of East Asia under her 'Monroe Doctrine'. Needless to say, such assertion and criticism are wholly groundless. That the United States has in fact kept the door of Latin America closed under her Caribbean policy cannot be refuted. Even if it is conceded for argument's sake that she has maintained the open door in her part of the world, the open door has always been and will continue to be maintained to the same extent, if not more, in East Asia, the Monroe Doctrine or no Monroe Doctrine.

Since it is clear that the Japanese 'Monroe Doctrine' is essentially the same as the original Monroe Doctrine of the United States, it must be freely admitted that the Japanese policy in East Asia

THE IDEAL CONCEPTUALIZED

is perfectly justified, if the American Monroe Doctrine was justified in its early stage. Thinking people in the United States who vindicate the Monroe Doctrine of their country as a matter of course should, from the standpoint of equity, recognize the justice of Japan's 'Monroe Doctrine' regarding East Asia.

The Monroe Doctrine is an effective manifestation of regionalism as against universalism. The United States which conceived this idea is really the originator of regionalism, which Japan is striving at present to establish in East Asia by following the example of that country. In claiming the 'Monroe Doctrine' for East Asia, Japan naturally expects sympathy and encouragement from the United States, a senior in regionalism, who for her best interests should lead and inspire her junior, Japan.

6
Greater East Asia Co-Existence Sphere

YABE Teiji, *a political scientist and critic, graduated from the Law Faculty of Tokyo Imperial University in 1926 and was appointed professor there in 1939. After the war he was president of Takushoku University. A member of the Japan Political Science and Economics Research Institute, he was an active member of the* Shōwa Kenkyūkai, *Premier Konoye's brain trust. He is the author of* Politics *and* The Essence and Value of Democracy. *He here argues for a Greater East Asia Co-Existence Sphere,* Dai Tōa Kyōzonken, *whose justification is defensive and economic, in a position paper prepared for the Navy Ministry in 1940.*

Greater East Asia Co-Existence Sphere

ONE of the essentials of Imperial defence and the national structure is to establish an autonomous defence sphere or economic sphere embracing Greater East Asia. How to define the sphere of Greater East Asia will be determined concretely and gradually; it should not be conceptualized abstractly and arbitrarily. But it is generally understood to include Northern Sakhalin and the Kuriles in the North, East Siberia,

Manchuria, Inner Mongolia, Outer Mongolia, China, and Tibet in the West, the Dutch East Indies in the South, and the ocean as far as the Hawaiian Islands in the East. Among these the order of priority must be determined according to the realities of the situation.

An autonomous defensive and economic sphere embracing Greater East Asia is not something already existing, but it should be established. An Imperial national defence structure is necessary now in order to create it. Therefore it is impossible to argue that the presently necessary national defence structure will be achieved based on the Greater East Asia Autonomous Sphere.

The nature of the Greater East Asia Autonomous Sphere will be based on the trend of world history and the situation in East Asia, with Japan as leader. It will exclude non-Asiatic invading powers and will eschew dependence on Europe and America. It will foster a new Oriental culture. It will avoid an imperialistic exploitative control structure. It will seek a defensive, political, economic, cultural and organic syncretic structure. It is especially necessary not to confuse the spirit of our country toward different peoples with Nazi racism .... This is fundamentally different from our traditional Imperial spirit which always embraces the world with morality and sees other nations as brothers. The object of the new world order is to make each nation play its proper role in the world. It can't be done through the idea of domination by force, believing in omnipotence. But we must consider several more practical policies to achieve the final goal of the New Order.

The Cooperative Defence of Greater East Asia

The Imperial Army should pursue its primary responsibilities. To do this it should secure the military bases necessary for land and sea operations over all of Greater East Asia. It should especially obtain control of the air and should prepare for a war of weapons appropriate to war in the various sectors. Thus, armaments should be vastly expanded. But because it will be very difficult, diversified operations should be pursued simultaneously through diplomatic activities, and, using the aims of the Axis Tripartite Pact, we should advance negotiations concerning several pending questions, especially demarcation of the

GREATER EAST ASIA CO-EXISTENCE SPHERE 33

whole border with the Soviet Union. We must hasten to readjust diplomatic relations with the Soviet Union in order to arrange a structure of sanctions against them (Britain and America). Therefore, if the Soviet Union does something in the area of the Near East and India, Japan will not interfere, and reciprocally, if Japan enters into a situation of conflict with Britain and America, the Soviet Union will not interfere. This kind of mutual neutrality pact should be considered. In this case it is possible to consider promising the Soviet Union materials from the South which the Soviet Union needs. So we believe that Japan should mediate [between the Soviet Union and Asia], and Japan should take full advantage of German pressure on the Soviet Union.

We can postulate that Japan might make an agreement about distant border areas of China as a *quid pro quo* for lessening Soviet support of Chiang Kai-shek. But it is dangerous to completely trust the Soviet Union, although such diplomatic relations between Japan and the Soviet Union may be readjusted. At least Japan should not neglect defence preparations. Japan should use this rather as a demonstration toward Britain and America. It is most necessary to attain the main aim without activating the third article of the Axis Tripartite Pact. In the distant future the completion of the Greater East Asia Autonomous Sphere might require the solution of the problems in Northern Sakhalin and the Maritime Provinces, etc. But it will be wise not to say anything about this for the time being. To speak further of these problems from the geopolitical standpoint will require full study of whether the future aims of the Empire should be based on continental or maritime nations or on both.

We must seek the military bases most effective and appropriate for confronting the Soviet Union in China in such a way that we won't make the Chinese people lose face. In order to maintain public peace in occupied areas, reorganization of the Chinese Army under the Wang government should be encouraged and guided to some extent. According to changes in relations with Britain and America it may become necessary to stop encircling operations around Chiang Kai-shek and make total peace. So we must fully prepare for that. As for French Indo-China, by the agreement previously reached we can make use of the Yunnan-Hanoi Railway and control the Burma road, and further, we should seek military bases in southern French Indo-China. We should promote friendly relations, especially with Thailand, and at the minimum prevent it from being used by Britain and America. We should consider further the possibility of making an alliance with it. Thus it is imperative to prepare for a British-American joint operation embracing Singapore, Hong Kong, the Philippines, Guam, Australia, etc.

Economic Unity

The foundations of the Greater East Asia Autonomous Sphere particularly dictate an economic cooperative unit. This economic unit should not be an imperialistic exploitative relationship but a cooperative relationship in co-existence and co-prosperity, bearing in mind the direction of the world's new order. Also there should be a more elevated mutual relationship between the sectors .... But in view of present requirements of the Imperial national defence structure, practical pressing requirements should of course also be considered. This is especially true when the need for the New Order in Greater East Asia is itself based on the need for liberation from dependence on Britain and America. The national defence structure for that purpose not only cannot presuppose dependence on Britain and America but also must anticipate every kind of pressure from Britain and America. In other words, if America dares to carry out a total blockade against Japan the Empire will face a very difficult situation regarding scrap iron, oil, especially fuel for airplanes, machinery, copper, molybdenum, vanadium, cotton, etc. And if Canada, Australia, New Zealand, India, British Malaya, the Philippine Islands etc. do not cooperate, Japan will have additional problems as to wool, cotton, rubber, pulp, nickel, lead, copper, bauxite, steel, etc. We have to anticipate not only an embargo but also to lose markets in these areas. So we must anticipate another problem: acquiring foreign exchange. Measures against these problems, and the use of raw materials and markets under our allies Germany and Italy, and under their influence the use of Soviet resources based on readjustment of diplomatic relations with the Soviet Union, of course should be reconsidered, as aforementioned. But above all it is imperative to encourage increased production and collection of raw materials, and development of resources and substitutes within the Empire. Expanded production in iron, copper, coal, aluminium, and magnesium, soda, industrial salts, pulp, cotton, wool, etc., especially in Manchuria and China should be emphasized and urgently needs to be carried out according to plan.

For example, with regard to oil, we must try to buy as much as possible from the Dutch Indies, Mexico, Arabia, Iran, Venezuela, Peru, Romania, the Soviet Union, etc. Also iron and copper from the Dutch Indies, Thailand, etc., nickel from New Caledonia, chromium from New Caledonia, the Soviet Union, Iran, bauxite from the Dutch Indies, copper from Brazil, and tin from the Dutch Indies are necessary. In this respect economic cooperation with friendly southern nations including Indo-China, the Dutch Indies, Timor, New Caledonia, and Thailand, is important. The purchase of a great deal of oil, rubber, tin, nickel, iron, etc., should not only be attempted, but also Japanese people should go there and work. Restrictions on business should be loosened. Entrepreneurial rights should be obtained. Markets should be developed. One can't help thinking that a military basis in these areas is necessary. However, aside from this we have to anticipate some decrease in productive capacity in the event of a blockade by America and Britain.

7
The Spiritual Basis of Asian Revolution and Unity

ŌKAWA Shūmei was a jurist, politician, and philosopher active in pre-war patriotic societies. He graduated from the Philosophy Faculty of Tokyo Imperial University in 1911. He served for a time as director of the Research Bureau of the South Manchuria Railway Company. He founded the *Yūzonsha** and *Jimmukai**, ultra-nationalist societies. He took part in the March Affair (1931) aimed at establishing a military regime. He participated in the May 15 Incident (1932) in which Premier Inukai was assassinated by young officers. He was arrested the following year and released (1935). After World War II, while on trial as a class A war criminal by the International Military Tribunal for the Far East, he became insane and his case was dropped. He was subsequently cured. He was an authority on Indian philosophy and author of numerous books. He felt revolution was necessary. His teachings were influential with the young officers and members of the *Sakurakai** who plotted the assassinations of the 1930s. He was a Pan-Asianist whose arguments were predicated on Asian spiritual and cultural unity. Here he explores the spiritual basis of the Greater East Asia Co-Prosperity Sphere. He suggests that Japan is the nation most representative of Asia and therefore is suited to leadership. This excerpt is

SPIRITUAL BASIS OF ASIAN REVOLUTION AND UNITY 37
from *The Establishment of the Greater East Asian Order* (1943),
(Dai Tōa Chitsujo kensetsu).

THE concept of the New Order in East Asia was not just a military slogan suggested following the China Incident, but was grasped firmly by several leaders at the time of the Meiji Restoration. It continued for three generations and has become the basis for Japan's continental policy. Finally we have come to see its realization during the Greater East Asia war. What area is meant by the so-called Greater East Asia Sphere? What various developments appear among the peoples and cultures of this sphere? What kind of relationship will Japan establish with the Greater East Asia Sphere? I have stated my beliefs concerning these problems. In my two volumes the phrase 'establishment of a New Order in Greater East Asia' is not just a simple slogan, but clearly includes the most serious life problems and real issues for the peoples of Japan and East Asia.

... Now we turn to Asia's poet-laureate, the Indian patriot Rabindranath Tagore, who twenty years ago was a special correspondent for *The Manchester Guardian.* Japan had unhesitatingly announced publicly her intention to become natural leader of Asia. I remember the following statement: 'There is nothing strange about Japan thinking she will really lead Asia and lead it as her national mission. The various nations of Europe, in spite of many differences among them, in their basic ideas and approach are one nation .... Take the Mongolian race who attacked part of the European continent, for example. In that case all Europe as a whole cooperated in repelling them. Japan cannot be isolated. Japan alone competing with the combined strength of the European powers would invite untoward disaster. It would be difficult for Japan to seek true allies in Europe. But it is natural that Japan seek those allies in Asia. Is there something strange in Japan cooperating with India, which will probably gain freedom, or with free Thailand or free China? Asia rising in cooperation — even excluding the cooperation of related peoples of West Asia — would be a union with real strength. Something like this will probably be natural in the distant future. There will no doubt be numerous difficulties

38   THE IDEAL CONCEPTUALIZED

in realizing it. Differences of language and problems in communication may become obstacles. Going from Thailand to Tokyo there are blood ties. From India to Japan there are connections through religion, art, and philosophy.' Even the most ardent anti-Japanese Chinese in the depths of their hearts would affirm the sincerity which imbued Tagore's words.

... There are some Japanese scholars who, fascinated by the richness of the Asian cultural area and by the diverse conditions of the various Asian nations, deny the existence of the East or Eastern culture. That is to say, in the West there has unfolded a single history, and a single culture has developed. Consequently, a single world has been formed. In the East this has never occurred. For the East, Eastern history has not had the same meaning as Western history; rather there has been only the history of various Eastern peoples: Chinese history, Indian history, Japanese history, etc. Consequently, some assert there is no world or culture which can be called Eastern. Thus the advocacy of 'one Asia' is called formalism and is ridiculed on grounds of naiveté. They say Asia with its varied political situations, diverse productive conditions and varied cultures can never be united, but will always be more pluralistic.

But of those who advocate one Asia none ignore the apparent complexity of Asia. The actual diversity of Asia is not something to be pointed to but is a fact which we hear and see... Asia's differences are recognized by everyone. It is only when we inquire about whether or not there is 'something Asian' lurking behind these distinctions that the theory of differences arises. For this reason the attitude of seeing the many as many, or stressing the many distinctions, and not endeavouring to deeply understand, should itself be called naiveté.

... In the Orient, through ideological and cultural interchange between China and India we saw the establishment of Eastern culture long ago in the T'ang period, and then in the Sung period Chu Hsi philosophy was born, and just as the Roman Pope was arbiter of the European spiritual world in the middle ages, so the Sung philosophy controlled the spiritual sphere of all Asia except India. The various Sung philosophies of Kegon, Zen, Confucius and Lao Tsu were a spiritual melting pot of Sung Confucianism and formed a great eclectic philosophical system. This was the leading principle of Asia everywhere. In our country too since the Kamakura Shogunate Chu Hsi controlled the spiritual sphere ....

...In recent times, when most Asian nations became Western colonies or semi-colonies Oriental culture was demeaned and history was neglected. Nations were deliberately left disrupted and in confrontation. This disruption naturally prevented Asian nations from understanding and recognizing each other... Intelligentsia in Asian nations were eager to learn about Europe and America but they came to have little or no concern for Asian nations....

...Europe and America have despised Asia. Therefore those who read their books came to think there was nothing good in Asia. Europe and America don't want Asia to awaken. Therefore they inhibit healthy thought about ancient times or reminiscences of national heroes. They are afraid that Asian nations will unite. Therefore they prevent [Asia] from remembering a common culture and ideology. This disruption itself was created by Europe and America. It was Japan's victory in the Russo-Japanese War that awakened from a long night's sleep this humiliated, disrupted, miserable, and numb Asia. Since then the dark night enveloping Asia has begun to break and the light of hope has shown from the East. The political awakening of the aspiration to be independent people free from European bondage rose suddenly in the peoples from Turkey to Annam. This awakening soon became a revolutionary passion and waves of the independence movements gradually gained strength and finally covered all of Asia. Who is to say that there is not oneness in Asia? Now Asia is on the verge of overturning European control everywhere and is about to destroy corrupt indigenous social traditions and to shed blood in building independent nations. First and foremost Asia now possesses a common political destiny. Needless to say a common political destiny can be a strong bond to unite Asian people. Besides, Asia obviously has something in common in a basic world view, a way of looking at the world and at life, and a way of understanding and interpreting them and living according to this understanding and interpretation, in spite of numerous superficial differences....

...Most of the Orient, as has been said, was enslaved by modern Europe, and its culture was degraded, its spirit became very corrupt, and the ancient spontaneity and soundness were lost.

But we cannot deny the Oriental spirit itself because of that. The traditional spirit of the Orient is very noble in essence. The revival of Asia means not only political independence from Europe but also resurrection of the ancient glory of the spiritual life of Asian peoples. Japan is fighting for this solemn mission, because the goodness and nobility of the Orient actually course with vitality through Japan, although they have become relics of past greatness in their native countries. It is unnecessary to repeat that Japan has long been learning many things from China and India. Our present spirit has long been cultivated by absorbing the thought and culture of both China and India. The thought and culture of the two nations, which have been the great centers of the East, are incorporated and integrated in our spirit.... Because we have been absorbing China and India into our lives through a thousand years of experience, Japan's spirit can be properly understood only as the Oriental spirit. Therefore those who reject the existence of the Orient or Oriental culture are self-neglecting people who cannot grasp or explore within themselves the most vital essence of Asia. In addition Japan called all Asia the 'three nations'... and has been constantly operating in this framework.... The daily life of the Japanese people is based on the consciousness of 'three nations,' or Orient-consciousness. Although China virtually ignored Japan, and India did not even know of the existence of Japan, our nation alone absorbed China and India within it.... This suggested that the day would come when Japan would bear the great mission and responsibility for Asia. That day has finally come. The spiritual basis for the New Order in East Asia about to be realized must be the 'three nations' spirit which has been inculcated through the experience of a thousand years. The Greater East Asia Co-Prosperity Sphere is the objectification or embodiment of the 'three nations' spirit.

8
Strategic Imperatives
in the Pacific

WILLIAM Magistretti did graduate work in Oriental Languages and Political Science at the University of California. In the only selection by an American in this section, Mr. Magistretti discusses immediate pre-war concepts of Greater East Asia, citing Western and Japanese authors. This is from an article in *Pacific Affairs*, vol. 14, 1941. Mr. Magistretti invokes the arguments of several Japanese military men and industrialists.

JAPANESE expansion toward the South Seas cannot be treated as wholly subsidiary to Germany's war on Britain. Obviously, Japan and Germany are working together; but it should be kept in mind that a Japanese move into the South Seas is not entirely contingent on a German victory over Britain. Rather it would seem that given sufficient confusion in Europe, enough to engage most of Britain's attention and most of the aid that America can give to Britain, Japan will move from the advanced bases which she has already established, to extend her area of occupation and penetration independently of Germany.

Although such movements should be considered from the standpoint of military and naval strategy, most of the material available to the civilian public reiterates only two arguments: 1) Japan's navy is inferior to the combined forces of the United States and Britain, and 2) her army has been severely strained by the protracted warfare in China; United States and British naval forces based in Singapore could readily cut Japan's line of communication. These arguments invite the obvious comment that Japan has been allowed to use diplomacy in very successful preparation for strategic advances, as in Indochina. With no risk whatever and almost no fighting Japan has established a semicircle of bases from Thailand to Saigon to Hainan to Takao (at the southern tip of Formosa) to Parao [sic] in the Japanese Mandated Islands. A possible extension of this semicircle is to Davao in the Philippines, where there is a very strong Japanese colony. The mere existence of this semicircle of bases ought to discount a great deal of the confidence of those who claim that it would be easy to cut Japan's line of communication. It may be that, on the contrary, it is now Japan that is in a good position to cut American lines of communication. It should be remembered that Japan's navy has scarcely felt the strain of the war in China and that Japan, like the other Axis nations, has a preponderance of light ships well designed for raiding.

These facts, and especially the complex movement of Japanese diplomatic and military action bear out the judgement that Japan's rapidly growing interest in a South Seas policy is more than the artificial production of a propaganda campaign. While the southward trend has undoubtedly been enhanced by the need to provide compensation for lack of success in the campaign in China and reinforced by the temptation to take advantage of the war in Europe, it also derives in part from the old and well established tradition that Japan has two major fields of expansion: one of the continent of Asia, in China and Siberia, and one in the South Pacific, at the expense of the colonial empires and interests of Great Britain, America, France, and Holland. These two fields are not necessarily alternative to and exclusive of each other. They may be exploited in combination. Thus Captain Otaku of the Imperial Japanese Navy in the October, 1940 issue of *Yuben*, after a historical summary of the Japanese, closes his eight page article with the following passage:

The spirit of embarking on great adventures abroad has been a characteristic tradition flowing in the blood of the Japanese people

STRATEGIC IMPERATIVES IN THE PACIFIC 43

from ancient times. Our Japanese race, raised in the temperate zone, is capable of expanding to either the north or south. It might be said that we are all like a mobile fleet which can be active in all quarters when necessity dictates. Cannot we thus assent to the intimate relation between Japanese overseas expansion and the Imperial Navy? I believe that this is a time for our seafaring nation, in view of the gravity of the present situation, to gather together more strongly and overcome our present difficulties by becoming a ball of steel and fire; that this is the time to establish the Greater East Asia Bloc and, in conjunction with the Continental Policy, advance in the direction of southward expansion.

It will be noticed that in this passage Captain Otaku, though speaking of Japan's ability to expand either to the north or to the south, also believes that Japan can be 'active in all quarters' and can combine southward expansion with the continental policy. A month earlier, in *Gendai*, a naval officer of higher rank, Admiral Sokichi Takahashi, published a longer and more explicit article on 'Japan's Advance and the Southern Pacific'. In this he put forward the following arguments:

Japan, who has been appointed the leader of East Asia, cannot possibly tolerate the crafty Far Eastern policy [of the European nations and the United States]. What is meant by Japan's going forward and constructing a New Order in East Asia is the construction on an economic bloc with the linking of Japan, Manchukuo, and China as independent countries in name and fact, rather than as semi-colonies. It means, moreover, the inclusion in this bloc of all the Southern Pacific region — Netherlands India, French Indochina, the Philippines, etc. It means the drawing together of all the northern and southern peoples, saving them from the colonial exploitation of Europe and America in order to establish an Asia for the Asiatic races. The objective of the New Order in East Asia is the well-being of all races. In other words, one cannot omit the South Seas from the New Order in East Asia. Japan, Manchukuo, and China, alone, are not enough, and if the South Seas is not included our objective will not be attained. This is the reason why we early attached importance to the South Seas and advocated the South Seas expansion theory.

Later articles by Japanese leave no doubt of the importance of the south in the expansion policy of Japan as a whole. Koichiro Ishihara, president of the Ishihara Industrial Marine Transportation Co. may be more outspoken than others, but he is not unrepresentative of the ideas and purposes of Japanese industry and finance. In an article in *Gendai* for January, 1941, he writes that the key to the whole of the China Incident is the southern regions. 'Without applying her hand to this [South Seas expansion] it will definitely be impossible for Japan to carry on a protracted war. On the other hand, if only this problem is solved, there will be nothing at all to worry about and the people can be made to entertain large aspirations. This is absolutely necessary for the prosecution of the war. Therefore I hope that we shall march forward as soon as possible toward this objective.' Ishihara supports his 'argument for management of the Southern region' by adding that once the mutual prosperity bloc is set up, the 15 billion yen favourable export surplus reported by the European colonies in 1935 would be converted into a tremendous and stimulating increase in Japanese industry. Once the bloc is set up, he observes, the economy of the various European countries will become dependent upon it; but so long as Japan fails to carry out this policy, so long will she be the victim of indirect British and American strategems, as in the deposition of the oil output of Netherlands India.

An even more important point, according to Ishihara, is that the China Incident, now magnified into the 'East Asia mutual prosperity bloc,' cannot be rounded out so long as Japan must bow to England or America for one or more of her strategic materials. Such outspoken writing raises a question which is of obvious interest but which cannot be directly answered: how far are the views of Ishihara and men like him the views of those in power in Tokyo? Do they also feel that the whole future of the 'continental' movement into which Japan has been pouring men and money for nearly four years depends upon the success of a 'maritime' expansion, still to be accomplished, which will bring the South Seas region into the mutual prosperity bloc? There seems little doubt that when influential Japanese now say that this is a 'matter of life and death' they are not speaking for purposes of propaganda alone. To a country impoverished by protracted war, and hard pressed for foreign exchange to purchase the sinews of continued war, the sight of abundant war materials in a geographically accessible region must be supremely tempting.

Ishihara's opinion of Japan's ability to take over and operate the Borneo oil fields is interesting in this connection. Much has

STRATEGIC IMPERATIVES IN THE PACIFIC 45

been said and written, outside of Japan, about thorough preparations to blow up the oil wells in Netherlands India and Borneo should the Japanese Navy appear over the horizon. Ishihara, far from considering this much of a problem, claims that the Borneo fields are the shallowest in the world, so that new wells could be bored in about two or three months, or a year at the most. This gives a special significance to the belief, which is very generally held, that Japan already has in hand a year's supply of oil. Ishihara even maintains that it would be extremely difficult to destroy all the wells in Borneo and Netherlands India.

Throughout the Japanese articles that have here been cited, there is manifested an unmistakeable attitude which the press outside of Japan has only recently begun to reflect: the attitude that 'the die is cast.' This attitude appears to be connected with the realization that expansion into the South Seas, far from being just an alternative to expansion in China, became inevitable from the very inception of the China Incident. This feeling appears to be reinforced by the fact that while Japan's commitments in China are now much too vast to be simply abandoned, all the expenditure in China has resulted in no satisfactory return flow of strategic materials. This again emphasizes the fact that while Japan's creeping movement toward the rich raw material areas of Netherlands India and Malaysia began to be ominously noticeable only after the outbreak of war in Europe, it was in fact inherent in Japan's steady extension of naval control over access to China from the very beginning of the 'land war' in China in 1937.

Japanese writers make much both of the 'righteousness' of their own expansion toward the South Seas and of the lack of righteousness of the present colonial owners of those regions. They point out, for instance, that the Dutch 'wrested' control of Netherlands India from the natives of the islands, and add that there is no time limit on the wresting process. Japanese writers now commonly regret the period of seclusion in Japan. They point out that prior to the Tokugawa seclusion Hideyoshi had some negotiations with the East Indies, while Nagamasa Yamada had established a high place for himself in Thailand. Some writers even claim a prior Japanese vested interest in the South Seas, under the argument that part of the racial stock of the Japanese was derived from the South Seas. It is not difficult to point out the logical inconsistency of an argument which both claims that there is no static point in history and at the same time lays claim to a region on the ground of racial descent. What is here significant, however, is not the faulty logic but rather the derivation of that logic from the feeling that Japan's foreign policy is geographically and racially predetermined.

In application and execution Japanese writers hold the view that the 'New World Order' will be composed of huge economic blocs. They place first the East Asiatic bloc, with Japan as the dominant power. Europe will form a bloc controlled by Germany. Soviet Russia will separately constitute a huge bloc. The continents of North and South America will form a bloc dominated by the United States. The last bloc will be that of Britain and her Commonwealth, deprived of influence on the European bloc but still formidable because of its widespread 'maritime' markets and sources of raw materials.

Under the title of 'The New Order in the Pacific' Hikomatsu Kamikawa defines in the August, 1940 *Nippon Hyōron* the following 'basic principles:' 1) construction of bloc or regional empires by the powerful races; 2) the granting of mutual autonomous independence to the weak and smaller races; 3) a world peace based on an inter-bloc balance of power, which will supersede the old racial or continental peace.

Kamikawa maintains that the tendency toward the emergence and establishment of these huge bloc-empires has long been evident. The European bloc will be the realization of the old Pan-European theory, with Germany and Italy as leaders and Germany the dominant power. The structure of the future Pacific bloc is not so simple. Kamikawa seems to think that since the Pacific region is not coterminous with a continent or continental area its fate may be to be divided between the Greater East Asia bloc, the American bloc, and the British Commonwealth of Nations. Thus the United States would dominate the Eastern Pacific and Japan the Western Pacific, with due allowance for Australia and New Zealand in the far South Pacific. The major problem of the New Order would be the disposal of the widespread Pacific Islands. The allotment of the French and Dutch possessions, and those of the British, should they be defeated, would present knotty problems for the 'Solomons' of the various blocs. The countries which would have a voice in the decision, according to Kamikawa, are Japan, Germany, Italy, America, and Britain.

The 'mutual autonomous independence' of the weaker and smaller races which Kamikawa lists as the second basic principle of the Far East is apparently to apply in the first instance to the Han race (the Chinese), and to the Indians. The Koreans, on the other hand, are overlooked, and so are the people of Formosa. This problem seems to be more realistically treated by Takanobu Murobushi, in his interesting book *A Prophecy for Japan*. Murobushi holds that the southern region, unlike the Asiatic continent, is very young and very new. Its peoples will therefore have to be guided in their early autonomous efforts. What would be more natural than that the dominant power in East Asia should guide them?

9
Japan as Economic Leader of Asia

TAKAHASHI Kamekichi, an economist, emphasized the idealism of Japan's position on the one hand and the insidious nature of Western capitalist-imperialism and propaganda on the other. He did not see any contradiction inherent in condemning Western imperialism and condoning Japan's expansion. Japan's Sphere, he rationalized, was justified as a peace-keeping mechanism in Asia. At the same time he admitted the Sphere was essential to Japan economically. Writing at the time of the creation of the Greater East Asia Ministry, he pointed to peace and stability as long-range goals of the Co-Prosperity Sphere and of immediate political, economic and strategic considerations. He viewed freedom of member nations within the Sphere as a major advantage. The excerpt here quoted is from *The Japan Times and Advertiser*, 2 November 1942.

SINCE Japan has determined to construct a Co-Prosperity Sphere in this part of the world, the Anglo-American nations, because of their own selfish designs, are deliberately disseminating fictitious information characterizing it as a deep-laid scheme to establish Japanese hegemony over Greater East Asia. They are purposely dissimulating the stern fact that Japan desires to evolve such a harmony in cooperation with each country of the sphere, because it is convinced in its mind that a mutual prosperity sphere cannot materialize unless its component units are permitted to play their legitimate parts for its development through an understanding of conjoint advantage with this country. In view of such a fundamental conception, it is obvious that the projected co-prosperous life aims at the creation of a new order in Greater East Asia for the common good and welfare of the entire region.

It is true that the realization of this objective is dependent on the solution of many problems arising out of the past colonial character of the southern countries. The first need is the organization of a new political and economic system in each country so as to stimulate the growth of regional consciousness. The next task would be to determine which nation should assume the leadership of the region. In this respect agreement shall have to be arrived at empowering the most developed and powerful nation with the authority to guide and advise the construction of the common prosperity fabric. The third problem requiring solution is the working out of an appropriate basis to accord each nation its just and proper place in terms of its intrinsic capability, economic potentiality, defence capacity and importance toward the maintenance and security of regional life.

Along with the solution of these problems, steps should be taken to construct the new order in Greater East Asia in such a manner that no difficulty would be experienced to make it fit in with the new order of the world now under development. This is necessary, because any scheme of setting up a new order in Greater East Asia, which is vast in area, cannot be considered separately from the world order. Whatever may be the final results of the current international hostilities, there is every reason to visualize that regional harmony will come to prevail in diverse parts of the universe. The white world is likely to have a common prosperity sphere in Europe and another in the Western Hemisphere. Also there may develop identical contiguities in other selected areas. But the point is that each of these spheres would naturally be of a different character, having varied duties to perform in order to suit the conditions of its racial, geographical, cultural, economic and strategic requirements. And the combination of these different Co-Prosperity Spheres will lead to the emergence of a new international order. This is the most important fact which should be borne in mind in promoting mutual prosperity in Greater East Asia.

No one can deny that Japan's position as a world Power entitles it to assume the leadership of Greater East Asia. Only with the assistance of this country can the southern nations reorganize their life to take their proper places in the Co-Prosperity Sphere. Now that the situation in this part of the globe has undergone a categorical alteration, and that Japan has taken steps to accelerate the fruition of mutual prosperity and harmony, it is evident that this country is propagating a new order as a contributive unit of the envisioned reformed international structure.

The old order of the world based on capitalist-imperialism is no longer tenable. National structures and political and economic systems require readjustment to create conditions for the speedy upsurgence of a new way of life divorced from capitalist-imperialist domination, but based on regional interdependence and international goodwill. In the past, scores of large and small nations, maintaining their independence on an equal footing, controlled the movement of international life. Though restricted by international treaties, each of them enjoyed the freedom of integrity and was quite at liberty to enter into arrangements detrimental to its neighbours. In Europe the existence of a number of small nations of that nature affected the equilibrium of the European order. In Greater East Asia, too, the perpetuation of alien dominations over the southern nations unnecessarily obstructed the natural growth of a greater East Asiatic order. As a reaction to these unnatural conditions, Japan has been compelled to shoulder the responsibility of creating a new order in Greater East Asia based on co-existence and co-prosperity while a similar policy is being pursued by Italy and Germany to establish a new order in Europe. It is, therefore, clear that the Italo-German new order in Europe and that of Japan in Greater East Aisa aim at liquidating the interference of an outside capitalist imperialism, so that the units of their Co-Prosperity Spheres would reciprocate mutual reliance for common benefit and security.

Broadly speaking, under the present changed conditions it seems an impractical proposition to allow a small independent nation to enjoy the right of overriding the policy of mutual reliance on a powerful neighbour State. If the latter has to depend on the economic resource and strategical points of the former for the maintenance of security and self-existence, it cannot possibly remain silent when an outside nation, coming from a different area, tries to control that small country. In that event, its national defence becomes valueless, especially when the destructive power of the modern weapons of war is tremendous. And if war breaks out, it at once becomes a total war, requiring the exertion of total energy on the part of either side. On account of this fact, it is just and proper that a world Power, standing firm on the principle of geographical propinquity, should demand that its neighbouring countries form a bloc of common existence with it to reciprocate mutual prosperity and security. Japan's present objective in Greater East Asia is fully in accord with this reasonable demand.

Quite apart from the political, economic and strategic questions, the construction of a Co-Prosperity Sphere in Greater East Asia is justified from the standpoint of maintaining the peace and stability of the region, thereby contributing to the peace and stability of the world. It must be remembered that, owing to the domination of Greater East Asia by Britain, America, and the Netherlands, and due to the imposition of third Power interference in the affairs of China, no durable peace and stability were established in this part of the world. Even Japan, which resented such an outside control, could not escape from its injurious effects. Because of this historic fact, Japan, having secured an advantageous position, is endeavouring its best to promote regional harmony in order to restore genuine tranquility without alien intervention. There can be nothing wrong in it, since it is conducive to the interest of the whole of Greater East Asia and then to the world.

It is a recognized fact that Japan in the past was greatly dependent on Britain and the United States to preserve its economic set-up. When a nation depends on another country economically, it is unavoidably subjected to more or less political restrictions. This is the reason why Japan had to put up with the political pressure of Britain and the United States disguised as economic blockade up to the days immediately preceding the outbreak of the current Pacific War. Up to that time, East Asia was not a full-fledged independent unit both politically and economically; in fact, it was subordinate to Britain, America and their allies. Now that East Asia has recovered its political and economic independence, it is obvious that Japan should try its best to reinforce that freedom by establishing a mutual prosperity sphere embracing Greater East Asia.

Although steps are being taken to strengthen the structure of the newly acquired emancipation of Greater East Asia, difficulties are being experienced to recast the various alien political, economic, racial, and cultural conceptions which have become stabilized owing to its long association with Western nations. Even in Japan, Western notions have not yet been fully eradicated, despite the fact that energetic efforts are being made to free it from such undesirable beliefs. So far as Greater East Asia is concerned, it is highly imperative that the Occidental way of thinking should be eliminated to regenerate Asianism in its true and vigorous form.

As for Japan it is gratifying to note that Western conceptions have substantially lost their brilliance due to the national determination to follow the course of the idealized past as a means of attaining a new Asiatic homogeneity in Greater East Asia. Still, there are some Japanese who are paying attention to Western conceptions. Some of them seem to think that certain phases of Japan's wartime economy have been modelled on the German pattern. As an instance they point out the price control system. That their view is incorrect is evident from the fact that price control has been in effect in Japan for a number of years, and that it formulated such a measure in conformity with the actual domestic conditions. The revised price control system now in operation has been enforced to suit the local conditions, and as such it cannot be compared to that of Germany which is different in character, having different obligations to meet.

Until the outbreak of the Manchurian Incident, Japan's political structure was under the influence of the 'democratic' liberalism of the West. Studious attention was paid to propagate parliamentarianism, while the bureaucratic tendencies of the government officials reflected the similar inclinations of the Anglo-American nations. But with the commencement of the Manchurian Incident, a new reawakening came to pervade the country, and as a result, national agitations were launched to build a new political structure compatible with the national ideologies and traditions. At the same time, far-sighted leaders and officials of the country urged the need of revamping the administrative system. Subsequently, when the China Affair ensued, a change became noticeable in the political and administrative set-ups, and

JAPAN AS ECONOMIC LEADER OF ASIA 53

with the protraction of it, Japan initiated steps to overhaul its political machinery and administration policies — steps which became concrete realities soon after the start of the Pacific War on December 8, 1941. Now a national single-dimensional politics and a one-way administrative system have been organized based on the principle of service to the State, which is in consonance with the political tradition and the spirit of the Japanese nation. Thus, Japan has eradicated the long-standing political and administrative influences of the West which found their way into the country in the Meiji era.

Since the national fabric of Japan is no longer dependent on any Western method for technique, albeit political, economic, or industrial, it is high time that it should create conditions under which it can independently judge the welfare of Greater East Asia and implement measures to that end. It is understood that, for the purpose of ushering in the era of Greater East Asia Co-Prosperity Sphere, the various committees of the National Policy Research Institute are studying all aspects of the economic, political and cultural problems affecting the entire region. As the political and economic structure of one unit is different from another, it is not possible to evolve a single type system applicable to all countries within the sphere. The same is the case with regard to the promotion of culture. Yet it is essential that the whole sphere must be reorganized into a single body as an organic unit.

Judging from this feature of Greater East Asia, it would be quite proper to evolve a complex system to suit the conditions of each nation. Nevertheless, unification remains the basic requirement for the smooth functioning of the Co-Prosperity Sphere, because such an objective can never be realized if different peoples were allowed to act freely without any restraint. Co-ordinated control is particularly necessary for attaining an economic anarchy; but it should be judiciously worked out in gradual stages to enable the southern countries to revise their respective economic systems, so that they would not feel any sudden reaction.

As the life of the Co-Prosperity Sphere is dependent on having highly geared defence organizations, it is vitally important that rigid collaboration should be maintained among the different defence structures with the main object of forming a Greater East Asian Defence structure under the aegis of Japan. In respect of international trade, production, distribution of industries, money and banking and diplomatic affairs, mixed control should be enforced; that is, there should exist a complete unity of purpose so far as the maintenance of co-existence and co-prosperity are concerned, and outside this limit each component nation should be given the privilege to shape its policies in the manner it thinks fit. For instance, certain kinds of industries and portions of international trade, material distribution and money and banking would come under the category of common control, while other arrangements would be left at the choice of the units themselves. In diplomacy, a common policy must be followed for the security of the Co-Prosperity Sphere, but beyond that the individual nations should be left free to handle their own diplomatic affairs in order to promote their international intercourse as member-States of the world order.

To Japan the Co-Prosperity Sphere represents its lifeline. Its self-existence is dependent on effecting good-neighbourly relations with the countries of Greater East Asia. That is why, in propagating the objective of co-prosperity, it does not entertain the ambition to become the ruling power of the region; instead, it desires to solemnize lasting partnership with it, expecting that Greater East Asia, under a new mutual reliance and cooperative order, would flourish peacefully without any outside interference, contributing at the same time its rightful share to the new world order, designed to restore international tranquility and stability on a durable footing.

PART II
Government Plans

1
Army and Navy Position Papers

WITHIN the Navy during the 1930s there were a number of research committees created to study various problems of national policy. Composed of military men, civilian authorities and scholars, these committees prepared position papers which in many cases influenced official policy decisions. Some of these Navy committees were notable for their relatively early concern with South-East Asia, by contrast with the Army's traditional preoccupation with Manchuria and north China as bulwarks against Russia. Beginning in 1936 the Navy committees began to insist on the signal importance of South-East Asia as a source of critical resources. The Navy's influence in drawing the Army's attention to South-East Asia is apparent in three documents here from 1936: Navy Headquarters' 'General Principles of National Policy' in April, followed by the 30 June statement by Army General Staff Headquarters and the 7 August formulation of national policy by the Five Ministers' Conference. This latter document shows South-East Asia assuming a place officially for the first time as an area of projected Japanese development and concern.

In a fourth document included here prepared by the Navy National Policy Research Committee under Yatsugi Kazuo the Navy again takes the lead in 'Summary Draft of a Policy toward the South'. The first three documents are from *Gendai shi shiryō*

(Materials on modern history), vol. 8, *Nittchū sensō* (Sino-Japanese war), vol.1. The fourth document is from the collection of Navy documents at the Daitō Bunka Daigaku's Tōyō Kenkyūjo, Supplementary, G., a copy of which is also in the Defence Agency's War History Library.

a. *General Principles of National Policy*

Navy Headquarters   about April 1936

The general principles of Japan's national policy are to expand the national government internally, and externally to ensure Japan's position on the continent. At the same time we will adopt as basic policy the development of the Southern areas and, planning the expansion of national power and national rights, establish peace in East Asia, advance the welfare of the people, and completely achieve a position as stabilizing power in East Asia.

Foreign Policy
1. Unification of formulation of foreign policy and its execution

The execution of the present national defence policy should be the keynote, based on the above-mentioned general principles of national policy. The essence of Japan's foreign policy must be to formulate various necessary policies autonomously and plan the expansion of our increasingly purposeful national destiny according to the world situation. Accordingly, to realize this we must centralize Japan's national policy. It is important to make it consistent. At the same time we should be careful not to stimulate the world powers unreasonably so as not to force them to use their power too early or to induce a situation forcing the world powers to unite against us.

2. Fundamental policy toward nations in an important relationship to us

(1) *toward Manchukuo*

Manchukuo, with the structure of an independent nation and the reality of an indivisible relationship with Japan, will be nurtured and fostered and, while having it achieve a self-supporting status economically, we will implant Japan's real economic power in both military preparedness and the economy and together strive to attain cooperative defence and cooperative existence.

(2) *toward China*

Through the combined mutual help of the three nations — Japan, Manchukuo and China, whose focus is Japan — the keynote should be to secure the stabilization of the area and to plan its development.

For attaining the above objective first of all we must have China recognize our three principles toward China and implement them. We should supervise and lead their implementation with both justice and mercy, in the sense of co-existence and co-prosperity. We should give economic and technical aid at the appropriate time and support their self-reliant regeneration. At the same time we should plan expansion of our power. Finally, we should induce them to be friendly, relying completely on Japan.

Regarding north China's five provinces and Inner Mongolia we should aim to make them special regions under Chinese sovereignty, which will facilitate the reinforcement of defence against Russia and economic development for both Japan and Manchuria. We will guide the government of China and local governments and have them take measures according to the real situation for completion of autonomous self-government. But in implementation we should not coerce them forcibly but progress by peaceful means.

China's traditional policy of controlling barbarians with barbarians, and the world powers' doubts about our continental policy may interfere with the implementation of our policy toward China or encourage Europe and America to present a united front against Japan. From the above consideration our policy should follow justice completely, and we should be careful not to provide an excuse for third powers to intervene. It is necessary to take measures to make the world powers understand our real intention — that we seek to ensure necessary and appropriate already-attained rights and interests and economic development, for the existence of Japan.

(3) *toward countries in the Southern areas*

The Southern countries are the areas we should regard as most important for strengthening our national defence and solving the population problem and economic development. The administration of this area is necessary to complete our policies toward Manchuria, China and Russia. That means it is our country's inevitable mission to expand our power, based on the Imperial spirit, in the Southern area, and to improve the peoples' welfare and realize co-existence and co-prosperity. For this Japan will devise the necessary agencies and discuss and establish unified means, and reinforce the administration of Taiwan and the trust territories. At the same time, regarding foreign countries, we plan to advance gradually in both areas, colonial migration and the economy. On the other hand, we should always be carefully prepared for pressure and intervention by Britain, the U.S. and Holland, which we should naturally anticipate. We must complete preparing our strength for any eventuality.

(4) *toward Russia*

In order to restrain Russia's advance in the Far East we should make necessary military preparations. At the same time we will determine appropriate limits for our administration on the continent. As the basic principle we should adopt a policy of active offence. For this we will be strictly watchful and on guard for Russia's policy of communization. We will take necessary measures to prevent it. At the same time we will improve the peaceful solutions we have been planning, and try actively to establish a friendly relationship.

(5) *toward Britain*

We will watch and be on strict guard against British maneuvers to bring pressure on Japan, using world power, especially America, Russia and China. At the same time we plan to advance our power as much as possible, utilizing the delicate political situation in each colonial area, and also making use of the unguarded movements of British rights and interests in East Asia. As for British possessions, we will form a close economic and cultural relationship in order to control Britain's anti-Japanese policy.

(6) *toward the United States*

In order to resist traditional American policy in the Far East we will make appropriate military preparations and we will get them to recognize our status in East Asia. At the same time we will try to establish a friendly relationship on the basis of a mutually dependent economic relationship.

b. General Principles of National Defence Policy

Army General Staff Headquarters, Second Section

30 June, 1936

1. Our national policy is to establish our status as protector and leader of East Asia. To do this we must have the power to expunge the pressure of the white races in East Asia.
2. It is necessary to strengthen requisite military preparations, especially sea and air power, in order to resist the pressure of Russia and Britain. At the same time it is necessary to complete all preparations to endure a war in the region of north China and Manchuria.
3. First we will devote all our strength to making Russia surrender. As preparations for waging war are insufficient in various respects today, it will be extremely difficult to execute a war against Russia unless we maintain (good relations) with the United States and Britain, at least with America. Concerning strengthening our military preparedness we will try to lessen Russia's resistance efforts by diplomatic means.
4. When strengthening military preparations and preparing for long range war are nearly complete, we will begin an active project to get Russia to abandon the policy of offence in the Far East. We will try to attain this aim immediately. Therefore, we sincerely hope to achieve our aim without leading to war.
5. If Russia surrenders, we will form a friendly relationship with Russia at an appropriate time and expel the power of Britain from East Asia.
6. Friendship between Japan and China is the key to administering East Asia, and the restructuring of China is our mission. However, it will be difficult to realize without sufficient power against the pressure of the white races. For war against Russia the political project in China should now be limited in scope to maintaining friendly relations with Britain and the United States, especially with the United States, as in other projects in the Southern area. During this time we will devote our energies to basic preparations for building a new China. When preparations to wage war in the region of Japan, Manchukuo, and north China have been made and Russia surrenders, we will begin the active project officially.

7. If Russia and Britain surrender, it will be an appropriate time to begin the basis of friendship between Japan and China. That means we will lead and cooperate with East Asian nations. We will plan a resurgent development of strength and prepare for a great decisive war against the United States.

c. *Fundamentals of National Policy*

Five Ministers' Conference   7 August, 1936

1. The nation should be administered according to justice. Domestically we will strengthen the foundation of the nation and externally we will expand our national destiny. Japan should be the stabilizing power in East Asia nominally and actually. Securing peace in East Asia, we will contribute to the peace and welfare of the human race. So the keynote should be to realize the ideal of the foundation of the nation. In view of the situation of Japan domestically and externally, the basic policy Japan should establish is to secure the position of Japan on the East Asiatic continent in both diplomacy and national defence, and at the same time to advance and develop in the Southern area. The fundamentals and general principles are based on the following:

(1) Realizing the spirit of the Imperial Way, we will avoid a political policy of world conquest and share pleasure and happiness mutually through mutual co-existence and co-prosperity. Our spirit of leadership should always be consistent with the development of political policies.

(2) We will strengthen military preparations for national defence necessary for peace and stability of the nation, protect its development, and secure Japan's position, which should be as stabilizing power in East Asia nominally and actually.

(3) We anticipate the sound development of Manchukuo, stability and solidarity of the national defence of Japan and Manchukuo, and removal of the threat of northern Russia. At the same time we will achieve a close tie between the three countries — Japan, Manchukuo and China for preparations against Britain and the United States. Our policy of economic development should be the keynote of political policy toward

the continent. Therefore in implementing it we will pay attention to friendly relations with the world powers.

(4) We plan to develop nationally and economically *vis-à-vis* the Southern area, especially the outer Southern area, avoiding stimulation of other countries as much as possible. We plan to expand our power by gradual peaceful means. With the development of Manchukuo we expect to strengthen our national power.

2. With the basic national policies above as the keynote, we expect to unify and devise domestic and foreign policies to regenerate the national government in response to the present situation.

(1) Regarding devising military preparedness for national defence:

(a) the Army's military preparations should be directed at resisting the armed strength Russia could use in the Far East. We will particularly improve our armed strength in Manchukuo and Korea in order to launch a major attack at the outbreak of war against the armed strength of Russia in the Far East.

(b) concerning the Navy's military preparations we will improve and achieve armed strength sufficient to ensure naval supremacy in the Western Pacific against the United States Navy.

(c) the first essential of our diplomatic policy is to realize our fundamental national policy satisfactorily. Coordinating and improving this, the military will devote itself to supporting them domestically in order for its activities to develop advantageously and satisfactorily. We will avoid superficial projects.

3. We will take suitable measures regarding the following items in order to revise and improve political and administrative organization and to establish financial and economic policies, having other administrative arrangements facilitate our fundamental national policy.

a. We will guide and unify public opinion in Japan and strengthen the peoples' readiness to solve the crisis situation.

b. We will suitably improve administrative organization and economic organization in order to promote essential industry and important trade for implementing national policy.

c. We will take suitable measures for stabilizing the people's livelihood, developing the physical strength of the people, and making the peoples' thought sound.

d. We will take suitable measures for the development of air and sea enterprises.

e. We will promote the establishment of self-sufficiency in important resources and materials essential for national defence and industry.

f. We will strengthen preparation for information and propaganda organizations, and at the same time create diplomatic organs and activate diplomatic functions and cultural development externally.

d. *Summary Draft of a Policy for the South*

Navy National Policy Research Committee   April, 1939

1. Relationship between the China Incident and Administration of the Southern Area.

Predicated on the China Incident, while the New Order in East Asia is being constructed, administration of the Southern area should be developed increasingly as part of it. The points we should carry out now are the following:

    a. securing materials necessary to promote productive capacity;

    b. promoting the maintenance of Japanese enterprises in the Southern area;

    c. promoting exports to the Southern area; controlling organization of trade to the Southern area;

    d. promoting the project for overseas Chinese in the Southern area;

    e. promoting friendship with each country in the Southern area.

2. Basic Policy of Economic Administration

We should promote industries in each region under our guidance, taking into consideration the whole economic sphere under Japanese guidance.

The outline of these enterprises is as follows:

    a. to promote necessary and appropriate industries in the Philippines, Siam, Netherlands Indies, Malaya, etc.;

    b. to make efforts to develop mines and smelting in Japan as much as possible;

    c. to make efforts for the development of agricultural production in the Philippines, Siam, Sumatra and the Celebes, etc.;

d. to develop undeveloped areas such as New Guinea, Mindanao, Borneo, etc.; At the same time to promote utilization and development of forests in the Philippines, Borneo, Celebes, New Guinea, etc.;

e. to develop fisheries increasingly;

f. to try to advance necessary techniques for development and utilization of resources in the Southern area and to arrange facilities relating to these;

g. to make an effort to foster regional commercial rights which would replace overseas Chinese in the Philippines, Siam, French Indo-China, Malaya, Netherlands Indies, etc.;

h. to develop our marine industries increasingly in the Southern area;

i. to extend our air routes in the Southern area immediately.

3. Political Policy

The political points we should note and for which we should work in the Southern area are as follows:

a. promotion of preparatory projects aimed at driving out British and French political and economic power in the future from the Southern area (corrected by the Chief of the eighth section to read: Promotion of research and investigation on French and British political and economic power as follows:) Concrete policies for this are as follows: (this sentence crossed out in eighth section correction)

(1) examination of the real power of Britain and France;

(2) gaining complete recognition of the native peoples of Japan's real power;

(3) conciliating the Muslims in the Southern Area;

(4) promotion and guidance for advancement and self-awareness of native peoples;

b. making an effort in the project of having the Dutch rely on Japan. For this we should conclude a cultural agreement or a non-aggression treaty, or approach them economically in buying products of the Dutch East Indies;

c. making a gesture toward giving sufficient support out of good will for Philippine independence (corrected to: taking an appropriate attitude out of good will for Philippine independence);

d. sympathizing with the policy of 'Siam for the Siamese' and supporting them if necessary (according to necessity);

e. making an effort to mitigate or abolish every anti-Japanese restriction;

f. trying to increase emigration to Southern countries as much as possible;

g. examining thoroughly the real situation of the overseas Chinese, and at the same time carrying out a conciliatory policy toward them;

h. regulating speech and actions which terrify the Dutch and Southern area unreasonably;

i. considering measures to utilize Catholics in the Southern area.

4. Cultural Administration Policy

Our main aim is good neighbourliness and co-prosperity, so it is important to have mutual familiarity and development of our cultures. This point is the greatest lag today. It is impossible to succeed in one day. It will require continuous efforts through the following policies:

a. introducing the true Japan by means of documents, films, sports, inviting tourists, and good will exchanges;

b. re-educating the Japanese people in the Southern area with the chief aim of appropriate activities in the countries they reside in, and at the same time completing the education of children of Japanese in the Southern area;

c. doing research relating to the humanities and physical sciences in the Southern area;

d. making an effort to foster young men who will be active in the Southern area in the future;

e. promoting friendship by academic research in these areas;

f. establishing and arranging cultural facilities for the endemic people;

g. making religious functionaries as active as possible;

h. devising a plan to invite foreign students (to Japan).

5. Expansion and Control of Facilities

Our facilities in the Southern area in every respect are presently very inadequate and their control is also very inadequate. At this time we should consider especially the following points:

a. expanding Foreign Ministry agencies in the Southern area, and at the same time trying to promote communication between each organ of government and the people in the Southern area;

b. making agencies for the Southern area — Taiwan Governor General's Office and South Seas Agency — exert themselves increasingly under the control of the central government;

c. expansion of diplomatic establishments in the Southern area:

(1) appointing ministerial rank people for consuls-general in Manila, Batavia, Hanoi and Singapore, and treating them appropriately for their rank;

(2) expanding and strengthening the organization of consuls-general in the Southern area. Posting people who have special knowledge so far as possible in and around the consuls-general in order to perform appropriate functions under the control of consuls-general;

d. raising legations in Holland (East Indies) and Siam to the status of embassy or posting ambassadorial rank people there and having them stay as long as possible;

e. having powerful civilians travel and stay in Manila, Bangkok, Singapore, Batavia, Amsterdam, etc.;

f. control and guidance, from the viewpoint of national policy, over powerful companies and banks concerned with the Southern area;

g. diffusion of banking facilities and guiding the people in industry by active protection. The government should support the above appropriately;

h. expansion and control of all research organs;

i. expansion and control of cultural friendship organs. For these agencies the government should seek the cooperation of civilians.

6. Arrangement of each facility and development of industry in Taiwan and the South Seas which will be the basis of advancement in the Southern area administration is very inadequate. Therefore it is necessary to promote these as much as possible to contribute to the development of the Southern area. The people of Okinawa prefecture constitute half the Japanese people involved in development of the Southern area. Consequently governors of that prefecture should be appointed by special order who have plans for administration of the Southern area. It is necessary to pay more attention to guiding that prefecture.

2
Konoye on The New Order in East Asia

PREMIER Konoye Fumimaro on 22 December, 1938 proclaimed The New Order in East Asia. The three-time premier has become the focus of diverse interpretations regarding his posture *vis-à-vis* the military in the years just prior to the Pacific War. Here Premier Konoye, in proclaiming the New Order, enunciated his principles for solution of the 'China Incident'. The New Order was a construct part way along a scale ascending in scope between the East Asia Cooperative Body and East Asia Co-Existence Sphere on the one hand and the Greater East Asia Co-Prosperity Sphere on the other. The New Order embraced Japan, Manchukuo and China, but not yet any of South-East Asia. Konoye's primary concerns were for security (against communism) and access to natural resources. This version of his proclamation comes from *The Japan Times*, 23 December 1938.

THE Japanese Government are resolved, as has been clearly set forth in their two previous statements issued this year, to carry on the military operations for the complete extermination of the anti-Japanese Kuomintang Government, and at the same time to proceed with the work of establishing a New

KONOYE ON THE NEW ORDER IN EAST ASIA

Order in East Asia together with those far-sighted Chinese who share in our ideals and aspirations.

The spirit of renaissance is now sweeping over all parts of China and enthusiasm for reconstruction is mounting ever higher. The Japanese Government desire to make public their basic policy for adjusting the relations between Japan and China in order that their intentions may be thoroughly understood both at home and abroad.

Japan, China and Manchukuo will be united by the common aim of establishing the New Order in East Asia and of realizing the relationship of neighbourly amity, common defence against Communism, and economic cooperation. For that purpose it is necessary first of all that China should cast aside all narrow and prejudiced views belonging to the past and do away with the folly of anti-Japanism and resentment regarding Manchukuo. In other words, Japan frankly desires China to enter of her own will into complete diplomatic relations with Manchukuo.

The existence of the Comintern influence in East Asia cannot be tolerated. Japan therefore considers it an essential condition of the adjustment of the Sino-Japanese relations as [sic] there should be concluded an anti-Comintern agreement between the two countries in consonance with the spirit of the anti-Comintern agreement between Japan, Germany and Italy, and in order to ensure the full accomplishment of her purpose, Japan demands, in view of the actual circumstances prevailing in China, that Japanese troops be stationed, as an anti-Communist measure, at specified points during the time the said agreements is [sic] in force, and also that the Inner Mongolian region be designated as a special anti-Communist area.

As regards economic relations between the two countries, Japan does not intend to exercise an economic monopoly in China. Nor does she intend to demand of China to limit the interests of those third Powers who grasp the meaning of the New East Asia and are willing to act accordingly. Japan only seeks to render effective the cooperation and collaboration between the two countries. That is to say, Japan demands that China, in accordance with the principle of equality between the two countries, should recognize the freedom of residence and trade on the part of Japanese subjects in the interior of China, with a view to promoting the economic interests of both peoples;

and that, in the light of the historical and economic relations between the two nations, China should extend to Japan facilities for the development of China's natural resources, especially in the regions of North China and Inner Mongolia.

The above gives the general lines of what Japan demands of China. If the object of Japan in conducting the present vast military campaign be fully understood, it will be plain that what she seeks is neither territory nor indemnity for the costs of military operations. Japan demands only the minimum guarantee needed for the execution by China of her function as a participant in the establishment of the new order.

Japan not only respects the sovereignty of China, but she is prepared to give positive consideration to the questions of the abolition of extraterritoriality and of the rendition of the concessions and settlements matters which are necessary for the full independence of China.

3
Proclamation of the Greater East Asia Co-Prosperity Sphere

Matsuoka Yōsuke was Foreign Minister during the signing of the Tripartite Pact in Konoye's second cabinet. The Foreign Minister's proclamation of the Greater East Asia Co-Prosperity Sphere on 1 August, 1940 followed by a few days a radio address by Premier Konoye on the same subject. Matsuoka spoke of Japan's mission and principles, settlement of the China Incident, and of the core area of Japan, Manchuria and China. Matsuoka equated the Co-Prosperity Sphere with the New Order and 'Security Sphere.' But by August his concept of *lebensraum* had broadened to include the Netherlands Indies and French Indo-China. This proclamation appeared in the *Asahi Shimbun* 2 August 1940.

SUMMARY: 1. The world-wide declaration of the Imperial Way (proclaimed by Foreign Minister Matsuoka) is the mission of the Empire, and if this policy is realized all people and all nations will prosper.

2. Our present foreign policy is to establish the Greater East Asia Co-Prosperity Sphere, but the Greater East Asia Co-Prosperity Sphere is the same as the New Order in East Asia

Sphere or the Security Sphere, and its scope includes Southern areas such as the Netherlands Indies and French Indo-China; the three nations of Japan, Manchuria and China are one link.

3. The process of establishing the Greater East Asia Co-Prosperity Sphere — that is, the first step — is to avoid all obstacles, tangible or intangible, which attend completion of dealing with the China Incident.

'To strengthen cooperation with friendly nations which support the Greater East Asia Co-Prosperity Sphere we must push ahead to establish our nation's principles and mission,' he proclaimed.

Speech: 'I asserted that the mission of Japan is to proclaim the Imperial Way toward the world in international relations. I believe many nations depend on the Imperial Way. That is, our present foreign policy will aim at establishing the Greater East Asia Co-Prosperity Sphere, linking Japan, Manchuria and China based on the great spirit of the Imperial Way. Because of this we may begin the process of contributing to establishing world peace and proclaim the Imperial Way decisively; but I believe that our people can avoid all our struggles, tangible or intangible, underlying this process. Moreover, we must achieve the mission and principles of our nation which are imposed by heaven, through unswerving courage toward the cooperation of concerned friendly nations. There is no time to say more. To establish the foreign goals of Japan it is the distinctive foreign policy of the present cabinet to frame a policy so as to create friendly nations. This is not to say the previous cabinet had a policy of cooperating with cooperative nations regarding the handling of the China Incident, excluding opposing nations. But it is necessary that Japan must create as many friendly nations as possible in the present international situation by operating actively toward many powers. We are not trying to please everyone at once. I am certain that Japan cannot try to please everyone. I hope you will understand our unswerving non-commitment policy for the moment. It is natural to include French Indo-China and the Netherlands Indies in the Greater East Asia Co-Prosperity Sphere.'

4
The Greater East Asian Sphere of Common Prosperity

MANY Japanese undertook officially and semi-officially to explain and defend the Greater East Asia Sphere concept to the rest of the world. One such explanation was made by Arita Hachirō, a professional diplomat who served as Foreign Minister in the Hirota, Konoye, Hiranuma and Yonai cabinets. Mr. Arita argues in this selection that Japan's goals in East Asia have been misunderstood abroad and that, far from monopolizing East Asia economically as European powers have done in the past, Japan seeks through its economic bloc in Asia to promote mutual prosperity, security and ultimately world peace.

This excerpt is from *Contemporary Japan*, vol. X, no. 1, January, 1941.

CONSIDERABLE misunderstanding seems to have arisen abroad regarding Japan's project for the creation of a sphere of common prosperity in East Asia. It is generally charged that Japan has suddenly seized upon this plan as a means of establishing her exclusive control over East Asia and that within this sphere Japan alone shall enjoy all benefits by virtue of monopoly. The idea of spheres of common prosperity, however, is not a Japanese invention. Nor is it an expedient by which Japan aspired to monopolize this part of the world to the exclusion of all others .... The proposed greater East Asian sphere of common prosperity is the outgrowth of a complicated historical process which has been manifested upon a world-wide scale. The present form which this historical process is assuming in East Asia is something devoid of national selfishness, aiming as it does at the universal welfare of East Asia and ultimately at bringing the movement into accord with the spirit of universal brotherhood, which by the way lies at the very foundation of the Japanese nation.

For about a hundred years up to the turn of the present century, when the principle of free trade was at its peak ... if any nation adopted a protectionist policy in contradiction to the free trade policy of the Anglo-American Powers, it was ostracized and considered a heretic by advanced countries. For many decades the less-advanced nations were not permitted to close their doors to the economic influences of Great Britain and the United States, and as a result, their industries were prevented from growing and attaining further development, being held back by advanced countries under political as well as economic pressure despite their will to progress.

Subsequently, Great Britain and the United States found that their industrial power could no longer check the industrial progress of the newly-risen countries and discovered that their long-held position of supremacy was tottering. They then promptly abandoned ... the free trade principle, which they had up to then forced upon other nations as the highest doctrine of international commerce, and adopted a protective trade policy, their governments and scholars being apparently oblivious of their former attitude and regardless of their sudden *volte-face* ....

Only a country like Great Britain, however, is in a position to act regardless of whatever criticism may be directed against it, because it contains within its own Empire such a vast population and such inexhaustible natural resources ....

When the doctrines of freedom of communications and trade prevailed the world over, enabling men and goods to move from one country to another with comparative ease, regardless of the status of their countries, it was possible even for small nations ... to maintain a respectable existence side by side with the great

GREATER EAST ASIAN SPHERE OF COMMON PROSPERITY

Powers .... Now, however, that such doctrines have all but disappeared with the great Powers' closing or threatening to close their doors to others, small countries have no other choice left but to strive as best they can to form their own economic *blocs* or to found powerful states, lest their very existence be jeopardized. There can be no just criticism condemning this choice of the small countries.

Accordingly, if Japan is now devoting its efforts toward the formation of an economic sphere, comprising Japan, Manchukuo and China, allowing them at the same time to maintain independence, enjoy freedom and display their strong points ... these are but the natural outcome of the action of the great Powers themselves, which, having both abundant raw materials and thriving markets, have tended to drive these countries to extinction by their exclusion policies, both political and economic.

Even if all nations were to revert to the doctrine of free trade, it is hardly likely that the idea of establishing economic spheres or powerful states will die out in view of the prevailing world situation. The reason is that a group of nations has not yet outlived the practice of considering it a right to impose its own will upon countries which it considers have committed wrong by meting out drastic forms of economic pressure....

Because of the existence of the idea of economic pressure, which does not seem likely to disappear, the countries which are not economically self-dependent will quite naturally try to find ways and means of defending themselves in anticipation of some crisis and in order to escape coercion in the form of economic pressure. They will consider the formation of economic *blocs* as a measure of economic self-defence, or the establishment of powerful states which can be self-sufficient both in times of peace and war.... There is no reason why economic self-defence, which is the same [as military self-defence] in its ultimate effects, should not be acknowledged as proper in international relations. If world peace is to be maintained, it is necessary, first of all, that the above principle be fully and frankly recognized. Secondly, since the confused existence of extremely large and extremely small nations is far from making for peace, there should be established a fixed number of regional units which are equally matched in military and economic power, so that no one can threaten the security of another. Such a happy state of affairs constitutes the very basis for the justification of the establishment of economic *blocs*....

When John Hay advocated the Open Door and Equal Opportunity, Great Britain and the United States themselves had not closed their doors to foreign goods. Sufficient justification existed, therefore, in the demand that China be opened equally to the trade of all nations. Economic nationalism, however, is now rampant throughout the world, with not the slightest vestiges of the free trade principle remaining. Self-sufficient countries like Great Britain, the United States and others keep their doors closed or are ready to close them to other nations. Thus a country like Japan, which is unable to obtain raw materials and markets within its own boundaries, has no other choice than to turn to nearby China in order to acquire... a market for Japanese goods and natural resources in which that country abounds, but which have not yet been fully developed. But even then, the Anglo-American Powers, although they have already discarded the free trade principle themselves, persist quite illogically in demanding that China be kept a common market for all nations throughout the world today, the principles of the Open Door and Equal Opportunity in China undoubtedly constitute a subject for serious re-examination.

Since Great Britain itself has a self-sufficient empire and the United States is assured of a similar position in the American continents, these Powers should not object to recognizing for Japan the right of attaining a self-dependent status in East Asia. So long as they practise economic nationalism...it is the duty for their statesmen who profess a love of peace to withdraw from China, the only region left for the development of Japan, thanks to their exclusive policies in their own countries as well as their economic spheres. This does not by any means imply, however, that Japan intends to monopolize China by abolishing the Open Door and Equal Opportunity. But it is essential and proper that the excessive rigidity with which the Anglo-American Powers have asserted these principles be at least modified and revised to suit the changed world situation. Through such processes, economic *blocs* may be smoothly developed, and since liberal economy has been replaced by economic nationalism throughout the world, it is fitting that such changes be made....

Apart from the question as to how many *blocs* should exist in the world, it can definitely be said that from the standpoint of

GREATER EAST ASIAN SPHERE OF COMMON PROSPERITY

Japan, a Greater East Asia — including the South Seas region — must constitute one of those regional *blocs*. The various regions of East Asia are geographically, historically, racially and economically so closely related that they are naturally destined to aid and minister to one another's needs and thus attain that co-existence and common prosperity which is essential to the successful practice of a regional *bloc*.

One of the common misunderstandings regarding the establishment of such *blocs* is that they are exclusive in nature. But it is utterly impossible to build a number of smaller worlds within the world. Even if it were possible to do so, it would only serve to retard greatly the progress of civilization and culture. In fact, the underlying idea of the *bloc* is quite the opposite; the establishment of *blocs* is the stage or method through which war is to be done away with and peace maintained, thereby assuring the advancement of world civilization and culture in general. Freed from economic pressure by other nations, the *blocs* will be able to develop economically, and, as they progress, they will naturally come into closer economic and cultural relationships with other *blocs*, thus making possible universal advancement in the economic and cultural fields.

...The *bloc* system as proposed by Japan for East Asia certainly promises greater security, because it proposes not competition, but co-prosperity and co-existence, as the principle of its establishment and as the objective of its efforts. It is a step forward for world peace, since it is an effort to find a more effective method of guaranteeing peace by abolishing those grave economic disparities which have so often been the source of conflict.

5
Tōjō on the Greater East Asia Co-Prosperity Sphere

PREMIER Tōjō Hideki, after the outbreak of the Pacific War and over a year after the proclamation of the Co-Prosperity Sphere, spoke to the House of Peers in the 79th Diet. By this time Japan had occupied Hong Kong, Malaya and the Philippines. Apart from defensive and economic goals, he spoke of liberation from Britain and America and of including Burma and possibly even Australia within the Sphere. His speech appeared in *The Japan Times and Advertiser*, 21 January 1942.

I am deeply moved with trepidation that, at the recent opening ceremony of the Diet, His Majesty the Emperor has specially granted the gracious Rescript. In humble obedience to the Imperial Wishes, I intend, together with you, gentlemen, to devote all my power to the performance of the duties and attain the object of the war, thereby setting the mind of His Majesty to rest.

It is indeed a matter for congratulation that, since the beginning of the War of Greater East Asia, the Imperial forces have crushed all enemies, continuously achieving brilliant victories wherever they went, and have already destroyed in a short space of time most of the enemy's strategic points.

The cardinal point in the War of Greater East Asia, which our Empire is now prosecuting, is to secure strategic bases in Greater East Asia and to bring the regions with important resources under Japan's control, thereby augmenting our fighting strength and, in close cooperation with Germany and Italy, to extend increasingly vigorous operations and to fight through until the United States and the British Empire are brought to their knees. The United States and the British Empire are, however, the countries which boast of their wealth and power as the greatest in the world, having for many years consolidated the foundation for their domination of the world. Even though they have suffered overwhelmingly defeat in the opening stage of the war, it is not difficult to imagine that they will stubbornly resist us and try to turn the tide of the war. We must, therefore, be prepared for difficulties of various sorts which may arise in the future and that the present war will become a protracted one. Accordingly this war remains indeed to be fought hereafter. In order to fulfill the purpose of the war, the whole nation must persevere in whatever difficulties and tribulations with a firm conviction of ultimate victory and thus serve the country. It is this very spirit of industry, thrift and reverence for valour and to sacrifice for the State that is absolutely indispensable to overcome the present crisis and also to assure the future progress and prosperity of our Empire.

Japan is now vigorously proceeding with the great task of establishing the sphere of common prosperity of Great East Asia, while prosecuting military operations on a gigantic and farflung scale, devoting the total strength of the nation. The basic policy of establishing the Greater East Asian Co-Prosperity Sphere has its origin in the great spirit which guided the foundation of our Empire, its aim being to enable each country and people in Greater East Asia to have its proper place and demonstrate its real character, thereby securing an order of co-existence and co-prosperity based on ethical principles with Japan serving as its nucleus. Its establishment extends over a vast area and is to be realized through mutual aid and cooperation with peoples of different races. The regions which will newly participate in this work of construction are those which, though they abound in various resources, have had the progress of their civilization and culture greatly impeded due to the ruthless exploitation by the United States and Britain for the past hundred years.

It is truly an unprecedently grand undertaking that our Empire should, by adding these regions, establish an ever-lasting peace in Greater East Asia with a new conception which will mark a new epoch in the annals of mankind, and proceed to construct a new world order along with our Allies and friendly Powers in Europe. The success of this great undertaking is a prerequisite condition for rendering our success in armed combat to an ultimate triumph.

It is the intention of the Government that in this construction, the areas which are absolutely essential for the defence of Greater East Asia be controlled and dealt with by Japan itself, while regarding other regions, appropriate measures be taken as the war situation develops in accordance with the tradition, culture and other circumstances of each people.

The Imperial Army and Navy forces have already occupied Hong Kong, secured the greater part of the Philippnes, brought nearly all of the Malay Peninsula under their control and recently occupied strategic points of the Netherlands East Indies. Of these regions, Hong Kong and the Malay Peninsula have for many years been the British possessions serving as bases for disrupting the peace of East Asia. Therefore, Japan will not only eradicate thoroughly the sources of such evil but on the contrary intends to convert these places into bulwarks for the defence of Greater East Asia. As regards the Philippines, if the peoples of those islands will hereafter understand the real intentions of Japan and offer to cooperate with us as one of the partners for the establishment of the Greater East Asian Co-Prosperity Sphere, Japan will gladly enable them to enjoy the honour of independence. As for Burma what Japan contemplates is not different from that relating to the Philippines.

As regards the Netherlands East Indies and Australia, if they continue as at present their attitude of resisting Japan, we will show no mercy in crushing them. But if their peoples come to understand Japan's real intentions and express willingness to cooperate with us, we will not hesitate to extend them our help with full understanding for their welfare and progress.

It is really regrettable that the Chungking regime is still continuing its meaningless resistance against us. Japan will thoroughly crush that regime. I am firmly convinced, however, that it is high time that all of the four hundred millions of the Chinese people saw the great change in the world situation in its true light and joined in the glorious task of constructing the sphere of common prosperity in Greater East Asia by discarding once and for all the time-old dependence upon the United States and Britain.

It is to be sincerely felicitated that the peoples of Manchukuo, China under the Nanking Government and Thailand, in unity with Japan, are putting forth ceaseless efforts for the construction of the Greater East Asian Co-Prosperity Sphere and that French Indo-China is also co-operating for the purpose.

The constructive undertaking contemplated by Japan will, in the early stages of war, be commended under military administration, beginning with those which are essential for the prosecution of the war. Meanwhile preparations will be made for future construction on a large scale and as the defence and maintenance of peace and order are firmly secured, the scope of civilian participation will be extended. In view of the fact that our plan of Greater East Asian construction is one that will determine the fortunes of the country for generations to come, it is necessary to perfect all preparations, leaving no stones unturned. The Government intends, therefore, to leave nothing desirable undone in the formation and execution of the plan by widely mobilizing the talents in Government and civilian circles and their wholehearted cooperation.

6
Foreign Minister Togo Opposes the Greater East Asia Ministry

TOGO Shigenori was Foreign Minister in the Tōjō cabinet. He resigned when the Greater East Asia Ministry was planned, for he believed it would invade the functions and powers of the Foreign Ministry. Speaking to the House of Peers earlier the same year (21 January 1942), he discussed Japan's historic mission to emancipate East Asia in a 'just war' and to create a new world order.

That Japan's wartime leadership was not a monolithic structure in complete agreement on important policy decisions clearly emerges in the selection included here from *The Cause of Japan* (Simon & Schuster, 1956) by Foreign Minister Togo. He delineates the nature of his disagreement with Premier Tōjō and other cabinet members over formation of the Greater East Asia Ministry. It was not simply that Togo resented what he felt would be incursions on the powers and functions of the Foreign Ministry; rather he differed fundamentally with the ideas of military control of Greater East Asia.

IT will be clear from what I have said that my East Asiatic policy was founded on allegiance to the principle of establishing relations of amity and neighbourly friendship with the countries of East Asia, with mutual respect for sovereignty and economic cooperation the keynote. Japan, as an advanced nation of East Asia, was to assist in the development of the other nations and the territory of this area, thereby bringing about through peaceful means the prosperity of all. This idea of mutual assistance left no room for any thought of control by military force. My foreign-policy speech to the Diet, on 21 January 1942, clarifying Japan's war aims, was an expression of these principles, as well as of Japan's intention not to exclude but to cooperate with non-Asiatic states in the development of East Asia. Naturally, in preparing my speech I had to give due consideration to the wartime atmosphere in Japan — it was a wartime speech — and to the views of my fellow cabinet members; but certainly the thoughts expressed by me conformed neither to the philosophy of military dominance nor to the concepts of bloc economy or of *Lebensraum*. It is clear that my position was discordant with the idea of a New Order in East Asia based on the idea of 'living space', and accordingly with the designs for the Greater East Asia as professed by Tōjō and his adherents.

I had noticed this discrepancy in our East Asiatic policy soon after entering the Cabinet, but the divergence naturally widened continually as the proponents of the New Order became increasingly drunk on the military successes. Tōjō himself, however, was rather cautious for some time, even after the war had actually begun. Thus, shortly after its outbreak the high command proposed to decide at once the future status of the Southern areas, for the convenience of military government of those areas after their occupation. When I objected that a decision of such importance should not be made when the war was still being fiercely fought and the situation fluid, Tōjō supported me, and the Liaison Conference decided in accordance with my contention.

There being these two currents of thought on East Asiatic relations, I had to endeavour to prevent the leadership in policy making from falling into the hands of those instigating establishment of the New Order. To this end, it was essential to keep management of those relations within the jurisdiction of the Foreign Ministry. Around May or June of 1942, however, I began to hear that there was under contemplation the creation of a new ministry, to be placed in charge of administration of the Greater East Asia area. With the passage of the days, the outlines of the scheme

GOVERNMENT PLANS

emerged. It contemplated that all overseas organs in that region (excluding only Korea, Formosa and Sakhalin) were to be directed and supervised by the New Greater East Asia Ministry; all political, economic and cultural affairs — everything but what was called 'pure diplomacy' — relating to Manchukuo, China, Thailand, French Indochina, and other areas (including the Kwantung Leased Territory and the mandated islands of the South Seas), were to be under the jurisdiction of the new ministry. The Manchuria Affairs Bureau, the Asia Development Board and the Ministry for Overseas Affairs would be abolished. The concept underlying this plan was said to be the treating of the East Asiatic countries as brothers, and the general mobilization of the material power of Greater East Asia, thus contributing to successful prosecution of the war.

Upon hearing of this, I told Tōjō that I was opposed to any such plan on the ground that the urgent thing was to mobilize our entire strength for carrying on the war and establishing ourselves in an impregnable position, and it was no time for play with organizational manipulation. I objected further that the plan as I had learned it not only would exclude the Foreign Ministry from the most important parts of diplomacy of Japan — thereby impairing the unity of our diplomacy — but would injure the pride as independent nations of the East Asiatic countries, rendering it impossible to maintain cooperative relations with them. Tōjō promised me to give careful consideration to my views.

Before I heard anything more about the Greater East Asia Ministry, bad news of the war came — it was disclosed that in June our Navy, which had been boasting of its invincibility, had suffered a defeat at Midway. ...Even more than theretofore, I became mistrustful of the Navy, and began to feel still more somber apprehensions over the future of the war, apprehensions which the enemy's landing on Guadalcanal shortly thereafter, evidencing the vigor of their counter-offensive, did nothing to lessen.

Then on 29 August, Hoshino, the Chief Secretary of the Cabinet, called on me at the direction of the Premier and showed me a draft of a proposal for establishment of a Greater East Asia Ministry, which Hoshino said it was the intention of the Premier to have adopted at the Cabinet meeting of 1 September. After glancing through the document, and seeing that the plan accorded

TOGO OPPOSES GREATER EAST ASIA MINISTRY   85

in general with what I had earlier heard rumored as its contents, I inquired of Hoshino the meaning of the 'pure diplomacy' which was to be retained by the Foreign Ministry; he answered that it comprehended international protocol and the formalities of concluding treaties. I told him that I considered the plan altogether improper, and requested that submission of it to the Cabinet be postponed till 5 September, to allow time for study of it. Hoshino left, but later returned to report that the Premier wanted to have a decision made without fail on the 1st. Meeting Tōjō after a dinner party on 31 August, I stated to him my grounds of objection to the plan, and requested postponement of the decision by the Cabinet, but Tōjō refused to agree to any delay.

The Greater East Asia Ministry plan was accordingly submitted to the Cabinet meeting of 1 September. For three hours at the meeting, from 10.00 a.m., I carried on an altercation over it, with Tōjō chiefly, no agreement, however, being reached in the end.

My opposition to the plan was based on five grounds:

1. According to this plan, Japanese diplomacy was to be placed under the jurisdiction of two independent ministries — one for East Asia and the other for the rest of the world — making it impossible to conduct a unified and consistent diplomacy.

2. The concept of 'pure diplomacy' was extremely odd; but the very fact that 'pure diplomacy' had to be left to the Foreign Ministry proved the plan to have serious legal defects.

3. The East Asiatic countries being treated differently from nations elsewhere, they would lose trust in Japan and come to entertain suspicion of her motives, and their pride would be affronted. The plan thus contravened the idea of respect for the independence of those nations.

4. It was evident that the activities of the Asia Development Board, having aroused the antipathy of the Chinese, had proved a failure. But the Greater East Asia Ministry plan looked not only to perpetuation of the board but to the elaboration of its organization and the extension of its activities permanently throughout the entire East Asiatic area, and its failure was therefore foreordained.

5. The pressing task confronting Japan was to build up her military potential and establish an impregnable position. Japan could not afford to waste time with such schemes as administrative reorganization.

The gravamen of Premier Tōjō's argument, in the course of our long controversy at this Cabinet meeting, was that the countries of East Asia should be treated differently from other countries, as being Japan's kin. General Suzuki, President of the Planning Board, kept protesting that, contrary to my contention, the Asia Development Board had by no means been a failure; I retorted to this that the failure of the board was notorious. Among the others, Overseas Affairs Minister Ino and Navy Minister Shimada argued in favour of the plan, and I took issue with them also. The Cabinet meeting recessed without coming to an agreement.

During the recess of the meeting Tōjō suggested to me that I should resign. I refused, saying that it was the Premier and the advocates of the reorganization who should reconsider their plan and, if there were to be resignations over it, should resign. The most serious ground of my opposition to the Greater East Asia Ministry — that suggested by the first of the points stated above — had been my fear that Japan's policy toward the countries of East Asia would, under the proposed ministry, be formulated by proponents of the Greater East Asia Co-Prosperity Sphere, a 'New Order' based on a bloc economy, thereby conflicting with my policy for foreign relations. Going beyond this narrow ground, however, I thought it necessary to make a stand to force, if possible, the resignation of the entire Tōjō Cabinet. The spectacle was exhibited of a government headed by a Premier who, with such principles of war direction as has been seen, laboured mightily at advertising the initial successes of the war but was guilty of flagrant nonfeasance in carrying out urgently needed moves for increasing fighting power; under such a Premier ultimate victory in the war was not to be hoped for.

When I had returned to my Official Residence after the recessing of the Cabinet meeting, Finance Minister Kaya called on me and asked in a friendly way whether I could find no room for reconsideration. Thereafter, General Satō and Admiral Oka, Directors of Military and Naval Affairs Bureaus respectively, together came with the same request, saying that establishment of the new ministry had the support of both Army and Navy. I rejected all these overtures. Finally, Navy Minister Shimada came to tell me that he had been summoned to the Court, and that it was the Emperor's wish that some compromise be effected, as the Court did not desire a change of cabinet at that moment. In view of this statement, I proposed to Shimada a compromise; this was in substance that the proposed ministry be abandoned, and while management of economic affairs only of Greater East Asia should be confided to a new organ, that organ should be preferably a ministerial committee. I was even willing that it be a ministry, with this limited function, if that was believed better by a majority of our colleagues in the Cabinet; control of diplomatic affairs of the Greater East Asia should, however, remain with the Foreign Ministry. Shimada left to report my suggestion to Tōjō, but returned shortly to say that the Premier would not agree to my proposal, nor was any form of compromise acceptable.

Although the Cabinet had not concluded its discussion at the recessing of the meeting, it had been evident that the general opinion favored establishment of the new ministry. Feeling that I could do nothing more to block it, and concluding that I should not cause anxiety to the Emperor by further complicating matters, I submitted my resignation. I left office that day, 1 September, and on the same day the Cabinet approved Tōjō's plan. On the following day I outlined the course of events to the staff of the Foreign Ministry, in the presence of Tōjō, who had taken over the Foreign portfolio temporarily in succession to me.

7
Tōjō Greets the Greater East Asia Conference

IN the first week of November, one year after creation of the Greater East Asia Ministry, delegates were invited from many nations within the Co-Prosperity Sphere to Tokyo. There were also delegates from the Free India Provisional Government, including Indian National Army commander Subhas Chandra Bose. In a speech of welcome Premier Tōjō spoke of expunging Western colonial exploitation from Asia and establishing in its place a New Order based on justice and peace. The purpose of the Conference, according to Tōjō, was to discuss successful conclusion of the war and creation of the New Order. He thanked the delegates for their cooperation in the common cause. The Joint Declaration of the Conference, drafted by the government, is also included here. These documents are found in the Gaimushō Gaikō Shiryōkan, volume: *Dai Tōa Sensō kankei ikken* (Matters relating to the Greater East Asia war), May-November 1943.

Address of Prime Minister General Hideki Tōjō before the Assembly of Greater East-Asiatic Nations

AS the representative of the sponsor nation, I have the privilege to extend to you the sincere greetings of the Japanese Government and to make a statement of their views.

Some time ago, the Japanese Government proposed the convening of an Assembly of the Greater East-Asiatic Nations for the purpose of holding frank deliberations on policies relative to bringing the War of Greater East Asia to a successful conclusion and to constructing a New Order in Greater East Asia. This proposal, I am happy to say, met with hearty approval on the part of all the countries concerned, and it is with a sense of great pleasure and profound gratitude that today at this gathering I bid welcome to Your Excellencies as representatives of the nations of Greater East Asia. I am also happy to say that this Assembly is honoured by the presence of His Excellency, Subhas Chandra Bose, the Head of the Provisional Government of Free India.

During the past centuries, the British Empire, through fraud and aggression, acquired vast territories throughout the world and maintained its domination over other nations and peoples in the various regions by keeping them pitted and engaged in conflict one against another. On the other hand, the United States which, by taking advantage of the disorder and confusion in Europe, had established its supremacy over the American continents, spread its tentacles to the Pacific and to East Asia following its war with Spain. Then, with the opportunities afforded by the First World War, the United States began to pursue its ambition for world hegemony. More recently, with the outbreak of the present war, the United States has further intensified its imperialistic activities, making fresh inroads into North Africa, West Africa, the Atlantic Ocean, Australia, the Near East and even into India, apparently in an attempt to usurp the place of the British Empire.

The need of upholding international justice and of guaranteeing world peace is habitually stressed by America and Britain. They mean thereby no more and no less than the preservation of a world order of their own, based upon division and conflict in Europe and upon the perpetuation of their colonial exploitation of Asia. They sought to realize their inordinate ambitions in Asia, through political aggression and economic exploitation; they brought on conflict among the various peoples; they tried to destroy their racial integrity under the fair name of education and culture. Thus, they have to this day threatened constantly the existence of the nations and peoples of Asia, disturbed their stability, and suppressed their natural and proper development. It is because of their notion to regard East Asia as a colony that they harp upon the principles of the open door and equal opportunity simply as a convenient means of pursuing their sinister designs of aggression. While constantly keeping their own territories closed to us, the peoples of Asia, denying us the equality of opportunities and impeding our trade, they sought solely their own prosperity.

The Anglo-American ambition of world hegemony is indeed a scourge of mankind and the root of the world's evils. Movements for emancipation have occurred from time to time among the nations and peoples of East Asia, but due to the ruthless and tyrannical armed oppression by America and Britain, or due to their malicious old trick of division and alienation for ruling other races, those patriotic efforts ended largely in failure. Meanwhile, Japan's rise of power and prestige was looked upon by America and Britain with increasing dislike. They made it the cardinal point of their East Asia Policy on the one hand, to restrain Japan at every turn and on the other, to alienate her from the other countries of East Asia. It was obviously unwise for them to permit either the rise of any one country as a great Power or the banding together of the various nations and peoples. These American and British methods became more and more sinister and high-handed, especially in the last several years.

Next, it is my desire to express to you the fundamental views of the Japanese Government regarding the construction of Greater East Asia.

It is my belief that to enable all nations each to have its proper place and to enjoy the blessings of common prosperity by mutual efforts and mutual help is the fundamental condition for the establishment of world peace. And I must furthermore say that to practise mutual help among the neighbouring nations in one region, fostering one another's national growth and establishing a relationship of common prosperity and well-being, and, at the same time, to cultivate relations of harmony and concord with nations of other regions is the most effective and the most practical method of securing world peace.

It is an incontrovertible fact that the nations of Greater East Asia are bound, in every respect, by the ties of an inseparable relationship. I firmly believe that such being the case, it is their common mission to secure the stability of Greater East Asia and to construct a new order of common prosperity and well-being.

This new order of Greater East Asia is to rest upon the spirit of justice that is inherent in Greater East Asia. In this respect it is fundamentally different from the old order designed to serve the interests of the United States and Britain who do not hesitate to practise injustice, deception and exploitation in order to promote their own prosperity.

The nations of Greater East Asia, while mutually recognizing their autonomy and independence, must, as a whole, establish among themselves relations of brotherly amity. Such relations cannot be created if one country should utilize another as a means to an end. I believe that they come into being only when there is mutual respect for one another's autonomy and independence, when all countries are willing to accept the principle of 'live and let live,' and give expression to their real selves.

A superior order of culture has existed in Greater East Asia from its very beginning. Especially the spiritual essence of the culture of Greater East Asia is the most sublime in the world. It is my belief that in the wide diffusion throughout the world of this culture of Greater East Asia by its further cultivation and refinement lies the salvation of mankind from the curse of materialistic civilization and our contribution to the welfare of all humanity. It is incumbent upon us all mutually to respect one another's glorious traditions and to develop the creative spirit and genius of our peoples and thereby to enhance even more the culture of Greater East Asia.

Furthermore, I believe that in order to promote the welfare of the people and to replenish the national power, the nations of Greater East Asia must carry on close economic collaboration on the basis of reciprocity and jointly promote the prosperity of Greater East Asia. Hitherto, Greater East Asia has been for many years the object of Anglo-American exploitation, but henceforth we must be also autonomous and independent in the economic field to gain prosperity, by mutually depending on and helping each other.

The new order of Greater East Asia which we are building is not exclusive unto itself, but rather it seeks positively to enter into cooperative relations with the nations of the world, politically, economically and also culturally, and thus contribute to the world's advancement. This differs completely from the way of the United States and Britain which, while advocating freedom and equality, oppress and discriminate against other nations and other peoples; which, while imposing the open door on others monopolize vast territories and natural resources, threaten the existence of others without compunction and retard the general advancement of the entire world.

The construction of Greater East Asia is being realized with a grim steadiness in the midst of war. In contrast, what are America and Britain doing in India? Britain's oppression of India grows in severity with every passing day; while America's ambition has recently asserted itself. Discord and friction between Britain and America on the one hand and the Indian masses on the other are aggravating, and the Indian people are being subjected to indescribable hardships and tribulations.... However, regardless of what the enemy may do, Japan is determined to follow, together with the other nations of Greater East Asia, the path of justice, to deliver Greater East Asia, from the fetters of America and Britain and, in cooperation with her neighbouring nations, to strive toward the reconstruction and development of Greater East Asia.

Today, the unity of the countries and peoples of Greater East Asia has been achieved and they have embarked upon the gigantic enterprise of constructing Greater East Asia for the common prosperity of all nations. This surely must be regarded as the grandest spectacle of human effort in modern times.

The War of Greater East Asia is truly a war to destroy evil and to make justice manifest. Ours is a righteous cause. Justice knows no enemy and we are fully convinced of our ultimate victory.

Japan is grateful to the nations of Greater East Asia for the whole-hearted cooperation which they are rendering in this war. Japan is firmly determined, by cooperating with them and by strengthening her collaboration with her allies in Europe, to carry on with indefatigable spirit and with conviction in sure victory in this war, the intensity of which is expected to mount from day to day. Japan, by overcoming all difficulties, will do her full share to complete the construction of Greater East Asia and contribute to the establishment of world peace which is the common mission of us all.

Joint Declaration of the Greater East Asia Conference

It is the basic principle for the establishment of world peace that the nations of the world have each its proper place, and enjoy prosperity in common through mutual aid and assistance.

The United States of America and the British Empire have in seeking their own prosperity oppressed other nations and peoples. Especially in East Asia, they indulged in insatiable aggression and exploitation, and sought to satisfy their inordinate ambition of enslaving the entire region, and finally they came to menace seriously the stability of East Asia. Herein lies the cause of the present war.

The countries of Greater East Asia, with a view to contributing to the cause of world peace, undertake to cooperate toward prosecuting the War of Greater East Asia to a successful conclusion, liberating their region from the yoke of British-American domination, and ensuring their self-existence and self-defence, and in constructing a Greater East Asia in accordance with the following principles:

1. The countries of Greater East Asia through mutual cooperation will ensure the stability of their region and construct an order of common prosperity and well-being based upon justice.

2. The countries of Greater East Asia will ensure the fraternity of nations in their region, by respecting one another's sovereignty and independence and practising mutual assistance and amity.

3. The countries of Greater East Asia by respecting one another's traditions and developing the creative faculties of each race, will enhance the culture and civilization of Greater East Asia.

4. The countries of Greater East Asia will endeavour to accelerate their economic development through close cooperation upon a basis of reciprocity and to promote thereby the general prosperity of their region.

5. The countries of Greater East Asia will cultivate friendly relations with all the countries of the world, and work for the abolition of racial discrimination, the promotion of cultural intercourse and the opening of resources throughout the world, and contribute thereby to the progress of mankind.

8
The Co-Prosperity Sphere Viewed from the West

ANDREW Grajdanzev, writing during wartime and several months following creation of the Greater East Asia Ministry, discusses the concept and reality of Greater East Asia. He notes that the scope of the term is imprecise. He quotes policy statements by several Japanese officials, military and civilian, as they attempt to rationalize and articulate Japan's goals. He notes the ambiguities in the status of the Greater East Asia Ministry. Grajdanzev was associated with the land reform program instituted during the occupation of Japan following World War II. This excerpt is from an article in *Pacific Affairs*, vol. 16, 1943.

THE term, Greater East Asia Co-Prosperity Sphere, appeared in Japanese publications during the third or fourth year of the undeclared Sino-Japanese War. It was an expression of hope for the Japanese people who had no clear idea of the purpose of the war and who were only gradually given to understand that the aims of the war are far beyond the immediate objective of the 'chastisement' of Chiang Kai-shek. It was also a slogan to combat the enmity of the Chinese and other peoples who, by force of arms or by threat of force, were included in this sphere. These

CO-PROSPERITY SPHERE VIEWED FROM THE WEST   95

peoples were to be convinced that their inclusion in this Co-prosperity Sphere was in their own interest; that not only Japan but also the population of the occupied regions would derive advantages from the occupation.

The term, Greater East Asia, lacks precision. For the time being it covers the Japanese Empire, Manchuria, China Proper, the Philippines, the Netherlands Indies, French Indo-China, Thailand, British Malaya, and Burma. Moreover, the Soviet Far East should be included. Writings of the Japanese militarists leave no doubt that, at the first possibility, the experiment of 1919–21, when the Japanese stood guard on Lake Baikal, will be repeated. In respect to other regions, we have more recent pronouncements: India, Australia, and New Zealand were to be included in the sphere. In May 1942 the Japanese Ministry of Agriculture and Forestry was not yet certain whether Australian wheat would be available in Greater East Asia during the war, but the Traffic Committee believed that large numbers of automobiles in use in Australia, New Zealand, and India (808,500, 276,000 and 123,000, respectively) 'may be mobilized for the smooth transportation of materials in the Co-Prosperity Sphere.' Among others, the Vice-President of the Nippon Yusen Kaisha wrote in the Oriental Economist (February 1942) that India 'should be included in Greater East Asia, which will then be self-sufficient and more complete and powerful than any of the other economic blocs which were to be formed after the restoration of peace.'

For the purposes of this article, however, attention will be concentrated on Greater East Asia as it is today and in particular on Japanese organization and policies in the territories of South-East Asia conquered or occupied by the Japanese since 7 December 1941, i.e., in the Philippines, French Indo-China, Thailand, Burma, Malaya, Netherlands East Indies, British Borneo, and Portuguese Timor — an area of 1.7 million square miles with a population of about 150 million. This area has large deposits of oil, iron, manganese, bauxite, chromite, zinc, lead, and tin ores. It is rich in rubber, rice, sugar, kapok, copra, teak, quinine, and many other products, and there are possibilities of cotton production. During his stay in Manila, Kazuo Aoki, the Japanese Minister for Greater East Asia, said that the establishment of any economic sphere necessitated three primary requirements—natural resources, scientific knowledge and technical development, and manpower — and that all three were found in Greater East Asia. However, this does not mean that a well-developed modern economy may be quickly built, especially in time of war. The war may end during the next five years, while the economic block which Japan envisages would, for the full realization of its potentialities, demand decades. The Japanese know this. Lieutenant-Colonel Tsukasa Kato, chief of the Military Affairs Bureau of the War Ministry, wrote in April 1942. 'The southern regions under Japanese occupation are very rich in resources, but, in view of the fact that adequate means of transportation are not available for the present, it is difficult to transport these materials in the quantities required at home'; and further:

> The development of southern resources is of vital importance ... this is all very well, but it is nevertheless very important that, in its enthusiasm over the south, it [the Japanese nation] shall not neglect vital interests nearer home which concern Japan, Manchukuo, and China. Very important though the southern regions are, they are, after all, a part of the Greater East Asia Co-Prosperity Sphere. It must always be kept in mind that Japan's national defence is fundamentally based on Japan, Manchukuo, and China.

This statement of the army specialists indicates clearly the direction of Japanese policy. Japan, Manchuria, and North China are to remain the economic foundation of Greater East Asia in this war, though the southern regions and other parts of China are to play an increasingly important role. The whole of Greater East Asia is to be divided into two parts: one suitable for large-scale Japanese emigration and one unsuitable. The suitable area comprises Manchukuo and some parts of China; to the unsuitable southern regions, only *leaders* of the natives will go. The Greater East Asia Personnel Training Committee was established in Japan with the purpose of training the personnel who will be 'leaders in the first line of the reconstruction work.' The Japanese have said that the winning of the war depends entirely on the ability of the officials to lead the natives in Greater East Asia. According to Dr. S. Naoki (writing in May 1943), Japan is predestined to reconstruct the south because '1) the Japanese love the nation; 2) the Japanese people are loyal and love their ruler, 3) the Japanese have patience; and 4) the Japanese also have very excellent health as has been proven in the present war.' Representing a mixture of southern and northern people, they can easily accommodate both in the north and in the south. 'This proves that the Japanese are the most capable race for the reconstruction of the south.' However, anyone who thinks that after the reconstruction of the south these leaders will leave, or that Japan would then stop her military preparation, is mistaken. In February 1943 Prime Minister Tōjō said in the House of Representatives:

'Even with the supposition that the war ends under certain [i.e., favourable] circumstances, it is not an easy task completely to equip a firm progressive power with the firm Greater East Asia unification, formed with Japan as the center of Greater East Asia, and to guard this so that it cannot be attacked from any point.... I am not considering the reduction of the Japanese military preparations which form our kernel, even in postwar time. Consequently... I believe that there should be no hesitation in wartime management with dreams of the past and with thinking that there will be an immediate reduction [in armaments] if the war should end in the near future.... The military preparations of Japan which are the pivot of Greater East Asia...will absolutely not be reduced.'

How is the new empire organized? There was no central organ in Japan which could direct Japanese and native activities in the vast area from the Amur River to Australia, but the need was felt more and more, and in November 1942 the Ministry of Greater East Asia was set up. This necessitated a reorganization of the whole system of Japanese government because the necessities of government in the southern areas demanded that many more officials be sent from Japan and her colonies. In June 1942 it was estimated that at least 30,000 officials with certain experience were required in the south, where the need was so great that many agents of the trade firms were compelled to carry out official functions in their free hours. Moreover, the rapid growth of the empire since caused many complications in the government, brought into existence many bureaus with parallel functions, overlapping and confusion.... It was decided that the new minister would administer all business affairs in Greater East Asia (including Kwantung Leased Territory and excluding the Japanese Empire), would take over protection of the Japanese interests within this region, would conduct business affairs concerning cultural problems, would appoint, direct and supervise all diplomats and consulates there, but it would leave 'purely diplomatic relationships' to the Ministry of Foreign Affairs. It is not clear what is included in these purely diplomatic relationships and how this system works in practice, but it is clear that the management of the new empire is concentrated in the Greater East Asia Ministry. There is very little diplomacy about it. At the head of the new ministry was placed Kazuo Aoki, a specialist in economics and finance.

The ministry was made up of the Minister, Vice-Minister, four advisors, and four bureaus, of which one was the General Affairs Bureau in charge of industrial and economic policies, compilation of statistics and other matters, while three others were in charge of geographical divisions of Greater East Asia. The administrative re-shuffle connected with the Greater East Asia Ministry affected 170,000 government officials and involved absorption or abolition of thirty-one bureaus and twelve departments.

The East Asia Development League serves as the body framing the policy and conducting research concerning East Asia. It antedates the formation of the Greater Asia Ministry. There were in Japan several organizations whose purpose was propaganda of conquest, or espionage, or formation of fifth columns in the southern regions. All such organizations, including the Greater East Association and *Kokuryūkai* (Black Dragon Association), were dissolved and their property transferred to the East Asia Development League which was to be affiliated with the Imperial Rule Aid Association. According to the official communiques, this new league was to 'exert itself to concentrate the total national strength on the unification of Asia, development movements at home and abroad, diffusion of Asia development thought, guidance of Japanese residents in the Greater East Asia regions with regard to their activities, organizations, etc., conducting research investigations.' Its president was a known militarist, former Minister of War and Prime Minister, General Senjuro Hayashi, and after his death the Vice President of the League, Rentaro Mizuno, was appointed to the presidency. For some unknown reason it was decided in May 1943 to dissolve the League and establish a new similar institution.'

9
Southern Policy Decisions and the Shōwa Kenkyūkai

THE late Kishi Kōichi was co-author with Professor Benda and Dr. James Irikura of a volume on *Japanese Military Administration in Indonesia; Selected Documents* and compiler of a documentary study on Japanese military administration in Indonesia. Mr. Kishi was a specialist not only on Japanese administration in Indonesia but also on modern intellectual history. In this excerpt from an article in *Tōyō Kenkyū* (Oriental studies), no. 7, February, 1964, he considers the discussions and writings of members of the *Shōwa Kenkyūkai* and weighs their relationship to government policy decisions regarding South-East Asia. He deals with attempts of the Shōwa Research Institute to halt the rise of the military in Japan during the late 1930s. He notes the discrepancy between this goal of resisting military control and the net effect of these writings by the intellectuals of the Shōwa Research Institute. The Institute was one of the early advocates of including the South Seas in an Asian economic bloc. This economic concern led to proposals that the U.S. and Britain be removed from political control of South-East Asia. Thus the development of the ideology of the *Shōwa Kenkyūkai* led them full circle to a point closely approximating military thinking on South-East Asia. He concludes therefore that the *Shōwa Kenkyūkai* did contribute to formulation of Southern policies adopted by the Army and Navy.

WESTERN pressure on Japan was increased at a time when Japan could not make any progress with its China problem. And in Japan the idea gradually gained force that Japan should not only repulse Western pressure but also take over Western colonialism by including East Asia in its sphere of influence. The development of this idea involved the problem of its policy of advance southward. The *Shōwa Kenkyūkai* began taking an interest in the policy of advancing southward in its discussions in the sub-committee on foreign policy. Also the subcommittee on foreign policy began expressing its views on the policy of advancing southward in discussions held with the East Asia Economic Bloc Kenkyūkai[1]....

The ideas in 'An Outline of the East Asian Economic Bloc from the Standpoint of Emphasis on Resources and Trade Relations' in 1939 by W. suggested that the East Asian Economic Bloc could not be formed merely by the supply and demand system of Japan, Manchuria and China. The bloc should include the South as well.... In conclusion, he said, 'It would be a kind of fantasy to realize a complete system of self-supply within Japan, Manchuria and China....'

The South Seas (the Philippines, Netherlands Indies, British Borneo, New Caledonia, French Indo-China, the Malay Peninsula, etc.) are not only geographically close to the above areas but produce abundant natural resources which are insufficient in Japan, Manchuria, and China. It is absolutely necessary to maintain a close relationship particularly with this area....

'Policy toward the Southern Area', as has been described earlier, was developed predicated on the rationale for an 'East Asian Economic Bloc.' It was developed on the basis of the rationale in the conclusion of the 'Outline of the East Asian Economic Bloc viewed from the Standpoint of Emphasis on Natural Resources and Trade Relations.'

The argument is further developed in the following statements: 'It is inevitable that this country, sandwiched between the two big nations, the United States and the Soviet Union, must advance to the South Seas in order to acquire the natural resources required for its survival in competition with these big nations. It would also be to the advantage of the countries in the South Seas to be included in the East Asian Economic Bloc and to have closer economic ties with Japan.' 'Furthermore, from the political standpoint of constructing a New Order in East Asia, it is absolutely necessary to remove these countries in the South Seas from the bloc of England and the United States.' The view expressed in these statements that Japan must advance into the South Seas in order to extricate herself from the status quo in which she is sandwiched between a hostile Soviet Union and United States and to compete with these nations reveals the tenor of the studies of the East Asian Economic Bloc. Furthermore, the argument that the countries in the South Seas will find it to their advantage to have economic ties with Japan and that it is necessary for Japan to remove these countries from the bloc of England and the United States and their allies reveals that the idea of an East Asian Economic Bloc had the primary aim of securing benefits to Japan rather than to the member nations of the bloc.

The studies of the policy toward the Southern Area indicated frankly that Japan's advance into the Southern Areas at the time had not achieved their economic goals. They pointed out as obstacles to these aims: (1) the low level of concern people had with the Southern Area and delays in the advance due to this lack of interest, (2) difficulties in conducting various operations in the Southern Area consisting mostly of territories subordinate to European nations, (3) the fact that the rapid advance of the Japanese into the Southern countries would cause social unrest there, (4) the low level of the native inhabitants' consciousness about their situation, producing only poor results for Japanese activities there, (5) the stiff competition with the Chinese immigrants established in the area and the lack of cooperation with these Chinese, (6) the low level of Japan's economic power, and (7) lack of concern with the national interests on the part of Japanese in the Southern Area, who pursued only their private gain.

These factors singled out as obstacles to achieving Japan's economic goals in the Southern Area clearly indicated that Japan's advance into the Southern Area was far behind the schedule Japan projected, and the problem was how to overcome these difficult conditions. In this argument, the report indicated that forcing one's way into the area by means of military invasion would not be to the advantage of Japan. It proposed peaceful penetration, particularly in the economic field. It pointed out that such peaceful penetration would be possible by overcoming the obstacles that retarded Japan's economic advance, described earlier....

The geographic areas selected for putting into practice the policy of advance into the Southern Area (the selection of the areas was the crux of the problem) were (1) Siam (Thailand), the only independent country in the Southern Area, situated between French Indo-China and British Malaya, and (2) the Dutch East Indies under the rule of a small nation in Europe, Holland. It should be noted that the proposal to select these areas was made about the time when military leaders were discussing the policy of advance into the Southern Area.

The report proposed a policy of assisting Thailand in the fields of government, economy and culture — a policy of carrot and stick to get Thailand out of the sphere of influence of England and France.

The report proposed with regard to the Dutch East Indies closer economic and trade relations in the main and also measures for preventing the European war from spreading into the area, and measures to be taken when this prevention was achieved. It further suggested that if war did spread to the area and if the area were placed under the joint control of the powers, measures should be taken so that such joint control would not jeopardize formation of a New Order in East Asia and an East Asian Economic Bloc....

This 'Southern Area Policy' was drafted in March, 1939, six months before the talks between Japan and the Netherlands began. It is quite conceivable that this 'Southern Area Policy' had some influence on the actual policy adopted in Japan's later advance into the Southern Area....

The proposals made by the *Shōwa Kenkyūkai* concerning Southern Area policy as described above may not have directly influenced later policy decisions, but the activities of the *Shōwa Kenkyūkai* probably had some influence on later developments.

Events, however, took quite a contrary direction from the opposition to the use of arms advocated in the Southern Area policy by the *Shōwa Kenkyūkai* following the entry of Japan into the Pacific War in December 1941. Nevertheless, we should note that the military also put emphasis on the occupation of French Indo-China and the Dutch East Indies in Japan's military operations, and thus the outcome was quite similar to the proposals made by the *Shōwa Kenkyūkai*. This does not mean that the *Shōwa Kenkyūkai* played the role of forerunners for the aggressive policy of the military, but we may conclude that it made at least a small contribution to the formulation of the rationale behind the policy adopted by the military.

I say this because I judge that the proposals made by the *Shōwa Kenkyūkai* had no small influence on the rationale behind the Navy's policy of advance toward the Southern Area. I suspect that it influenced the formulation of the theoretical framework for the implementation of military administration in the occupied areas which the Navy secretly prepared before it occupied and began military administration in the Dutch East Indies. It appears that the proposals made by the *Shōwa Kenkyūkai* had particular relevance to policy decisions after the talks between Japan and the Netherlands concerning the Dutch East Indies began. In other words, I suspect that the Navy, which showed an unusual enthusiasm for strategic occupation of the Dutch East Indies, paid particular attention to the discussions by the *Shōwa Kenkyūkai* in which arguments were focussed on the Southern areas.

[1]One of the many subcommittees of the *Shōwa Kenkyūkai*.

Part III
Policy Implementation in the Field:
The Reality

1
The Case of Korea

BORN in Manchuria, Professor Lee Chong-sik has studied Japanese colonial policies in Manchuria and Korea. He has worked for the Rand Corporation and has taught at Dartmouth. In this selection Professor Lee expresses the negative view of Japanese colonial administration in Korea that is shared by most Koreans. While he sees no positive results from Japanese policies of cultural assimilation, conscription and suppression of liberalism, at the same time he believes Japan provided Korea a model for technological development. The Japanese presence, he feels, provided both a positive and negative stimulus to Korean nationalism. This selection comes from *The Politics of Korean Nationalism* (University of California Press, 1962).

THE principal aide to Governor-General Terauchi up to 1914 was Lieutenant-General Akashi Motojirō, who had studied the colonial policies of Russia while he was military attache in St. Petersburg between 1902 and 1904. Terauchi, an army general and Minister of the Army at the time of his appointment to the governor-generalship, was no expert in colonial administration. It is reasonable to assume that Akashi played a major role in shaping his policies in Korea.

Akashi came to Korea in 1907 as commander of the Japanese

gendarmerie. After carrying out for a year the not too difficult mission of subjugating insurgent Koreans, he was appointed director of the police affairs for the regency-general. The success of the Japanese government in annexing and maintaining its rule over Korea, and the accompanying 'unscrupulous and brutal oppressions,' are in great part attributed to this 'authoritarian despot.'

Governor-General Terauchi arrived in Korea in July, 1910, to begin his rule in the new territory. With the assistance of Akashi, he introduced oppressive measures into politics, industry, communications, and other phases of life, to the extent that the 'entire Korean peninsula was turned into a military camp' and his 'extreme military dictatorship gave the impression that Korea had returned to the medieval authoritarian regime.'...

The suppressive policy of Terauchi and Akashi can be accurately described as hysterical. By 1911 the activities of the Righteous Armies were coming to an end, the army and gendarmerie had killed thousands of Korean rebels, and order was restored, but the Koreans were still far from convinced that the presence of the Japanese was desirable and necessary for Korea's future. Terauchi and Akashi seem to have decided that this conviction could be implanted through fear. They decided, therefore, to arrest the most vocal elements in the northern provinces and show them what the Japanese were capable of doing. These provinces were chosen because Christianity was strong in the north, and also because the New Peoples' Association *(Shinminhoe)*, a secret organization established by An Ch'ang-ho, Yi Kap, Yi Tong-hwi and others in 1908 to promote industry and advance educational standards, was influential there....

Within a few years about 76 per cent of the farm population became tenants, partly or wholly, in the modern sense, deprived of their old, near-hereditary rights to the land and attached to it only by short-term contracts. They were required to pay fees to the landlords as before, but with a new burden created by the change from a predominantly barter to a predominantly money economy....

To Korean political and economic discontent there was added resentment of the behaviour of Japanese residents. Koreans, particularly members of the elite, were proud of their ancient traditions, culture, and observance of Confucian propriety; in their view the Japanese civilization was somewhat inferior to their own. Although their country had deteriorated economically and politically, they prized the quality of their culture. The Japanese, in general, despised the peculiarities of Korean civilization. Further, despite the official status of Korea as a part of Japan, most of the Japanese regarded the annexation as a conquest and displayed the arrogance of conquerors. The Koreans saw them as such and regarded their rule as a transitional one to which no complete submission was justified.

In an effort to secure total support for the war the Japanese government initiated the 'Movement for the General Mobilization of the National Spirit.'... This elaborate network of *han* ('squads'), *kumi* ('teams'), and *cho* ('streets') in each administrative unit served both as a controlling mechanism over the people and a rapid and sure system of communication. As a means of attaining spiritual unity, all the population was coerced into marching to Shinto shrines periodically to pray for the victory of the Japanese armed forces. Since food rationing was administered through the 'patriotic groups,' the system operated with maximum efficiency....

Although the policy of Japanization had been pursued ever since the annexation in 1910 the Koreans were still far from being assimilated. The international and domestic situation of Japan after the outbreak of the war demanded an intensification of the policy. Japan needed not only the material resources and strategic position of the Korean peninsula, but also the native manpower
....

The government had, of course, a choice of more than one way of conscripting Koreans. There was the precedent of the British in India during the First World War, when independence was promised as a reward for submitting to conscription. But this alternative was not very attractive. The promise of independence would only enliven the nationalist movement, as it had done in India, and complete independence of Korea after the Japanese victory would weaken the empire.

The only practicable alternative was to accelerate the assimilation process. In 1938, therefore, the government abolished Korean-language instruction in all secondary schools. Soon the elementary schools ceased to teach Korean, and the use of Japanese became mandatory.... School instruction began with 'worship toward the east,' reciting the 'oath of the Imperial subject,' and veneration of the shelf for Shinto tablets installed in every classroom. Students were taught to believe in the 'spirit of Yamato' and the superiority of the Japanese race, of which the Korean people were to be deemed a part. Of course, these daily programs were not confined to the schools. All government agencies, factories, 'patriotic groups' and public gatherings of any kind had to begin their activities with the same standard procedures.

An essential part of the stepped-up program for assimilation was the permission granted to the Korean people to change their monosyllabic surnames to multisyllabic Japanese forms. They were free to choose whatever surnames they preferred, so long as these were not distinctly Korean....

The final step in the assimilation program was the recruitment of Korean young men for military service. The process of recruitment began soon after the outbreak of the war. Before adopting actual conscription, however, the government announced in February, 1938, a euphemistic program, the 'Korean Army Special Volunteer Troops System.' The government and the government-inspired press played up the theme of the 'grace of the emperor,' proclaiming it a great and distinct privilege to serve in the Imperial Army. Administration of the program was entrusted to the police. Since more volunteers from a jurisdiction meant a better record to show to their superiors, police officials exerted pressures to bring in as many recruits as possible. There were 2,946 volunteers in 1938 and 12,348 in 1939. In August, 1943, when the war had become world-wide, full-scale conscription was put into effect and the facade of the volunteer system was abandoned.

Thus Korea went into another 'dark age' after 1937. Restriction of freedom and the imposition of totalitarian rule were not confined to Korea, for all political parties and liberals in Japan suffered the same fate; but it is important to note that such expansionist generals as Minami Jirō and Koiso Kuniaki were governor-generals of Korea after 1936. What, then, was the attitude of the general public in Korea toward the expansionist policy of the government after 1937?

The nationalist leaders of the earlier period showed varied reactions. There were some who chose or were persuaded to collaborate with the regime. Some of these were genuinely impressed by Japanese strength and wished the Korean people to share the fruits of expansion; some others merely paid lip service because of police pressure. Owing to the prestige of the veteran nationalist leaders among the Korean masses, the government resorted to all possible means to get their support. Those who participated in the government's campaign for closer ties between the Japanese and the Koreans urged young men to enlist in the Imperial Army and their elders to donate money to the government, to help bring about Japanese victory. A police report in 1938 stated that about half of the formerly nationalistic or socialistic organizations still existing at that time — youth, athletic, labour, farmer, etc.—either collaborated with or paid lip service to the government policy.

Another noteworthy characteristic was the influence of the students who attended Japanese universities. Because of the fact that the nationalist movement within Korea was of a reformist nature, the number of leaders from the older generation was not very significant. As time passed, the older leaders gradually ceased activity and surrendered leadership to younger men. The most active elements in the nationalist and Communist movements after the 1920's were, therefore, from the generation that attended secondary and higher institutions in the decade beginning in 1910. Since Korea did not have modern colleges and universities until much later, it was only natural that students who attended universities in Japan and other countries between 1910 and 1919 came to positions of leadership, having had the benefit of the best available modern education. Since Korea was seeking new knowledge and culture of the West, these students came to hold more prestige than any other element in Korean society....

Japan, through her conquest and rule of Korea, awakened and sustained Korean nationalism. Japan provided the negative and yet the most powerful symbol for Korean nationalism, a national enemy.

...The continuing presence of the Japanese in Korea had both positive and negative impacts upon Korean nationalism. The large number of Japanese officials and prosperous Japanese migrants constantly reminded the people that Korea was an enforced dependent. The attitude of the Japanese wounded

Korean pride. The strong competition offered by the Japanese in the fields of industry, commerce, and agriculture under government protection may not have damaged the economy as a whole, but it disturbed settled practices and was seen by Koreans as a hindrance to their getting a livelihood. In these ways antagonism toward Japan was sustained and Korean nationalism was intensified.

But it is also possible to see the presence of the Japanese as enlightening. Although not many Koreans were benefiting from the rise of new industries and enterprises, the people could observe the ways in which the Japanese approached certain tasks and also their materially more advanced mode of living. In technology they offered a model for the Korean population to follow. It is certainly possible that the better standard of living enjoyed by the Japanese made the Koreans envious and inspired them to desire independence so as to seek the same advantages.

2
Principles for Administration of Southern Areas Adopted by the Liaison Conference of 20 November 1941

THE late Professor Harry J. Benda was Director of South-East Asia Studies at Yale University and during 1968–9 was Director of the South-East Asia Institute at the University of Singapore. From his broad perspective of South-East Asian history he pioneered the field of Japanese military administration in South-East Asia. He has authored numerous studies on Indonesia, including *The Crescent and the Rising Sun: Indonesian Islam Under Japanese Occupation, 1942–5* (1958). Dr. James K. Irikura was formerly Professor of Japanese History at Kent State University. Mr. Kishi Kōichi was research specialist at the Institute of Economic Affairs in Tokyo. Together they have edited and translated *Japanese Military Administration in Indonesia: Selected Documents* (Yale University South-East Asia Translation Series, 1965), from which these excerpts are drawn.

a. Objectives and Principles

FOR the present, military government shall be established in occupied areas to restore public order, expedite acquisition of resources vital to national defence, and ensure the economic self-sufficiency of military personnel.

The ultimate status of the occupied areas and their future disposition shall be separately determined by the Central Authorities.

As Imperial policies relative to the occupied areas progress, the administrative organs of military governments shall be gradually integrated into, coordinated with, or transferred to the new administrative machinery to be established by Government.

Principles governing the implementation of the first paragraph of the above objectives are as follows:

1. In the implementation of military administration, existing governmental organizations shall be utilized as much as possible, with due respect for past organizational structure and native practices.

2. Occupation forces shall take measures to promote the acquisition and development of resources vital to national defence so far as military operations permit.

Important defence resources developed or secured in occupied areas shall be integrated into the Resources Mobilization Program of the Central Government in Tokyo. In general, resources required locally for the self-sufficiency of occupation forces shall be allotted in accordance with the allocation system of the said Program.

3. The Army and Navy shall render all possible assistance in the transportation of these resources to Japan. Further, they shall endeavour to make optimal use of ships requisitioned for this purpose.

4. Occupation forces shall maintain control of railroads, shipping, harbours, aviation, communications, and postal services.

5. Occupation forces shall regulate foreign trade and exchange. In particular, they shall prevent the outflow to the enemy

PRINCIPLES FOR ADMINISTRATION OF SOUTHERN AREAS

of especially important resources such as petroleum, rubber, tin, tungsten, and cinchona.

6. In general, local currency shall be utilized as much as possible; where this is not possible, military scrip shall be issued in denominations of the foreign currency used in the respective areas.

7. Economic hardships imposed upon native livelihood as a result of the acquisition of resources vital to the national defence and for the self-sufficiency of occupation troops must be endured; and pacification measures against the natives shall stop at a point consistent with these objectives.

8. American, British, and Dutch nationals shall be induced to cooperate with the military administrations, and appropriate measures, such as deportation, shall be taken against recalcitrants.

The existing interests of Axis Power nationals shall be respected, but the future expansion of such interests shall be restricted as much as possible.

Chinese residents shall be induced to defect from the Chiang Kai-shek regime and to cooperate and align themselves with our policies.

Native inhabitants shall be so guided as to induce a sense of trust in the Imperial forces, and premature encouragement of native independence movements shall be avoided.

9. Japanese nationals wishing to enter the occupied areas after the start of military operations shall be carefully screened beforehand, and preference shall be given to former residents now residing in Japan and desiring to return to these areas.

10. Measures to be taken in connection with the implementation of military administrations are as follows:

a. Important matters pertaining to local military administrations shall be determined through the Liaison Conference between Imperial Headquarters and the Government.

Decisions of the Central authorities shall be transmitted by the Army and Navy to their respective local commands.

b. For the present, planning and control relative to the acquisition and development of resources shall be undertaken by the Central authorities centering in the Cabinet Planning Board.

Decisions thus reached shall be implemented as prescribed

in the preceding paragraph. Personnel in charge of military administration, especially civil administration, shall be selected through consultations among the Government agencies concerned.

c. Policies previously determined shall continue for Indo-China and Thailand and no military governments shall be established there. Further measures necessitated by drastic changes in either country shall be separately determined.

d. Details shall be cooperatively determined by the Government agencies concerned.

b. *Economic Policies for the Southern Areas adopted by the Liaison Conference of 12 December 1941*

1. The primary objectives shall be to fulfill the demand for resources vital to the prosecution of the present war, to establish at the same time an autarchic Greater East Asia Co-Prosperity Sphere, and to accelerate the strengthening of the economic power of the Empire.

2. The present policy outline is designed for the Dutch East Indies, British Malaya and Borneo, and the Philippines (all in Area A); and for French Indo-China and Thailand (both in Area B).

3. Policies relative to Area A are divided into two stages as primary and secondary policies, and shall be based on the following objectives:

(1) Primary policies

a. Emphasis shall be placed on the acquisition of resources, particularly those essential to the prosecution of the war.

b. Every effort shall be made to prevent the outflow of indigenous resources from the Southern Areas to enemy nations.

c. In acquiring resources, strenuous efforts shall be made to secure the full cooperation of existing enterprises in order to reduce the burden on the economy of the Empire to the absolute minimum.

(2) Secondary policies

To hold to the objective of completing the economic self-sufficiency of the Greater East Asia Co-Prosperity Sphere and to work for its permanent consolidation.

PRINCIPLES FOR ADMINISTRATION OF SOUTHERN AREAS 117

4. Policies relative to Area B shall be based on previously determined objectives and shall be conducted so as to achieve their fruition as soon as possible. And depending upon changes in the situation in Area A, increasing pressure will be exerted in planning for the fulfilment of our requirements, such as vital resources, especially in food resources, and others. Objectives shall be separately altered in the event of abrupt changes in the situation....

3
Plan for Leadership of Nationalities

MARQUIS Tokugawa was a personal friend of the Sultan of Johore, north of Singapore in southern Malaya, and was regularly invited to hunt tigers with the Sultan in pre-war Malaya. During the war the Marquis collected and preserved many documents relating to the military administration of Malaya. These documents are preserved in many volumes in the War History Library of the Defence Agency in Tokyo. This plan for a nationality policy is among the Tokugawa Papers.

Plan for Leadership of Nationalities in Greater East Asia, General Staff Headquarters, 14th section
6 August 1942

Foreword:
1. This guideline is aimed at contributing to the control of the occupied areas in the South temporarily. We here specify the ideal of leading the nationalities.
2. Emphasis will be placed on the Southern nationalities in this guideline; we refer only to ancillary matters regarding the others.

1. *Policy*
Under the leadership of the Yamato people morality shall be the foundation, and we will try to mutually develop the peoples of

Greater East Asia. We anticipate the prosperity of Greater East Asia and will realize the great ideal of *hakko ichiū.**

2. *Main Points of leadership*

(1) We will realize the preordained view of Asia for the Asiatics. On the basis of the common ideal of development of Asia we anticipate the strong unity of all peoples. For this all peoples of East Asia are in a relationship of one inseparable body by preordination. We will have them complete an organic people's cooperative structure whose nucleus is the people of Yamato.

(2) In guiding and fostering each nationality we will not stress the individual advancement of each nationality. Our main goal is to try to develop a sound people's cooperative body. To do this we will restrain or expand their power according to each nationality's distinctive character. We will have each nationality participate in the responsibility of building Greater East Asia according to their respective status. We will obliterate the former European and British superiority complex and American and British world view. We will raise the Imperial Way. But we will value highly the distinctive culture and tradition of the respective nationalities.

3. *Allocation of missions for each nationality and their relationship*

(1) *Yamato people*

a. As the pivot of the Greater East Asia Peoples' Cooperative Body Japan will have the central role in military, political, economic and cultural spheres. To other people Japan has the duty of leadership. As the keynote of Greater East Asia defence we will control domestic national defence.

b. We will strengthen the foundation in Manchuria and North China. At the same time the important Southern Area will be the basic area of Yamato people's activities, and we will build Japanese people's society. In choosing these areas we will consider carefully the nationalistic, military, economic and climatic factors. In order to secure for the Japanese people in perpetuity the leadership of the Co-Prosperity Sphere we will take special measures to guide the education of the Japanese people and to provide cultural facilities. This is also to prevent the lowering of quality.

c. As Japan has the qualifications to be the leading nation it should try to develop and improve in quality and quantity. We should especially maintain the purity of blood.

(2) *Korean people*

We will advise them to go abroad to the Southern Area in groups and restrain their advance into Manchuria and China. Their destinations should be chosen from areas where native society is not so strong and is separated from society generally. They will have the responsibility for part of defence.

(3) *Manchurian people*

For the building of Greater East Asia from the viewpoint of their status we will try to develop a sound defensive perimeter in the northern area.

(4) *Mongolian people*

As one sector in the building of Greater East Asia we will try to develop them in unity and strength and have them become a defensive wall in the north-west.

(5) *Han people*

First we will extirpate the anti-Japanese enemy character and, using the people's ability, have them devote themselves to the prosperity of Greater East Asia.

The pressure of their nationalism should be directed against the West. We will stop their advance into Manchuria or the South.

(6) *Each nationality of the Southern Area*

(a) *Native peoples*

In decisions on jurisdiction of occupied areas from now on we will change the main points of leadership and determine the ordering of peoples in each area. We will liberate them from colonial status and try to raise their consciousness as peoples of Greater East Asia. We will expand the power of nationalities suitably as an important facet of the prosperity of Greater East Asia. We will have them contribute to the building of the Southern Area. We will have them assume charge of part of the defence of the Southern Area. In fostering or leading them we will discipline ourselves to be generous and dignified and kind, not uncontrolled. At the same time we should study the real situation of the peoples. It is necessary to act according to this situation. We should avoid immediate Japanization. So long as it does not interfere with our control we will respect old customs and religion and the native language as much as possible. We will try to expand the Japanese language as the common language of Greater East Asia.

(b) *Overseas Chinese*

Regarding Chinese who swear loyalty to Japan and hope to become Japanese they will be Japanese nationals. But those who do not will be driven out of the Southern Area or will be treated as temporary residents. Therefore even regarding the Chinese who are Japanese nationals, their power will be gradually restrained. We will prohibit new immigration from China.

(c) *Indians*

We will treat Indians just like the Chinese people. But we will consider the India project.

(d) *Europeans and Americans*

We will generally treat them as temporary residents, and gradually restrain their power or expel them. But it is necessary not to give an excuse for a racial war.

Note: Relation between rights and duties in the order of nationality.

Shūjin minzoku (master peoples), As a rule they have all the rights and duties;

Yūjin minzoku (friendly peoples). Though they have similar duties and rights to the master people we will reduce them commensurate to status and capability;

Kigū minzoku (guest peoples). As a rule we will recognize their right to hold public office and the right to own land. They will register for business, announcement of wills, holding meetings and forming groups.

4
Military Idealism in the Field

FUJIWARA Iwaichi was a professional military man, at the outbreak of World War II a major in intelligence assigned to the 8th section, Second Bureau of Imperial General Headquarters. He was sent on a mission to Bangkok in October 1941, assigned to liaison with overseas Chinese and Indians in Malaya and Thailand, and with sultans in Malaya. With an Indian POW, Captain Mohan Singh, he helped organize in the jungles of Malaya in December the first Indian National Army to fight for Indian independence. The sincerity of Maj. Fujiwara's commitment to the goal of independence for India is reflected in this excerpt from his *F Kikan-chō no shuki* (Memo of the F Kikan chief, 1959). Based on notes made during 1941, a revised edition was published under the title *F Kikan* (Hara Shobo, 1966). The '*F Kikan*' or 'F' Agency, was the liaison agency which acted between the Japanese Army and the Indian National Army. After World War II Fujiwara became commanding general of the First Division of the Ground Self-Defence Forces. He represents Pan-Asianism in the Army at its most idealistic in this excerpt.

WITH both enemy and inhabitants alike who have been pressed into cooperation with the Japanese Army amidst gunpowder and smoke we must forge the basis of a new friendship and peace. We must spread this among the enemy and find allies among the enemy. So long as the Japanese Army fights we will not tire; we must go on adding enemies to our allies among the inhabitants. Japan's war will truly liberate inhabitants and POWs. Unfortunately they have to be made to realize that it is a righteous war in which the aspirations of the people will be achieved, and we will have their sympathy. Defeat in this ideological war, even though we achieve military victory, would mean that we could not attain complete victory. Regardless of the significance of the war, people who participate in this kind of work behind those in the independence movements of various nationalities must have enthusiasm and faith in the movements. And we must be humble and modest....

If this area becomes the battleground of Greater East Asia, Japan's ideal must be to establish the goal of prosperity and harmony which transcends all conflicts and rivalries. There must be no consciousness of control or pride of victors or conquerors. All peoples of Greater East Asia must build a peaceful sphere wherein, after being released from control and oppression, all nationalities' political aspirations and cultural traditions will be enhanced in a free and equal relationship, and wherein the prosperity and progress of all Asia will be promoted. The Japanese people, shouldering the duty of becoming leaders, must achieve this. The faiths, manners, customs and way of life of all peoples must be respected without exception. Furthermore, we must avoid insisting subjectively on our own way.... Our actions must accord with personal examples of the ideal of cooperation, and our sincerity and passion will thus secure friends of all races and elicit their sympathy....

Our mission must be executed through assisting the independence movements of comrades of different races who sympathize with Japan's ideals. There must be no hint of constraint or intervention, no thought of using them or suggestion of their being puppets. Without artifice we must do our duty with sincerity. The most important thing for the achievement of our duty is that we cherish toward our comrades of all races in the South and in India the same kind of sacrificial spirit of friendship and for liberation which we cherish for our own people. Furthermore, the important point is that we mediate between them and the Japanese Army, and see that no heartless conduct occurs toward the inhabitants or toward POWs such as has been criticized in China....

The plan which was thus sketched in my mind was that, simultaneous with the outbreak of war we should assist the Indian Independence League,* dash behind enemy lines, and directly enlist comrades within the British Indian Army. Then we should expand the political activities of the IIL rapidly among all Indian peoples, starting with Thailand and Malaya. After the outbreak of war we should move toward the two objectives of the IIL movement, among the Indian soldiers in the British Indian Army and among Indians generally. The policy toward Indian soldiers in the British Indian Army would be for *F Kikan* members themselves to protect Indian POWs, to make them aware of IIL ideals and of propaganda on Japan's true aims, to rapidly promote the establishment of a brave army for Indian independence ... and thus to enlist the Indian soldiers of the British Indian Army. The policy toward the Indian people generally would be for the IIL and *F Kikan* themselves to protect the people who were suffering amidst the smoke of gunfire and to communicate the true aims of the IIL and the Japanese Army; also for the people to join the IIL movement, to expand the IIL movement on all battlefields, and to diffuse (our aims) among the people within the sphere of enemy army control....

An indomitable will is necessary which will inform Indians of our aims and passion. Not only must the Japanese Army refrain from illegal actions toward Indian residents and Indian POWs, but it is particularly necessary that they have understanding and warm feelings about protecting their lives and property and freedom. The IIL is an autonomous movement of Indian patriots and we must cherish the ideal and policy of helping all Indians without any racial or religious prejudice. Futhermore, it is necessary for Japanese, especially for heads of the army and government, to have knowledge and understanding of proper good will toward India, Indians, and their independence movement. (The Japanese awareness of India and Indians is extremely weak)....

I explained to them [Indian POWs captured in Malaya] repeatedly from the standpoint of the Japanese Army the real aims of the Japanese Army regarding its aid to the independence of India, and the procedures of the Japanese Army cooperation with the IIL. I also revealed to them my own views concerning the achievement of Indian independence. I pointed out the sorrow and disgrace of the subjugated peoples. Also I stated my conviction that in my judgement the independence of India could not be completely attained without the rise and struggle of the Indian people themselves. Further, I emphasized that the Greater East Asia war which had followed the second European War is the sole and last chance for the Indian people to rise and win the glory of their freedom and independence....

The defeat of England will necessarily be decisively influenced by the attitude of India. Excitement over the present progress of the war in Malaya and Penang and Singapore was useless. A policy of embracing India in the Greater East Asia camp was to be hoped for in the near future. The progress of the war to achieve this will be slow. Furthermore, the military strength of Japan needed to embrace Burma would probably be excessive. If we assume for the sake of argument that Japan's military strength will positively not extend to India, even if Japan should make an attack on British power in India, the Indian people would probably strongly resist.... Japan should adopt a policy of cutting India adrift from England — but not depending on the unreliable method of Japanese military power — and getting cooperation in accordance with what Japan advocates. Toward this end we must eschew a Machiavellian policy and, standing on the basis of freedom and equality, assist with all our strength the attainment of Indian independence, and urge the cooperation of the Indian people in the establishment of the New Order in Greater East Asia. In all dealings Japan must have no sinister designs on India, and interference and constraint in the substance of their political movement must be prohibited....

The Indian people and of course the IIL and INA members are watching from evidence of personal practice in Burma, Penang and other areas occupied by Japan what form the New Order in Greater East Asia will assume in the future. We will investigate the inclinations of 350 million Indian people on this point. Japan should demonstrate by personal example in Burma, Penang, and other occupied areas the ideals of the New Order which Japan professes.

5
Occupation in Burma

DR. Ba Maw, lawyer and the first Premier of Burma after separation from India, was also wartime Premier under the Japanese. He attended the Greater East Asia Conference in Tokyo in November 1943. He was tried and interned in Sugamo prison in Tokyo after World War II as a war criminal. He was detained more recently by General Ne Win's military regime in Burma. In his wartime memoirs, *Breakthrough in Burma, Memoirs of a Revolution, 1939–1946* (Yale University Press, 1968), Ba Maw describes the impact of Japanese military administration on Burma and particularly on élite groups. In this selection he discusses the idealistic policies of Bo Mogyo, or Col. Suzuki Keiji, who, in a role analogous to Fujiwara's, organized the Burma Independence Army. He also deals with some Japanese miscalculations in dealing with the B.I.A. and ultimately with all Burma.

SO the Burma Independence Army (B.I.A.) was born during those last five days of 1941, with all the stars and omens favouring it; all except one, which lay dormant then because it was lodged deep within Suzuki's personality.

I have already described Suzuki, or Bo Mogyo as I shall call him from now on, and some of his conflicts with those above him. He was an incongruous character in many ways, a rebel by temperament and a conformist by upbringing, an individualist who had with difficulty learnt to live with others, intensely ambitious and pragmatic yet ready to throw everything away for a dream. As I have said before, the dream at that moment took the form of a conviction that he alone as the Japanese head of the Burmese forces of liberation could unite and complete the victory of the two peoples; in other words, he was the man of destiny in Burma. All his plans had gone without a hitch till then, and that turned his belief in himself into a fixation. He claimed to derive his authority directly from the Supreme Command, at whose head was Prince Kan In, the Emperor's uncle; that is, from the Emperor himself, as he insisted. Consequently, his was an independent and parallel campaign, a Burmese war fought side by side with that of the Japanese to secure Burmese as much as Japanese objectives. He wanted recognition for his Burmese army on that basis. For the Japanese the claim sounded almost like a challenge. It brought Bo Mogyo into a head-on collision with the Japanese Army Command in Burma. Soon he drew into this collision the new-born Burmese army and thus the first seeds were sown of the conflict that in time developed between the Japanese and the Burmese as the war dragged on.

Bo Mogyo aroused fear, distrust, and jealousy among the other Japanese in Burma. He reciprocated that ill-will in most cases. Before long these strained relations spread to the B.I.A. forces and their partisans, who had always eagerly picked up his ways and words. That, among other reasons, led the Japanese to turn against the B.I.A. itself in a large number of places, and the Burmese army; and the masses that followed it retaliated with a secret hostility. So the rift began between the two peoples, and with time and growing strains and the certainty of defeat hanging over all of us in the latter days, these worsening tensions became one of the biggest problems we faced.... The problem, of course, was far more complicated, and I have shown how it began in yet another way, by the process of emotional transference as I called it loosely....

Nevertheless, they were right about Bo Mogyo. 'He created our little army and we were completely in his hands,' one of the thirty comrades explained to me after thinking over the matter for some time, 'and as we say in Burmese, we feared him from our youth, and we also loved him. So his ways with the Japanese army became ours. Moreover, we liked it so, because it made us share Bo Mogyo's independence and importance and feel that we were fighting for our own cause and not that of the Japanese'. I remember most particularly their phrase about their fear of Bo Mogyo beginning from their youth; Aung San used the same phrase to me when in June 1942 I suggested to him that it was time for Mogyo to leave and a Burmese, meaning him, to take over the B.I.A., which had become a national army, and he agreed with divided feelings.

The words of the comrade I have just mentioned reveal that Bo Mogyo's independent ways taught the Burmese much that was essential and timely. It is true that they created a lot of friction and even chaos in those first days, but at the same time Bo Mogyo, by his example, stiffened the backs of the Burmese in dealing with the victory-flushed Japanese armies. It turned out to be an essential lesson at the time, one that had to be learnt before it would be too late. I have also mentioned a little further back that Tokyo did not take Bo Mogyo and his thirty comrades very seriously. But Bo Mogyo did, and he made others do it. It was largely this man's will and vision that had created the tiny force and later gave it a place in the vast story of the Japanese invasion and conquest of South-East Asia.

I am dwelling at length on Bo Mogyo because, balancing everything, he was the most vivid and dynamic force at that juncture of our story. Both for good and for evil his attitudes shaped those of the B.I.A. and the masses who flocked to his name, and they in turn shaped the general feelings in the country, notably those of the youth. Therefore to follow this part of the story we must understand Bo Mogyo and the appeal he made to the masses during that brief period. It ended when he left in June 1942, but while it lasted it was phenomenal. Colonel Hiraoka, the Japanese officer who was then in charge of relations between the Japanese and the Burmese, told me that the Japanese army regarded Bo Mogyo as its toughest problem in hand. 'Your people are following him like children, and that may not be good for them in the long run,' he explained to me at our very first meeting. I had not yet met Bo Mogyo, but Hiraoka's words first put the idea into my head of doing something to replace Bo Mogyo with a Burmese officer.

In his book *'Burma under the Japanese'* U Nu has recorded what Bo Mogyo told him when they met for the first time in May 1942.... 'Don't be worried about independence,' Bo Mogyo said. 'Independence is not the kind of thing you can get through begging for it from other people. You should proclaim it yourselves. The Japanese refuse to give it? Very well, then; tell them that you will cross over to some place like Twante and proclaim independence and set up your own government. What's the difficulty about that? If they start shooting, you just shoot back.' U Nu, of course, doubted Bo Mogyo's sincerity; but then, since Japan's defeat U Nu does not believe that any Japanese is ever sincere or can be so. Furthermore, he was writing in 1945 when that was the propaganda line of the victor powers.

To find out the truth, I have asked several of the thirty comrades who knew Bo Mogyo most closely for their view of him. They assured me that what he told U Nu truthfully reflected his attitude; even more, that was the attitude of all the Japanese they knew in the *Minami Kikan*.* The Japanese instructors in Hainan had to take an oath to fight for Burmese independence. Let Ya remembered that it was Kawashima who read out the proclamation of Burmese independence when their unit entered Tavoy. Other comrades likewise remembered similar incidents. 'Bo Mogyo proved his sincerity by all he said and did,' was the sum of their statements. 'He showed his independence of the Japanese armies and even defied them at times. He was sent away from Burma because of that,' which, by the way, was not quite true, as I know. On the other hand, they readily admitted that he had many ugly edges, that he was brusque, domineering, even shrill and brutal at times and easily provoked, but beneath all that 'he was a soldier as well as a dreamer pursuing a dream and making others do so too; and a good part of that dream was to lead a Burmese army of liberation to set Burma free'.

...In planning the campaign of the Burma Independence Army Bo Mogyo naturally kept close to the Japanese plan for the invasion of Burma. At the same time he had certain clear purposes of his own. The first of these was to keep the Burmese army and its final objectives as separate and Burmese as the pressures created by the Japanese invasion would allow. It would be a Japanese-created army, but Burmese in spirit, fighting to gain its own objectives as a part of the larger objectives of the

Asian war. His next purpose was the practical one of ensuring the safety of this tiny army still in the making. To achieve this it would have to follow the Japanese armies as they advanced and cleared the enemy out of the way.

Thus the B.I.A. would be able to grow in safety behind the Japanese armour and to move forward and gather the fruits of the Japanese victories, and to use them to win over the Burmese masses. As a third purpose it would learn its first lessons in active combat by engaging in small mopping-up operations here and there behind the Japanese advance. Lastly, there were the civilian tasks the B.I.A., as a Burmese force, would be most fitted to perform, such as winning the cooperation of the people, bringing back peace and order to the conquered areas by setting up local administrative bodies, and generally acting as the Burmese face of the Japanese war. The attainment of these purposes, Bo Mogyo calculated, would enable him and his army to realise their final dream of a Burma liberated and ruled by men working hand in hand with that army. It was with such careful designs that Bo Mogyo had sent his first small batch of troops to three border towns, and they were told to hang on closely to the Japanese advance across Burma....

The new Burmese pride had the makings of a psychosis with all its disturbing symptoms. In fact, it might even be said that the deeper problem between the Burmese and the Japanese was psychotic. It could be viewed as a clash between two psychoses: that of a late-coming strong race trying to impress a weak race with its new strength and superiority, and that of a weak race trying not to be impressed in order not to expose its weakness. The final truth, or a good part of it, perhaps lies there.

The B.I.A. too, on its side, was watching every move the Japanese were making. Many in it who knew something about Korea and Manchukuo saw the Japanese action against their army in Moulmein as being much more than what the Japanese said it was. They traced a deep design in it which fitted in with increasing reports of Japanese highhandedness and brutality towards the Burmese. This view soon spread among the troops, and then among the people till it became so firmly lodged that there was almost no way of dispelling it. And it seemed that the Japanese militarist clique did not have the slightest interest in dispelling anything. In fact, even I, who worked closely with them as the head of the state as well as of the government, could not detect any sign that they were even aware that such a universal feeling existed; nor, as I have said, did they seem to care. I found this to be one of the most baffling aspects of the character of the Japanese militarist, which to the Burmese was baffling enough as it was. This was yet another way in which the problem of the relations between the Japanese and the Burmese began....

But, for the B.I.A. in those days of its first contact with the Japanese army any Japanese troops happening to cross its path appeared to carry the authority of the whole army. The Burmese leaders who had kept aloof from the Japanese High Command under Bo Mogyo's orders were responsible for this blunder.

Another blunder they committed was in giving a party character to the B.I.A. and its local administrations and keeping all the other parties and communities out or nearly so. Because of this rebuff many turned to the Japanese. And so the B.I.A. and its civil administrations found themselves dealing with the local Japanese forces actually as just a single party, of dubious reputation, and not a whole nation. The Japanese High Command did not recognize the B.I.A. as a Burmese national army or even as an army, and the B.I.A. on its part did not seek such recognition; so no relations existed between the two armies, and in all administrative matters the B.I.A. was regarded as a charge of the Kempeitai. This was roughly how the new situation arose.

6
Occupation in the Philippines

DR. Teodoro Agoncillo is professor of history at the University of the Philippines. His speciality is the development of Philippine nationalism under Spanish, American, then Japanese rule. This excerpt is from his two-volume study, *The Fateful Years, Japan's Adventure in the Philippines, 1941–5* (2 vols., R. P. Garcia, 1965). He discusses here the Japanese attempt to reorient the life of the Filipinos and to impose thought control on both the people and officialdom. Among Japanese measures to achieve these goals was the liquidation of political parties and creation of the *Kalibapi** Association, which Professor Agoncillo characterizes as a qualified success to which the Filipinos responded in a way which saved them from a worse fate.

THE forced liquidation of the political parties in December 1942 marked the overt and undisguised attempt of the Japanese military authorities to eliminate all possible sources of irritation that had plagued the Military Administration since it took over the reins of government on 3 January 1942. While to all appearances political parties since the date of abolition had remained quiescent and immobile because of the natural fear of Japanese persecution, yet in the eyes of the Japanese military those parties still exerted an influence and were a stumbling block to the formation of a climate of opinion friendly to Japan or at least not hostile to the creation of a Greater East Asia Co-Prosperity Sphere. The Japanese knew that the Filipinos, under the guidance of the Americans, had gone into politics with as much alacrity as the latter and had learned all the tricks and nuances of that democratic institution. Consequently, the military authorities, in order to re-orient the Filipinos to a way of life that was in consonance with the 'new order,' took steps to stamp out all vestiges of American influence and to substitute these with Japanese ideology in order to make the Philippines a pawn in Japan's war politics.

The Executive Commission, a Japanese creation, was the most important tool that was fashioned out of Philippine materials to bring about the changes in the thinking and actions of the Filipinos. Through the Commission, the Japanese succeeded in curtailing the basic freedoms and in imposing their will upon the people and their hapless officials. The press, or what was left of it, was gagged. Not satisfied with censoring the press, the Japanese military placed all the newspapers under the management of the Manila Simbun-sya operated by the *Osaka Mainichi* and the *Tokyo Nichi Nichi*. With the press completely in their hands, the Japanese began to exercise thought control. The significance of this step was not lost on the people when they read the Japanese explanation, or rationalization, for their act. 'The new company', it was announced, 'has been established for the purpose of further clarifying the invulnerable position of the Nippon Empire, now in the midst of the creation of the New Order in Greater East Asia, of making more thoroughly understood the purpose of the Military Administration in the Philippines, and of propelling with greater force the materialization of the New Philippines.'

But more potent than the Executive Commission in carrying out the Japanese mandates was the KALIBAPI, created by Executive Order No.109 on 4 December 1942. Article II defined the purposes of the Association, as follows:

'1. To render such services as will bring about the rapid reconstruction of the Philippines and the rehabilitation of its people, for which purpose, it shall strive a) to secure the unification of the Filipino people of all classes through the development in them and among them of the conviction that the permanent security, well-being, and happiness of the Filipinos depends on the permanent security of the Philippines; and b) to coordinate all activities and services of organizations or individuals that are or may hereafter be concerned with the development or promotion of the welfare of the people socially, spiritually, physically, culturally, economically or otherwise;

'2. To insure a stable foundation for the New Philippines by fostering a) the cultural, moral, spiritual, and economic advancement of the people by giving encouragement to the abovementioned activities and by invigorating in them such oriental virtues as hard work, faith, self-reliance, loyalty, bravery, discipline, and self-sacrifice; and b) the development of a more sturdy and vigorous race of Filipinos by attending to the physical development of the people through a wise supervision of physical exercise and wholesome recreational and outdoor activities, particularly sports, and athletic meets and contests;

'3. To assist the Filipino people in fully comprehending the significance of, and to strengthen their adherence to, the principles of the Greater East Asia Co-Prosperity Sphere;

'4. To secure for the new Philippines its rightful place in the Greater East Asia Co-Prosperity as a worthy member thereof;

'5. To adhere strictly to the policies of the Imperial Japanese Forces in the Philippines in their administration and to render service in the establishment of the Greater East Asia Co-Prosperity Sphere; and

6. To do any and all acts which will facilitate the reconstruction of the New Philippines, and contribute to the advancement of the Greater East Asia Co-Prosperity Sphere.'

The Association was supposed to be non-partisan, but its duties were such as to edify and promote Japan's war efforts. Benigno S. Aquino, who was unceremoniously removed from the Department of the Interior, was given the task of directing the affairs of the Association as Director-General. With the creation of chapters in the provinces, the KALIBAPI's tentacles reached into almost every home. Under Aquino's indefatigable leadership, the Association staged meeting after meeting in different parts of Luzon, telling the people that the 'new order' was here to stay. Aquino, always heading a platoon of able speakers, almost always spoke against the guerrillas and, in one instance, wondered why the 'pernicious guerrilla activities continued' in spite of the fact that the 'Philippines was not at war with Japan.' Handbooks, published by the Department of Information of the Imperial Japanese Army, were printed and distributed to apprise the people of the KALIBAPI's 'noble aims.'

...On 18 May, 1943, Vargas issued Executive Order No.156 amending the Kalibapi charter in order to provide for the organization of the Junior Kalibapi. The Kalibapi leaders felt that the young citizens of the land 'should be mobilized with a view to preparing them for unified and integrated service to the country and thus keep the work of the Association continuous.'

The noise created by the Kalibapi increased in volume and tempo until the Japanese became convinced, or pretended to be convinced, that it was a potent weapon in their efforts to isolate the discordant voices in Philippine society or to make them sing in unison with the leading tenors of the huge chorus. Aquino, more than any other Filipino, was responsible for the success of what was then called the 'Kalibapi movement.' A fiery orator and a seasoned politician, he swayed, or seemingly swayed, the masses to the Kalibapi way. That huge masses of people attended Aquino's meetings and affiliated with the Association was, however, no indication that the people believed in him or in the Kalibapi's avowed aims. Actually, the people were merely curious what the Association was all about. Aquino himself must have divined the peoples' thoughts, but the play must continue and he as director must make it appear to the Japanese that the Filipinos were behind him and applauding his stage act. The Japanese authorities, on the other hand, were so thoroughly convinced of Aquino's role that they could not bring themselves to believe that he was merely acting. Thus General Wachi Takaji, the Director-General of the Japanese Military Administration and at the same time Chief of Staff of the Imperial Japanese Army in the Philippines, wrote in his reminiscences of the war that the Association's activities were aimed at 'spreading the influence of the Japanese Army even to provincial districts' and that it was a 'body patronized by the Japanese military.' While to all appearances many people attended the meetings of the Association, they were nevertheless wary of it and expressed their true convictions only in private conversations. It was this make-believe attitude of the people that perhaps saved them, to a certain extent, from further Japanese brutalization.

7
Occupation in Indonesia

THE late Mr. Kishi Kōichi was a research specialist with the Asian Economic Research Institute and spent several years studying Japanese military administration in Indonesia. Mr. Nishijima Shigetada of the North Sumatra Petroleum Company collected many documents on military administration in Indonesia; this Nishima collection is now in the Ōkuma Institute of Social Sciences at Waseda University. Messrs. Kishi and Nishijima edited, under the auspices of the Ōkuma Institute of Social Sciences, *Indonesia ni okeru Nihon gunsei no kenkyū* (1959). The volume was then translated by the U.S. Department of Commerce Joint Publications Research Services under the title *Studies in Japanese Military Administration in Indonesia*. Excerpts included here are derived from the translation. The emphasis is on the impact of Japanese attempts at political mobilization and social change.

THE Japanese military administration provided strong factors for the changes in the Indonesian social structure. Naturally, these forces stemmed from the strong compulsion with the Japanese sword of the military forces in the background.

We have already seen that the Japanese military administration strongly shook the social structure of Indonesia. It was expressed

OCCUPATION IN INDONESIA 137

in the form of mass mobilization. The interests of the masses in political trends were hardly seen at all under the Dutch colonial system. The political movement of the Indonesian masses was a nationalist movement of the elite with the political leaders as the central figures. Political parties were for these small number of nationalist movement workers. Under the Japanese military administration all political movements were prohibited and suppressed. However, the growth of the military administration required cooperation not only from the small number of political leaders but also from the masses, and many measures were adopted for the realization of growth. The nationalist movement in Java grew from a movement of the elite society to the mass movement by the process of the Triple A Movement,* the *Poetera* Movement,* and the Java Patriotic Service Association,* which were structured by the Japanese policy. It may be regarded [sic] that the growth of such nationalist movements appeared as a result of the structural changes of the national society.

Furthermore, the impacts of the military administration are also manifested as a result of the trisection of the military administration. The Japanese military administration recognized the position of the Indonesian language as the unifying language of the people. It also utilized Islam as the central religion. However, these two cultural policies did not appear as the result of consistent policies in the three areas of military administration. There were several ethnic groups in Java and Sumatra, and many in Borneo, Celebes, in the Lesser Sundas, and in the Moluccas, and they all had different languages. Therefore, when these three areas of military administration needed a common language, a language policy was adopted to force the Japanese language, to prohibit the Dutch language, and to encourage the Indonesian language. As a consequence of this an opportunity for linguistic unification arose. However, in other policies, especially in the economic policy, the trisection of military administration was strongly reflected. The remarkable instance could be said to have been expressed in the result of the attempts of recolonization of Indonesia by the Dutch after September 1945. The Poetera Movement of Java and the Java Patriotic Service Association contributed to inciting the Javanese masses' enthusiasm for independence. However, the general masses in Sumatra, Borneo, Celebes, the Lesser Sundas and Moluccas heard the trends in Java only as the voice of the wind, and wished they could join the movement themselves someday. However, the leaders in these areas overestimated their positions granted by the occupation forces as the supreme leaders as equal to the positions of the leaders in Java. On the other hand, Japan, based on the basic principle that the nationalist movement was not to be prematurely incited, oppressed all nationalist movements as independence movements in Sumatra, with its abundant oil resources, and in the Navy areas that Japan attempted to possess permanently, and suppressed the popular trends to follow the practice in Java. The result was that by the Dutch attempt to recolonize beginning in September 1945, Outer Territories gradually seceded from the Indonesian Republic and came under the protection of the Netherlands, and local leaders in all areas were appointed prime ministers and ministers, and they extolled their good fortunes.

On the other hand, there was the formation of the New *Priai** class against the old so-called *priai* class, which was thought about as a result of the Japanese policy to attain their own objectives. Under the Japanese military administration, a policy to respect and utilize Islam was adopted, especially in Java, and as a consequence Kiai* and Ulama* emerged among the elite classes; furthermore, as a result of the formation of the Military Auxiliaries and the Volunteer Corps to aid in defence, soldiers appeared as new elites; and out of the youth stratum who engaged in the practical activities for the declaration of independence in August 1945 a new political leadership elite came into being.

These foregoing factors are to indicate that the military administration resulted in accelerating the structural change in the social strata. However, the military administration did not stop at merely leaving such impacts. Economically, it devastated the livelihood of the populace by the forcefulness manifested in the rice delivery and labour requisition, by the unlimited issuing of military payment certificates, and by the deprivation of consumer goods. The consequence, together with the four years' military resistance against the Netherlands, was that it left deep scars.

We have described the circumstances of the declaration of independence, on 17 August 1945, in Chapter 7. Yet, the fact that the true picture of this glorious one page in the history of struggle for independence as described by Indonesians is not always accurate is implicitly recognized by the Indonesians who happened to be at this historic moment. That in the execution of the declaration as a step for the formation of this extremely glorious state many difficulties were broken down by a small number of Japanese was a hidden fact. More than ten years after the formation of the state bringing this fact to light would not soil the history of the Indonesian people. Rather, when we think of some Japanese who tried to check cooperation in making this moment of formation of the state, we regarded it necessary to quote the description in the history of struggle for independence and to clarify the new circumstances of the declaration by quoting from the descriptions in the history of that struggle written by Indonesians, and by further adding comments to these descriptions concerning the real conditions of the bona fide cooperation by a small number of Japanese, we dared attempt this. Throughout this essay, we have intended to clarify that there were conflicts between the Army and Navy on the Japanese side, and also on the Indonesian side there was criticism of the collaborator group with Japan by the Sjahrir group, and the conflicts between the two.

Finally, to add, the 1945 Constitution formulated as a result of the declaration of independence was never practically and peacefully put into practice afterwards owing to the emergency status in the struggle against the Netherlands for independence, and was evolved into the 1949 Temporary Constitution, or the current Constitution. This 1945 Constitution was formulated with the intervention by the Military Administration Department in the stage of the Preparatory Committee for Independence, and it was much influenced by the American Constitution, the Dutch Laws of State Organization, and the Constitution of the Greater Japanese Empire. It remains an extremely interesting problem to speculate what impact this Constitution would have had on the present-day Indonesian politics had it been enforced.

As we have described, the Japanese military administration in Indonesia was developed to satisfy their own national ambition; yet we have analyzed the fact that the forcefulness for the Japanese forces 'own expediency in the process of its development resulted in letting the Indonesians realize that their own capability was not less than other world peoples'. Therefore, it cannot be generalized that the world position of the present-day Indonesians is a result of the training given by the Japanese military administration as generally believed, although it was a result of the Pacific War.

However, as we added as a final note, if the present political situation were controlled by the 1945 Constitution, it might be said that the military occupation administration by Japan left an unexpected bastard after over ten years.

8
Occupation in Malaya

PROFESSOR T. H. Silcock has spent many years in Malaya, and Singapore, where he was professor of economics and has been particularly concerned with problems of development. He has written *The Commonwealth Economy in South-East Asia* (Duke University Press, 1959). Dr. Ungku Aziz, Vice-Chancellor of the University of Malaya, studied in Japan during World War II at the personal invitation of Marquis Tokugawa, receiving his Ph.D. from Waseda University. Here Professors Silcock and Aziz discuss the atmosphere of Japanese Pan-Asianism in which Malayan nationalism was nurtured. The authors maintain that in fostering Malayan patriotism within the Co-Prosperity Sphere, the Japanese encouraged what became a weapon turned against them.

THE invasion of Malaya by the Japanese in December 1941 produced many different effects on nationalism in the peninsula. Among the Malays the important effects were shock and upheaval, and also the learning of the habits of violence and of staged mass demonstrations. Among the Chinese the Occupation meant guerrilla activity, a sense of insecurity and a reversion to habits based on personal accommodation to an atmosphere of violence; the psychological effect on their attitude

POLICY IMPLEMENTATION IN THE FIELD

to the British was also very important. Among the Indians the organisation of the Indian Independence League and the Indian National Army was probably the dominant factor. But on all the peoples of Malaya, brought up in an atmosphere in which government had been run by an alien people, on the whole accepted as friendly, and in which politics was definitely not respectable, the sudden change of masters and the impact of violent Japanese nationalism and pan-Asianism was a most intensive school for nationalist feelings and thoughts about political questions.

The principal technique of the Japanese was one of stirring up anti-European feeling and emphasizing that they were an Asian people. They were not concerned with efficient or progressive administration. Moreover they were dependent on the existing government services for local effect by promoting to the top people who had previously occupied comparatively junior positions. The early days of Japanese rule were a time of opportunity for the young and ambitious, especially among the Malays.

The civilian administration was in the main a facade. Such activities as education, medical services and public works were starved of funds, material and personnel. The actual work in-, volved was improvisation rather than creative development. But in some cases it was done well; and it gave a sense of power and consequence until the Japanese themselves arrived to take over. One of the effects of having local men as directors and administrators in services in which formerly they had been assistants, was to stimulate local professional pride. The Malayan population acquired new self-confidence and the Japanese acquired a reputation for being in earnest about their pan-Asianism. Similar results developed in the non-Malay technical services.

It may be questioned how far the responsibility exercised by Malayans at this time was genuine. In some cases, particularly in the early days, there can be little doubt that it was. Senior men, whose initiative had to some extent atrophied under constant European supervision, in conditions in which quite junior Europeans had access to confidences that were denied to them, were able for a few months to exercise genuine control. The return to subordinate positions, first under Japanese and later under British superiors, inevitably made these men feel bitter and frustrated.

OCCUPATION IN MALAYA 143

There were, however, others who were given status and authority in return for political services during the campaign, but were not in effect given any real administrative work to do. The effect on them, if they were intelligent enough — as many were not — to avoid being shot by the Japanese, was to give a wholly false idea of the nature of the administrative work. In essence, they merely occupied positions in which they did what they were told, and others did what they told them to do, because of the framework of a police state effectively controlled by the *kempeitai*, the Japanese military police. The difficulties of controlling clever and ambitious men were much simplified in an atmosphere in which any awkward customer would simply be executed. And the problems of drawing lines that would create the least sense of injustice and frustration were easily solved in a situation where the general environment was saturated with frustration and fear.

It can hardly be doubted that the experiences of this time have profoundly affected current Malay attitudes. Those whose training consisted largely of indoctrination with patriotic sentiments on behalf of Malaya, the Co-Prosperity Sphere, and Japan, no doubt feel that they have unused talents, but their attitude to power is likely to be unconstructive, and their knowledge of the possibilities of the situation very vague. But the more senior men whose local knowledge enabled them in the early days to perform genuine functions may have a better grasp of the situation....

In fostering a patriotism for Malaya within the Co-Prosperity Sphere, the Japanese fostered something that ultimately turned against them. The highly emotional cult of the Emperor did not make many converts among the Malays; but it stirred up feelings that could later be transferred to Malaya, in a way which the more reserved British expressions of national feeling could never do....

Some Malays had formed a fifth column to aid the Japanese against the British. Before and after the fighting this was known as the *Kesatuan Muda Melayu* (K.M.M.), or Malay Youth Movement.

During the campaign of 1941–2 it came under the control of Major Fujiwara and its members wore an F armband and were known as 'F men.' Other Malays, including the Sultan of Pahang and many men in important positions under the Japanese, organised an anti-Japanese movement on the side of the United

Nations. In some cases the same men served in both movements; and though this may denote political incompetence it would be unjust to condemn it as mere treachery and self-interest. Certainly it is not always regarded as such among the Malays themselves.

It is a fact of considerable importance to the subsequent history of Malaya that no Malay guerrillas were trained by the British to operate against the Japanese....

The effects of the Occupation on the Chinese were far more complex. To begin with, there was a very considerable massacre of Chinese by the invaders. So far as can be ascertained, the Japanese were concerned to kill three classes of Chinese: active supporters of Kuomintang, active Communists, and those who had fought in the Volunteer forces and not surrendered....

Those who were genuinely pro-British in their attitude and who succeeded, by keeping out of the limelight, in escaping with their lives if not their property, expected to be rewarded for their loyalty when the long-awaited liberation arrived. When the British returned and treated all inhabitants in very much the same way they felt bitter and frustrated. It is probably this as much as anything that accounts for the intensely bitter feelings generated by any real or imagined instances of racial discrimination such as were inevitable in a situation in which the Japanese had treated Asians in one way and Europeans in another. And it is probably this that put an end to the propaganda of loyalty to the British Empire, such as was frequently voiced before the war through bodies like the Straits Chinese British Association....

The group most affected by the war and the Japanese Occupation was the Indian community. From being depressed and uninterested inhabitants of a political backwater, the Indians of Malaya became, in their own estimation at least, the spearhead of a movement to liberate India. For it was in Singapore that the Azad Hind Government was set up, and it was in Malaya that most of the personnel for the Indian National Army were recruited.

Very soon after the coming of the Japanese Army, Indian Independence League branches were set up in every major centre in Malaya. Their aim was to spread propaganda, to collect funds, and to recruit and train workers and troops for a fighting movement to liberate India.

The original organizer of the movement was Major Fujiwara, a senior intelligence officer on the staff of General Yamashita. Though he had to work through interpreters he was extremely efficient in picking enthusiastic Indian personnel, and giving them enough freedom of action to convert the former Indian Associations into active political bodies....

It is important to emphasize that, though the Japanese no doubt intended the movement for Indian Independence to be merely another puppet in their pan-Asianism, this was strongly, and to a limited extent successfully, resisted by the Indians themselves. There can be little doubt that the leaders felt they were using the Japanese almost as much as the Japanese were using them.

By making some concessions to Indian opinion and giving some genuine freedom of action the Japanese were able to revive the Indian National Army and use the Indian Independence League for their own purposes....

Echoes of the Indian National Army still linger in Malaya. The Indian community learnt the use of arms, learnt how to organise politically, and learnt some of the techniques of political bargaining. But even more important for the future was the fact that it learnt a sense of consequence. The Congress Party accepted the Indian National Army as heroes and in many parts of India they are honoured today. Whatever may be the future of the Indians in Malaya, these facts will not be easily forgotten.

9
Goals and Methods in the Sphere

DR. A. J. Grajdanzev first studied Japanese agriculture in 1930 when he made his first visit to Japan. During World War II he was a member of the research staff of the Institute of Pacific Relations. During the occupation of Japan he served as Chief of the Prefectural Branch of the Government Section in General Headquarters, SCAP. He has authored several books on Korea, Formosa and Japan. Here Dr. Grajdanzev deals with the identity of goals but diversity of forms and techniques employed by the Japanese throughout South-East Asia. He discusses the Japanese attempt to work through local elites but also the sponsoring of 'Nazi-type organizations'. Writing in the midst of war, he spoke of Japan's economic needs and ideological predilections as major determinants of Japanese policy. Fear of communism he regarded as a weak point in the Japanese system. This excerpt comes from an article on the Co-Prosperity Sphere in *Pacific Affairs*, vol. 16, 1943.

IN each region a military administration was established under the supervision of the supreme military commander of that area. In this respect there is no difference between the Philippines, Burma, Malaya, Netherlands Indies, and Hongkong; even in Thailand, French Indo-China, and Portuguese Timor the military commander on the spot is the master of the situation. This

GOALS AND METHODS IN THE SPHERE 147

military commander may be an army man or a navy man, depending upon which arm of the service is entrusted with defence of that region. Under the military commander there are departments of general affairs, of industry, of finance and of transportation, then prefectural and branch offices. In all these offices there is a certain number of military men whose duty it is to maintain the unity and consistency of the policy, and many civil officials, Japanese and natives. The heads of the departments and the governors in Malaya, Hongkong, and Netherlands Indies are Japanese; in the Philippines and partially in Burma the Japanese are advisors or vice governors but with the real power in their hands. No figures are available for the army, but in September 1942 the navy had in South-East Asia 327 chief administrators, 2,953 administrators, 2,123 engineers and about 15,000 other officials....

But though the names of the governing bodies, the number of used Quislings, and the number of bureaus and departments have varied, fundamentally the structure is the same — a Japanese military regime. The Japanese are too few to rely exclusively upon Japanese military force in governing the newly acquired territories. The use of the old administration made their task easier. But the Japanese went further and attempted to organize the natives politically. In every occupied region they formed, or helped to form, a political organization or party. In Burma it is the Dobama Sinyetha League with many thousands of members. The Japanese established quotas for every locality to supply so many members, but they claim enthusiasm on the part of the natives was so great that these quotas had to be raised. For Rangoon the quota was raised from 5,000 to 10,000. Many of the members were priests, and it was said that many itinerant priests held meetings throughout the country. In Java it was the 'All-Java Cultural Movement' with 20,000 members in October 1942, and with prospects of reaching 200,000 in the near future. In December 1942, the Japanese military administration announced the establishment 'in the near future' of a new organization, the 'Java Leaders Patriotic Society,' which was expected to 'greatly enhance the independence spirit.' It is not clear what relation these patriotic leaders were to have to the Cultural Movement, but, in as much as only one party is permitted in all places dominated by the Japanese, either the new society will absorb the old, or the old one was stillborn. In the Philippines the organization is the Kalibapi, a 'popular movement' for the reconstruction of the new Philippines. It was said that the Kalibapi is an instrumentality of the central administrative organization.

Thus all these bodies are organized along Nazi lines, with only one party, the purpose of which is to strengthen the grip of the government over the population....

Besides political organization of adults, an attempt has been made to organize youth as well. Persons who are trained in obedience from childhood can be good servants in the new empire. We hear, for example, that a 'federation of youth and boys throughout Greater East Asia is to be formed, starting with ceremonies here [Tokyo] 30 March, 1943, in which representatives of youth of Japan, Manchukuo and China will discuss plans and methods. Later the youth and boys of Burma and Thailand will join.' Earlier, in October 1942, there was a discussion of militarization of the youth movement in the Netherlands Indies.

Religious matters have not been forgotten in the construction of Greater East Asia. At the beginning, the policy toward religion was only that of toleration. The officials and military men were reminded by Tokyo that local religions should not be molested by the armies of occupation. However, the Japanese later decided that even non-Shinto religions can be put to good use. In March the representatives of 'ten million' Moslems of Malaya and Sumatra decided to meet in Shonan (Singapore) and 'this is expected to have wide effect on the attitude of the entire Moslim world. They [the Moslims] have so well understood Japan's war aims. Mohammedans have cooperated closely with the Japanese forces in military operations and reconstruction work.' In April 1943, the same kind of ability to understand was shown by the Christians, and, on occasion of the forty-second birthday of the Emperor, the inaugural ceremony of the newly created Friendship of the Japanese and Overseas Catholics was held at Koishikawa Catholic Church in Tokyo. It was asserted that the new organization 'aims at the union of 30 million Catholics within the Greater East Asia Co-Prosperity Sphere and was organized as a party in response to a suggestion advanced by the Japan-Philippine Catholic Society'. It is not clear where the Japanese could find 30 million Catholics in the Greater East Asia Co-Prosperity Sphere, but the purposes behind the move are clear. Finally, in May 1943 the inaugural ceremony of the Buddhist General

Council of Greater East Asia was held at the Chingan Temple, Shanghai, 'attended by many Japanese and Chinese. The object of the council is to unite the Buddhists in the Greater East Asia Co-Prosperity Sphere into a single body to assist prosecution of the war and foster development of the Buddhist spirit and relief work.' ... We see that no stone is left unturned in the reconstruction of Greater East Asia, no moss-covered institution is forgotten, no scheming politician is neglected; sultans and government secretaries, Moslems and Buddhists, Christians and itinerant monks, old and young — every one is to be pressed into the service of the Greater East Asia Co-Prosperity Sphere by the Tokyo planners.

At the same time efforts are made to spread Japanese propaganda by all means; radio, schools, newspapers, cinema. The teaching of English or Dutch has been forbidden, being replaced by the Japanese language.... Japanese language schools sprang up everywhere, and the Japanese universities and colleges now discuss the best methods to be used to convert and guide their students from Greater East Asia....

As to the economic development of the southern countries, little is yet known, but from the articles and speeches of the military and civilian leaders it can be seen that the Japanese do not plan immediate rapid development of these regions. It is emphasized that, however important the development of South-Eastern Asia may be, the center of gravity of Greater East Asia remains in the 'inner zone' — Japan, Korea, Manchuria, and North China — and it is these latter regions which are to be developed most intensively. The task of South-East Asia is to supply needed raw materials for the 'inner zone' and to supply necessary foodstuffs and materials for the Japanese armies stationed in the respective southern countries. Japan, preoccupied with production of war materials, has little to offer to these countries during the war; hence a policy of self-sufficiency is planned for each of them, so that there will be no need to import foodstuffs, textiles, and other necessities. In this way the demand on shipping will be reduced and some of the idle equipment in Japan (spindles and looms, for example) could be used profitably in South-East Asia. As a rule, no general industrialization is attempted, but some occasional industrial developments may follow as a result of such a policy....

These considerations show clearly that South-East Asia is to be energetically and ruthlessly exploited on the basis of the available resources and equipment. The resources and equipment that fell into Japanese hands are enormous. The area was an important supplier of raw materials for the whole world. It had a good network of railways, harbours, some processing capacity, relatively well-developed public utilities in centers where raw materials were collected, sorted, and stored in expectation of shipments and where white masters and native bourgeoisie could live in comfort...

The advantages received by the Japanese from the occupation of South East Asia are undoubtedly great. It is a mistake to think that the farther the Japanese advance, the more thinly they spread their forces and that they will be choked with loot.

In March 1943, Major-General Kenryō Satō declared that the communists in China number between 500,000 to 600,000 and continues:

'As for ideological war against communism, the Chinese National Government [of Wang Ching-wei in Nanking] is achieving such success, that great results are expected, and the army is guarding against the appearance of communists in the south... If the principles of Japan's *Hakkō Ichiū** are transmitted fully to the people in the south, I believe that there will not be the least need to fear that the various regions will become hotbeds of communism.... Measures are being taken by the military against communism. With sufficient practical application of such measures by the leaders of the empire in these various southern regions, all these areas will be handled so that they will not become red.'

This fear of communism shows clearly a weak spot in the Japanese system. The Japanese are relying upon reactionary forces: landlords, sultans, priests, native bureaucrats are recruited as their allies; old customs are resuscitated, spying is in full force, chauvinism is encouraged. But in all these countries there are millions of persons who can gain nothing from such a regime; their economic position has been undermined; they are likely to be in a receptive mood for Allied propaganda, especially if that propaganda can offer them something better than merely the return of their former rulers.

PART IV
Evaluation and Retrospect

1
Post-War Implications of the Sphere

ROBERT S. Ward discusses Japan's goals, methods and propaganda, particularly its emphasis on Asian 'liberation'. He suggests that Japan's real objectives in Asia extended far beyond the time limits of World War II, though Japan did not really anticipate victory. Mr. Ward's argument gains relevance and import in view of Japan's post-war economic posture in South-East Asia. This selection is from *Asia for the Asiatics? The Techniques of Japanese Occupation* (University of Chicago Press, 1945).

THE first five points [of the Greater East Asia Declaration] asserted that Asia was no longer to be a colony or 'semi-colony' of the Anglo-Saxons but was to be 'delivered from alien aggression and exploitation and restored to the Asiatics.'

The second point was to the effect that Asia 'should arise again; there should be constructed a New East Asia of sovereign and independent countries.' The third pledges the signatories to the defence of the now 'liberated areas' and sets forth that they would regard it as 'intolerable for the peoples of East Asia if their territories which have been liberated at no small cost should be made again the object of aggression and exploitation.'

The fourth point asserted that the conferees stood for 'free access to natural resources, freedom of communication and trade, and unrestricted cultural interchange.' The fifth demanded that the 'principles of equality and reciprocity should be extended to govern international relations throughout the world' and particularly condemned race prejudice.

From the day of its promulgation to the present time, the five points of this Greater East Asia Declaration have been a constant theme of Japanese propaganda throughout the occupied areas. Continual references are made to them in Diet interpellations, in the statements of Japanese and puppet leaders, and in the controlled press from Rangoon to Harbin. It would perhaps not be exaggerating the importance which the Japanese have attached to this declaration to say that they are attempting to make it one of the principal instruments of their political warfare.

The immediate purpose of the declaration is obvious: Japan hoped, by a formal pronouncement of her aims in Asia, with which the puppet leaders of the subject peoples had associated themselves, to procure more widespread support in the decisive battles of the Pacific war that still lay ahead. But the apparatus that was employed, and even some of the words that were used, suggested that the Japanese were more intent upon a subtler purpose, one for the accomplishment of which the declaration and correlated courses in policy which were subsequently taken were even better adapted. That purpose is the projection of the political struggle in Asia beyond the issue of the present war.

To achieve that purpose, it would be necessary to create a situation in which the most overwhelming victory of the United Nations in Asia would seem to be only the ultimate vindication of the Mikado's leadership of the valiant struggles of his warriors against impossible odds. Then the victory of the West in whatever year would only lead it on more infallibly to a subsequent and inevitable defeat whenever the bells of destiny should toll again.

Many of the basic lines for such a trap had already been laid. A major shift in Japanese policy toward the occupied areas began to be manifest early in 1943, when it was clear that at best the war was to be a long one, and a Japanese victory was coming to seem more and more questionable. This shift was followed by a series of manoeuvres which in a sense had their culmination in the declaration: a conciliatory policy toward the puppet regime in China, and the whole 'China question,' was adopted; Burma was 'granted' her 'independence' on August 1, 1943; the 'Provisional Government of Free India' was set up in Singapore; and on October 14 of the same year the 'government' of the Philippine Commonwealth was declared to be 'free and independent.' These acts cost Japan nothing; no actual change occurred in the condition of the subject peoples, and, were the war to end in her victory, she could easily enough allow these 'independent governments' to slide quietly into oblivion. But only a very naive person could believe that they were set up in contemplation of such a victory; rather they looked toward defeat and were calculated to make history plead the cause of Yamato before the bar of the East at some later judgement day....

The official statement of 'the aim of the Japanese war operations in China which are now in progress' issued by the Imperial Government on July 5, 1944, at the opening of the great offensive to reduce the whole of China to the status of a secure rear base, shares this characteristic dual motivation; it is a move which may help to win the present contest and at the same time a gambit to fend against defeat in the longer game. Essential to both these services was the widespread publicity which it was given, particularly in China. Typical portions of it read:

'Since the outbreak of the War of Greater East Asia, Japan is actuated solely by her earnest desire for the liberation and stabilization of Greater East Asia and for the establishment of a new World Order and has been fighting vigorously to defeat the vile designs of America and Britain in cooperation with the various countries and peoples of the region.... On the Chinese continent...America and Britain are manifesting even more nakedly their sinister design of aggression and domination. By taking the initiative, however, the Imperial Japanese forces have captured enemy bases in various areas and are everywhere dealing shattering blows to the hostile forces.'

'The aim of our military operations in China now in progress being simply to frustrate the attempts of America and Britain at aggression and domination, the Chinese people are, it goes without saying, our friends, and even the armed forces under the Chungking regime who are opposed to cooperation with America and Britain are not our enemies. What Japan earnestly desires is to bring to a consummation a permanent relationship of good neighbourliness and friendship between Japan and China on the basis of respect for sovereignty and independence in conformity with the Japanese-Chinese pact of alliance and the Joint Declaration of the East Asiatic Nations.'

2
Inversion of Japanese Goals

DR. Ba Maw here argues (again, in *Breakthrough in Burma*) that Japan's good intentions and policies, even her success in liberating Asia from white domination, were betrayed by Japanese militarists and misunderstood by the Asians Japan helped. It was the racism and short-sightedness of the military that was responsible for this tragedy; but political obsession and short-sightedness also distorted the Burmese vision.

AS for the Japanese militarists, few people were mentally so race-bound, so one-dimensional in their thinking, and in consequence so totally incapable either of understanding others, or of making themselves understood by others. That was why so much of what they did during the war in South-East Asia, whether it was right or wrong, always appeared to be wrong to the people there. The militarists saw everything only in a Japanese perspective and, even worse, they insisted that all others dealing with them should do the same. For them there was only one way to do a thing, the Japanese way; only one goal and interest, the Japanese interest; only one destiny for the East Asian countries, to become so many Manchukuos or Koreas tied forever to Japan. These racial impositions — they were just that — made any real understanding between the Japanese militarists and the peoples of our region virtually impossible.

The case of Japan is indeed tragic. Looking at it historically, no nation has done so much to liberate Asia from white domination, yet no nation has been so misunderstood by the very peoples whom it has helped either to liberate or to set an example to in many things. Japan was betrayed by her militarists and their racial fantasies. Had her Asian instincts been true, had she only been faithful to the concept of Asia for the Asians that she herself had proclaimed at the beginning of the war, Japan's fate would have been very different. No military defeat could then have robbed her of the trust and gratitude of half of Asia or even more, and that would have mattered a great deal in finding for her a new, great, and abiding place in a postwar world in which Asia was coming into her own. Even now, even as things actually are, nothing can ever obliterate the role Japan has played in bringing liberation to countless colonial peoples. The phenomenal Japanese victories in the Pacific and in South-East Asia which really marked the beginning of the end of all imperialism and colonialism, the national armies Japan helped to create during the war which in their turn created a new spirit and will in a large part of Asia, the independent states she set up in several South-East Asian countries as well as her recognition of the provisional government of Free India at a time when not a single other belligerent power were permitted even the talk of independence within its own domains, and finally a demonstration by the entire Japanese people of the invincibility of the Asian spirit when they rose out of the ashes to a new greatness, these will outlive all the passing wartime strains and passions and betrayals in the final summing-up of history.

...Rightly or wrongly, the Burmese obsession with their own political aims was total, and it often distorted their vision by making them see only the side of a truth that fitted into the obsession.... They saw what the Japanese were taking from them to carry on the combat, but not what they were getting back from the Japanese in return....

3
Inadvertent Stimulus to Nationalism

WILLARD H. Elsbree, professor of political science at Ohio University and former delegate to the United Nations Economic and Social Council, is best known for his classic study, *Japan's Role in South-East Asian Nationalist Movements* (Harvard University Press, 1953), from which this excerpt is drawn. Professor Elsbree stresses the initial Japanese propaganda appeal and reasons for its ultimate failure to capture South-East Asian-nationalist sentiment. Nevertheless, Professor Elsbree counts the growth of nationalist movements throughout South-East Asia one of the significant by-products of Japanese rule. Similarly, greater political participation by native population was a signal feature of Japanese administration.

A few days before the fall of Singapore, an Indian member of the Malayan civil service declared that 'although his reason utterly rebelled against it, his sympathies instinctively ranged themselves with the Japanese in their fight against Anglo-America'.... Similar sentiments, often less mixed, were widespread among Asians. In many instances the entry of Japanese soldiers assumed the air of a triumphal procession. At the very least, they were greeted with indifference on the part

EVALUATION AND RETROSPECT

of the local population, and only the Chinese communities can be said to have offered anything approaching active resistance.

Anti-Westernism, the basic cause of this reaction to Japanese victory, provided the Japanese with their most effective propaganda weapon. They used it unsparingly and often with telling results, but with diminishing returns. As the Report of the Government of Burma indicated, the old slogans about British imperialism became badly frayed from constant use as answers to new problems. The evils of the past did not entirely erase those of the present which had to be dealt with in different terms. That the Japanese failed to meet the challenge of these new problems can be illustrated by the contrast between the welcome accorded their arrival in South-East Asia and the conditions under which they departed. In the Philippines they were beset by guerrillas everywhere, in Burma they were under attack by a Burmese army, officered and manned by their recent collaborators, in Indo-China and Indonesia they found safety only in numbers. Even if there was a noticeable lack of enthusiasm for the white man's return, scarcely a hand was lifted in support of the Japanese. They clearly had failed to identify the interests of the South-East Asians with their own.

There are many reasons which can be given for this failure — two of the most obvious are the cruelty meted out to the native population, and the privation due to the economic dislocations which accompanied the war. This study has been concerned with a rather different cause of their failure, namely their inability to capture the loyalty of the national movements with which they came in contact. In many instances they received considerable support from nationalist parties and succeeded in attracting the cooperation, sometimes nominal, but often active, of nationalist leaders who spurned (and were spurned by) the previous colonial regimes. There never developed, however, a real unity of interests between the two parties, there was no overwhelming despair on the part of the Asians at Japan's defeat, no feeling that they must have Japanese support to stand on their feet.

The idea of linking forces with the national movements was a sound one. It was by no means original with the Japanese but the circumstances under which they launched their effort gave them a unique opportunity. They fumbled it, and one basic

INADVERTENT STIMULUS TO NATIONALISM 161

cause was their own faulty conception of the national movements in Asia. The view came dangerously close to being one according to which the 'native blokes' were given a few trappings of authority, rather as playthings to keep them amused while the Japanese devoted themselves to essential matters.... The idea of Japanese superiority was implicit in their estimates of the national movements, cited in the opening chapter; it was borne out in all their actions during the occupation. The notion of guidance was always that of leading a little child by the hand, there was no inkling of a relationship in which mutual problems would be discussed on equal terms. The process by which one nation transmits to another the fruits of its own experience is an exceedingly complex one, particularly if some respect is paid to elements of the old society of the recipient; perhaps there is no very satisfactory method, but it is certainly true that the Japanese violated most of the rudimentary principles of such a relationship. They saw what a useful instrument nationalism could be in their plans for a Co-Prosperity Sphere, but they failed to draw all the necessary consequences from this realization, for if nationalism was a force strong enough to be of use to them, it would require more consideration than they were prepared to give. No second rate status but some measure of real equality, not the mere trappings of power but authority actually exercised were the minimum requirements which they would have had to meet.

This study has tried to show, in some detail in the case of Indonesia, the gradual awakening of the Japanese to the fact that nationalism was a stronger and more developed force than they had imagined and demanded greater concessions than they had anticipated. They gave ground grudgingly and, like the colonial powers a few years previously, came close to meeting the demands of the nationalists only when defeat was staring them in the face.

If the Japanese found nationalism a less pliable instrument than they had anticipated, the nationalists found that Japanese promises far outstripped performance. Each seeking to use the other as an instrument in his own plan, was disappointed, and yet each reaped some benefit from the association. There is no question but that the acquiescence of the great part of the people and the active cooperation of many of the leaders made Japan's occupation task much simpler and, at the same time, provided a fine weapon in the propaganda war. On the other hand, this period saw a marked development in the nationalist movements everywhere in South-East Asia. Japanese policy was responsible for this only in part, in part it was the result of the general situation, but these movements were certainly more powerful in 1945 than they had been in 1941.

As illustrations, two important developments which occurred during the occupation of Indonesia have been considered in this study — the increased role of the native population in administrative affairs, and the strengthening of the forces of national unity. The Japanese, having at first assumed practically all of the important administrative positions themselves, gradually gave ground before Indonesian pressure for a greater hand in administering their own affairs. Particularly through the system of appointing Japanese advisers, they tried to maintain actual authority in their own hands while nominally giving it to the Indonesians. In this they were not altogether successful for the pressure of events, especially in the closing stages of the war, brought positions of real power into the hands of the Indonesians and, moreover, the divorce between real and nominal authority was often not as complete as they intended. Probably too much cannot be made of the technical experience gained by the Indonesians as a result but they did receive a psychological fillip which strengthened their determination to resist the return of colonial rule at the end of the war.

Just as the pressure of events forced the Japanese to make concessions in the field of administration, so it led them to pay more heed to the aspiration for national unity. From 1944 onward in particular, they geared their organizational and propaganda facilities to the task of fostering national unity. As the Allied counter-attack gained momentum it became more and more urgent for Japan to win the active support of the local population if she were to hold her conquests. This situation enhanced the bargaining power of the nationalists. The story of events in Indonesia shows the widened latitude given nationalist spokesmen, the heightened effectiveness of their work due to the facilities of communication and transportation provided by the Japanese, and the increased audience which they were able to reach. Under the occupation the movement was centralized as it never had been before the war, and under the leadership of men determined to unite all of the Indies under one government. The organizations sponsored by the occupation authorities, both civilian and military, were a more effective means of carrying on nationalistic work at the local level than anything previously known. Not only was a new audience tapped but new cadres were being trained and, at the same time, there was a uniformity in program and propaganda that helped break down the isolation of the villages from central authority. The educational system, as it functioned during the occupation, was another instrument of centralization and unification. All of these developments, in conjunction with the overthrow of the old colonial system and the disruption of life occasioned by the war, were catalytic agents in the dissolution of the old order; they were paving the way for the construction of a modern system....

One question raised in the Introduction has not been considered. Did the Japanese occupation give totalitarian forces the upper hand over a nascent democracy? No answer will be attempted here but it should be noted that, although the Japanese gave encouragement to extremist and militaristic elements, there were anti-democratic forces in the colonial regimes and in the native societies which provided as good a model for totalitarian development as did the occupation....

For the West, however well-intentioned its motives and circumspect its conduct, there is a special problem. Nationalism in South-East Asia retains its strong flavour of anti-imperialism which in its most frequent and powerful manifestations, is equated with anti-Westernism.... The West is not likely to duplicate the Japanese mistake of underestimating the strength of nationalism but it must constantly remain aware of the limitations which this strength imposes on both the range and effectiveness of its actions.

4
Critique of the Greater East Asia War

SOME Japanese scholars — Marxist and otherwise — have recently taken issue with apologists for Japan's role in World War II. One of these critics who specifically takes issue with Hayashi Fusao's *Dai Tōa sensō kōteiron* (Affirmation of the Greater East Asia War) is Iyenaga Saburō. He argues here in excerpts from *Taiheiyō sensō* (The Pacific War, Iwanami, 1969) that Japan's military actions in China — beginning with the Manchurian Incident in 1931 and continuing until World War II — all constituted a continuous fifteen-year war. The moralistic slogans which Japan proclaimed in Asia had, Professor Iyenaga maintains, little relation to the brutal inhumane realities in Japanese-occupied Asia. He takes issue with apologists further, charging that Japan's role in liberating Asia from Western imperialism was really a negative and inadvertent one, resulting mainly from the resistance struggle against Japan in occupied areas.

    The author is Professor at Tokyo University of Education and Instructor at Tokyo University. He was awarded the Japan Academy Prize in 1948 for his study on Japanese painting. He has authored a number of books on Japanese ancient history.

CRITIQUE OF THE GREATER EAST ASIA WAR

ALL the wars since the 'Manchurian Incident', whose beginning was the Lukouchiao Incident in September 1931... were continuous acts in a series.... In fact in Konoye Fumimarō's memorial to the Emperor in February 1945 he clearly stated 'We caused the Manchurian Incident and the China Incident and expanded them, finally leading to the Greater East Asia War.' Actually, in the explanation of the Prime Minister, when the outbreak of war with Holland, Britain, and America was decided, at the Imperial Conference on December 1, 1941, there is one paragraph which states that if we accept America's demand 'we will be forced to retreat in the whole situation from the continent. As a result, our status in Manchuria will surely change. In this way our completion of the China Incident will be destroyed fundamentally.' It is clearly stated that the outbreak of war against the United States and Britain can't be avoided to preserve the achievement of the Manchurian Incident, Manchukuo. Here we can see clearly the fact that the ultimate goal of the nation officially recognizes that the 'Manchurian Incident' was the beginning of the Greater East Asia War.

Next, the war in wartime was actively supported and praised in Japan as a 'sacred war.' Many people believed that from the bottom of their hearts. A few insisted it was an 'imperialistic war,' and some others displayed a critical or negative attitude for other reasons. But such views of the war were thoroughly quashed by the authorities....

Undoubtedly it is especially important to pay attention to the social structure of Japan among the factors that caused the Pacific War. As we have stated...it is true that the aggression doctrine began prior to creating Japan's capitalist economy. It is also certain that such a tradition affected the onset of the Pacific War. But in the long range view such reasons as: the modernization of farming villages was not advanced and the standard of living of farmers was low, and consumer purchasing power was low — made Japanese capitalism turn abroad from the early states, when capitalism had not yet reached the stage of imperialism. After Japan reached the stage of imperialism the tendency was more pronounced. Besides, there were the restrictions of an absolutistic system.... Japanese capitalism faced severe danger in the great world panic of the 1920s, and they took the path of aggression abroad as one policy for solving the dilemma. We can't deny that these social and economic conditions were the most important causes encouraging war....

The aims of the Sino-Japanese war were varied, and we cannot deny that the desire for economic control was an important element. But the minimal demand which was manifest through the peace negotiations was maintaining 'Manchukuo' and the stationing of troops to prevent Communism. When we consider the fact that Manchukuo had a large role as a military advance base against Russia, we must conclude that this war was strongly characterized as an anti-communist war. In May 1931 Itagaki Seishirō said 'If we occupy Manchuria our military superiority over Russia will be decisive'.... In the report of the young Army staff officer Katakura Chū, in January 1934, it is suggested that 'separately in secret we plan to destroy the hinterland', while concluding a mutual non-aggression pact with Russia. In December 1935 Kwantung Army Headquarters said critically, 'What we can't allow the Nanking Government to do is revive the policy of recognizing Communism and express a pro-Soviet attitude, neglecting the so-called Communist movement toward the Shensi area.' At a meeting of the Privy Council investigating committee for discussing conclusion of a basic treaty with the Wang government on 20 November 1940, Premier Konoye answered, 'The significance that this incident is a sacred war should be most clear in preventing Communism, so we are resolved to maintain prevention of Communism to the end, despite our relationship with Russia....'

Anyway, Japanese war power devoted itself at times to war with China and at others to the death struggle against the U.S. and Britain because of tactical necessity. There was no room to consider other matters. They were forced to adopt a policy of diplomatic relations with Russia, but the following fact should be noted particularly: that on the basis of the war goals, the idea of destroying Communism was there, visibly or latent, from beginning to end, including the aggression in China. The basic criteria for differentiating bourgeois democracy and fascism is that fascism does not compete ideologically with Communism but tries to destroy Communism by force. This being so, the war Japan continued was a fascist war and it corresponds closely to the oppression of Communism by force in Japan's domestic policy. So I believe we can call the fifteen-year war the international application of the law for maintaining peace and order at home. I add this particularly as I think this was an important point in considering the historical character of the war....

The slogans which Japan proclaimed to the world in the name of justice were not necessarily logically consistent.... Frank expressions of Japan's national interests, called defense of rights and interests, were mingled with Pan-Asian slogans of Asian solidarity. When at last the advance to South-East Asia took place, 'building the Greater East Asia Co-Prosperity Sphere' was emphasized as the highest ideal. They spoke of liberating Asian peoples from the oppression of 'American and British imperialism'. For example, in 1943 they had Burma and the Philippines declare 'independence', and in Singapore steps were taken to establish the Indian Provisional Government. In November the same year the Greater East Asia Conference was held, assembling the heads of state of 'Manchukuo,' Wang's government, Thailand, the Philippines, and Burma. The phrase 'Greater East Asia War' itself was chosen to demonstrate such an intention, but as expected, in the region of East Asia which fell under Japan's control and occupation, can we see the reality of 'liberation' and 'co-prosperity' commensurate with the slogan? To clarify the nature of this war I believe it is necessary and very urgent to study concretely the reality of the Greater East Asia Co-Prosperity Sphere.

First of all, in the phrase 'Greater East Asia Co-Prosperity Sphere' there is no solidarity of the various peoples of East Asia in a position of complete independence and equality; rather they said 'Japan occupies the position of political leader.' 'Concerning peoples who do not possess the ability for independence', and 'we will preserve our preferential position regarding raw materials for national defense in the region above.' The position of leadership was arranged on the premise of Japan's privileged control. Thus, in the publication of the announcement of the Imperial Rule Assistance Association in March, 1941, 'the idea of leadership of the Greater East Asia Co-Prosperity Sphere' declared that 'even if we speak of East Asian cooperation, it should by no means be based on the automatic notion of people's equality, losing sight of the founding spirit of the nation.' When the literary assembly planned to hold a writers' conference, inviting cultured people of the Greater East Asia Co-Prosperity Sphere, one of the planners, Nakayama Shozaburō, criticized the statement of Kaneko Mitsuharu, who wondered whether it wasn't unreasonable to try to elicit understanding from cultured people of other countries of '*Hakkō Ichiū*' and the Japanese spirit. He attacked him saying, 'It isn't a matter of cultured men of other nations, but rather people of the Co-Prosperity Sphere who gather under the Emperor's virtue'. And in the post-occupation policy for the South in the Imperial Conference of 5 November, 1941, there was the explanation, 'We must disregard local economic chaos for the time being and press on to the end.' At a Liaison Conference on the 29th of the same month in the decision on a 'Draft for Administration of Occupied Areas in the South' there was the phrase: 'We will have the people endure the pressure, and we can't avoid affecting the people's livelihood because of the need to gain resources for national defense and self-support of local armies of occupation. The demand for pacification should be within the limits of the above goals.' Further, 'toward local inhabitants we will avoid giving premature encouragement to independence movements'. On 14 March 1942, at the Imperial General Headquarters Government Liaison Conference, Chief Cabinet Secretary Hoshino Naoki said, 'Since enemy nations took the possessions they wanted, there is no reason for our hesitation in taking them away'. And Planning Agency Director Suzuki Teiichi and Kaya Okinori asserted strongly 'Military administration must be carried out for a long time. We should not indulge them by promising independence too early.' In the same month in the items on geographic requisites for military government in occupied areas it was decided that 'Various measures will be taken to foster industry in the local areas, with the idea for the present of the Southern areas supplying resources to us and serving as markets for our manufactured goods,' and 'wages for labour should be maintained at as low a rate as possible'. The policy of recognition was always couched with the stipulation that when Burma and the Philippines became independent, military matters and diplomacy would be handled completely by Japan. We should note that this demonstrated that the national policy was to use the Southern Areas as Japan's colony just as with Korea and 'Manchukuo.'

...The reality of the East Asian region under military control in which Japan sought to justify her war power using beautiful words was substantively as I have related. The above should be recognized as the destruction of each peoples' independence and livelihood by intensive military pressure and economic exploitation which was quite different from the 'Kyōdōtai' and 'Kyōeiken.' Some people appear who insist on the *Dai Tōa sensō kōteiron* (Affirmation of the Greater East Asia War) with the logic that Asian people's independence 'owes much to Japan's Pacific War, so we should evaluate the war highly.' It is true that Japanese military control disrupted the control of Europe and America and resulted in weakening the power of the former controllers, but that was an inadvertent result of the transition from European imperialism to Japanese imperialism. As is clear from the above statement, Japan did not liberate the Asian people, but each people began the struggle to attain independence in the midst of the process of the resistance struggle against Japan. Asian people did not become independent through the power of Japan, but they attained independence in resisting Japan. That was Japan's disgrace. If they boast of it as Japan's achievement, it must be regarded as an inverse evaluation contrary to the truth....

War where open murder is carried out not as a crime but as a duty has an essentially misanthropic character. The past history of war clearly demonstrated that war is apt to induce brutal behaviour which exceeds the bounds of necessity. The increase in destructive power of weaponry and the development of the total war style which obliterates the distinction between military men and non-military men has made war increasingly cruel. In the Second World War many brutal incidents which had never occurred before in human history occurred. That fact was conspicuous in the behaviour of the Japanese Army. In an earlier chapter I introduced some typical examples which occurred in Japanese-occupied areas. But I would like to take up this aspect again as the theme in this chapter and to clarify concretely the 'Greater East Asia War' whose pride in morality of beautiful phrases actually was a 'dirty war' filled with brutal and inhuman behaviour....

If men feel a psychological resistance to brutal murder they won't be able to carry out wars, so war has the power to transform men into inhuman beings. In a death struggle, whether a man kills the enemy or is killed by the enemy there are many instances when he can't remain alive unless he is thorough in inhumanity against the enemy or third persons, or even against a man on his own side. That applies to an individual or a group or a nation. First of all it is necessary to note the fact that brutal behaviour was repeated not only toward enemies or other peoples under control but toward Japanese ourselves. First, we should consider it the greatest brutality that they began a war in which there was no possibility of victory and that they didn't try to end the war even after defeat was clear, and that they had a war policy which sacrificed many people without reason. In June 1945 an army commander in Osaka stated carelessly, 'It is necessary to kill all the old, the infants, and the ill, as food has run short in all Japan and Japan will soon become a battlefield. Japan cannot die with them.' This can be regarded as revealing the real mentality of the promoters of war. This should be condemned morally as inhuman behaviour. Besides, we may interpret it as culpability for murder according to criminal law....

5
A New Asian Approach to Asia

MARUYAMA Shizuo was a wartime correspondent who covered much of the action in Burma. He accompanied the Indian National Army in Burma in 1944 and observed Japanese military rule in many parts of South-East Asia. He is presently an editorial writer for *Asahi Shimbun*. He has written on World War II in South-East Asia, on the war in Vietnam, and on Japan's contemporary role in South-East Asia. Here (in an article from *Chūō Kōron*, April 1965) Mr. Maruyama presents the case for Japan not only as liberator from Western imperialism and stimulus to nationalism and political participation but as architect of a new style in dealing with South-East Asian peoples.

DURING the Pacific War what kind of policy and attitude did Japan adopt toward the various Asian nations? What kind of influence has Japan's colonial policy had after the war on the liberation, independence and national organization of these various countries?...

In Asia similarly the plan was to create a new order with Japan as the focus, which would replace the colonial empires in Asia. However, in setting forth the theories of liberation of peoples and the new order, the authorities did not consider very thoroughly what political status the liberated peoples would have in the new order....

There were nearly always three views asserted in policy decisions. One argument focussing on the aspirations of the local inhabitants was that, based on the purposes of the declaration of Greater East Asia cooperation, we should liberate the oppressed peoples, achieve the independence of the people, and assist them wholeheartedly. The independence of all Asian peoples, beyond realizing Japan's just war aims, must be complete and free and based completely on the fundamental ideas of the people. But if some impression should arise of being Japan's puppet wouldn't Japan's war aims be lost with control exercised over the people?...

Another view was the theory that we should adopt as our aim the ideal of establishing a 'new order' centering around Japan. So long as this war professes the establishment of a new order it must abolish western European-style democracy and parliamentary government and adopt as its keynote the '*Hakkō Ichiū*' spirit in which the new principle of leadership in East Asia will flourish.

Third was the theory of the campaign first, focussing on the military aspect. The Army judged that this war would become protracted, and that the Army must itself secure Dutch oil, Malayan rubber and tin. From this arose the strongly worded theory that we should annex them as dominions.... If Japan operates from the sound principle of the 'campaign first' it is imperative to establish the prestige of the Army and to create a system which reflects the Army's principles. This was in essence the argument for military rule, and for free use as military bases....

Policy and action, rather than being decided through a compromise of these three views, gave priority to the theory of military reality.... The Army always stood on the principle of the 'campaign first, and, without developing independence at all, we will develop the possibility of cooperation of the volunteer army'. For this goal they sought to reduce the *Minami Kikan** and seize the power of the volunteer army. The *Minami Kikan* was originally created as a cooperative project of Imperial General Headquarters and Army Headquarters, but in October, 1941, jurisdiction was transferred to the Army, next to the Southern Army, then to the Burma Area Army. Formed as a powerful political project, it was sold for a period of service to the field army. When the period as a political project ended it entered a phase of purely military intrigue which was unavoidable, but through the arbitrariness of the Army on the march it managed

A NEW ASIAN APPROACH TO ASIA 173

to defeat the project and to distort the genuine people's project....

The co-existence and co-prosperity argument was a reordered version of colonialism. Behind the series of ideas and decorative words to what degree was there any substance to Asian liberation? How can we withstand this sort of criticism definitely? However, taking a long-range view it is impossible to say that all Japan said and did in wartime Asia was mistaken or invalid.... This would also distort reality.

In the last analysis I think we had something of a new approach toward various Asian peoples which could not be attained by Western European colonialists or by China or the Soviet Union.

There are probably at least three reasons for this. I think one was that we stood for sympathy and a sense of equality as Asians and we practiced it. This was our comprehension of nationalism. At least this was recognized among those who participated in front-line projects. They shared their well-being and feelings of defiance and resistance against Western European control and white domination, and rejoiced at being liberated from a subjugating system. This means that some Japanese took the side of the popular movements and independence movements to the end....

What I wish to stress particularly is that in the process [of liberation] those concerned with the projects did not have the mentality of rulers....

Another factor is that although they could not be said to be of the same race, there was a way of thinking and attitude on the part of the Japanese that signified they should be considered one in the cultural and political areas....

Besides this, everywhere we saw the people united with us as one and we addressed them as equals. When under West European control the people had absolutely no connection with politics. They were first mobilized then gradually their attention turned to politics. We cannot overlook the fact that the soldiers, through organizing volunteer armies and defense armies, and young men through experience in the practice of independence movements, grew in stature as new political elites.

I think this can be considered a kind of change in social and political structure.... And I don't think we can overlook the fact that there was some influence extending to the shape of nations. I think the influence of Japan's nationality policy must be considered by country, but we can see this especially in Burma and Indonesia. In Indonesia at the time of independence the '1945 Constitution' was enacted, and later they shifted over to the provisional constitution, but now they have reverted again to the '45 Constitution. The '45 Constitution was enacted originally at the 'suggestion' of the military government supervisory bureau, and referred to the constitutions of America, Holland, and Japan. It gave strong powers to the president.... I cannot help but feel that there is some legacy remaining from Japanese military administration and Japan's nationality policy which gave birth to these nations.

Thirdly, while we cannot generalize, there was some sort of decision to respect the traditions and customs of Asian peoples.

Premier Satō used what he termed an 'Asian approach' as his argument for a method of advancing Asian diplomacy. I think this may be ultimately aimed at creating harmony of tradition and modernity and creating unity out of the diversity of Asia, and at understanding nationalism. This is the antithesis of the Western colonial mentality and policy of divide and rule. This will be one way of modernizing Asia analogous to Communist revolution.

Glossary

Biruma Kenkyūkai	Burma Research Association, partially Navy funded
Burma Independence Army	Japanese-trained forerunner in 1941 and early 1942 of the Burma Defence Army, Burma National Army, and Patriotic Burmese Forces
Dai Tōa Kyōeiken	Greater East Asia Co-Prosperity Sphere
Dai Tōa Kyōzonken	Greater East Asia Co-Existence Sphere
'F' Kikan	Also *Fujiwara Kikan* or agency, the liaison agency which contacted the Indian Independence League in South-East Asia and helped create the Indian National Army
Gen' yōsha	Dark Ocean Society, earliest (1881) patriotic or ultra-nationalist society in Japan
hakkō ichiū	'whole world under one rule', a phrase commonly used in wartime to refer to Japan's leadership in Asia and the world generally
Indian Independence League	Organization of the Indian independence movement in South-East Asia during and before World War II
Java Patriotic Association	Japanese-fostered political mobilization movement in Java

GLOSSARY

Jimmukai	The Jimmu Society, referring to the legendary Emperor Jimmu; nationalist group
Kalibapi Association	Abbreviation for Association for Service in the New Philippines, a Japanese-sponsored mass organization to foster co-operation with Japan
Kempeitai	Japanese military police
Kesatuan Muda Melayu	Malay Youth League, supported by Japan
Kiai	Muslim religious teachers and scholars whose status rose as a result of Japanese policies in Java
Kokusaku Kenkyūkai	National Policy Research Association, a Navy-funded group
Kokuryūkai	Amur River Association, or popularly, Black Dragon Society, founded 1901
kyōdōshugi	'cooperation-ism', a concept and phrase used often in Japan's Pan-Asian constructs of the 1930s and World War II
Liaison Conference	Chiefs of Staff of Army and Navy, Army and Navy Ministers, Prime Minister and Foreign Minister meeting together to coordinate views of the military and cabinet, established 1937
Mahayana	'The Greater Vehicle', or Northern branch of Buddhism which spread from India northward to North and East Asia
Manshū Teikoku Kyōwakai	Manchukuo Imperial Harmony Society
Mantetsu Chōsakyoku	South Manchuria Railway Company Research Office
Minami Kikan	'Southern Agency', Japanese intelligence agency in Burma headed by Colonel Suzuki Keiji
Nan'yō Kyōkai	South Seas Association, under Navy sub-contract
Poetera	Or Putera, abbreviation for Center of Peoples' Strength, a Japanese-sponsor-

GLOSSARY

	ed political mobilization organization
Priai	Old aristocratic class in court towns such as Jogjakarta and Surakarta; the Japanese fostered a new counter-*priai*
Sakurakai	Cherry Association, whose members included young officers in the conspiracies of the 1930s
Shina rōnin	China '*ronin*', a variety of idealistic, romantic and other Japanese adventurers in China
Shinjinkai	New Man Society, a student group at Tokyo University in 1919
Shinminkai	New People's Society
Shin Taisei	New Structure, referring to mass mobilization of the Japanese populace in wartime
Shōwa Kenkyūkai	Shōwa Research Association, braintrust of Premier Konoye, including influential civilians of many ideological persuasions
Shōwa Restoration	A nativistic and nationalistic harking back to the Meiji Restoration as a period of security, strength and propriety
Sōgō Kenkyūkai	General Affairs Research Association, under Navy contract
Tōa Kyōdōtai	East Asia Cooperative Body
Tōa Renmei	East Asian Federation, the brain-child of Colonel Ishihara Kanji and Miyazaki Masayoshi
Tōa Shin Chitsujo	New Order in East Asia, proclaimed by Premier Konoye in 1938
Triple A Movement	Or 'Tiga A' Movement, propaganda movement proclaiming Japan the light, saviour and leader of Asia, in Java
Ulama	Muslim scholars in Java whose status rose as a consequence of Japanese policies
Yūzonsha	'Yet remaining' Society, led by Kita Ikki and Ōkawa Shūmei to establish Kita's 'revolutionary Empire of Japan'

Who's Who

Japanese

Akashi Motojirō

Army General and intelligence officer attached to the Japanese Embassy in St. Petersburg, where he aided Lenin and others in anti-Tsarist activities. Continued intelligence during and before the Russo-Japanese war. Commanded military police in Korea. Governor-General of Taiwan in 1918.

Aoki Kazuo

Finance Ministry bureaucrat, president of the Planning Board. Member of the Foreign Policy Committee of the *Shōwa Kenkyūkai*. Adviser to Wang Ching-wei's regime. Greater East Asian Affairs Minister. Class A war criminal, released without trial. Post-war member of the House of Councillors.

Arita Hachirō

Graduate of Tokyo Imperial University. In the Foreign Ministry served in Germany, Austria, Belgium, China. Foreign Minister in Hirota, Hiranuma, Konoye, and Yonai cabinets. After the war ran unsuccessfully in Tokyo gubernatorial election.

Fujiwara Iwaichi

Intelligence officer in Army General Staff Headquarters before the war. Assigned to South-East Asia as head of an intelligence mission, the *F Kikan*, in which capacity he helped create the Indian National Army and to encourage Indian independence aspirations. After the war Commanding General of the 1st

Division of the Ground Self Defence Forces. Ran unsuccessfully for the House of Councillors in 1971.

Harada Kumao
Secretary of Prince Saionji Kinmochi, last surviving *genrō*. Harada was best known for the *Saionji-Harada Memoirs*, used by the International Military Tribunal for the Far East against the defendants.

Ishihara Kanji
Lt. General. Served in Germany and Manchuria. Staff officer in the Kwantung Army who engineered the Manchurian Incident. Later as Operations Bureau Chief, General Staff, he opposed Japan's military actions in China and was relieved of his post and transferred back to the Kwantung Army. One of the best theorists in the Japanese Army. Organized the East Asia Federation. Noted for studies of Napoleon and Frederick the Great.

Iyenaga Saburō
Professor at Tokyo University of Education. Wrote a critical analysis of Japan's role in the Pacific War. His high school text was rejected by the Education Ministry; Iyenaga sued the government over the case. Winner of the Japan Academy Prize (1948) for a book on Japanese painting.

Kamikawa Hikomatsu
Professor emeritus of Tokyo University where he taught international relations. Awarded the Japan Academy Prize for a three-volume history of diplomacy. Has written several volumes on international relations.

Katō Tsukasa
Army staff officer in the Military Affairs Bureau; also staff officer in military administration in the Southern Army until 1943. With Colonel Ishii Akiho, Katō formulated an over-all military administration policy for the occupied Southern Area.

Kawashima Takenobu
Army Captain who studied at the Army Intelligence School. A leading member of the *Minami Kikan*, he was instructor of the Burma Independence Army in all phases, from the 'thirty comrades,' through the Burma Independence Army, Burma Defence Army, Burmese Officers Staff School, and also trained sixty

Burmese officers at the Army Staff College in Japan. Since the war he has been with the Burma Reparations Mission in Tokyo.

Kaya Okinori

Finance Ministry bureaucrat and Finance Minister before and during World War II. A member of the standing committee of the *Shōwa Kenkyūkai*. After the war was classified as a Class A war criminal and later released. An influential senior statesman of the Liberal Democratic Party and member of the House of Councillors.

Kishi Kōichi

Specialist on Indonesian affairs. During the war stationed in Java as a member of the East Asia Research Institute. After the war research staff member of the Institute of Developing Economies. Author and editor of several volumes on Japanese military administration in Indonesia.

Koiso Kuniaki

Army General. Chief of the Military Affairs Bureau when the Manchurian Incident occurred. Served as army commander in Korea, Minister of Colonial Affairs, Governor-General in Korea, and finally Premier (1944–5). Tried as a class A war criminal. Published his memoirs.

Konoye Fumimarō

Graduate of Kyoto Imperial University. President of the House of Peers and Privy Council. Also President of the Imperial Rule Assistance Association and East Asia Research Institute. Premier three times between 1937 and 1941. Used the *Shōwa Kenkyūkai* as his brain trust; was the focus of civilian hopes for peace in 1941. Named a class A war criminal; committed suicide in 1945.

Maruyama Shizuo

Editorial writer for *Asahi Shimbun*, Japan's largest newspaper. As a war correspondent covered Japanese campaigns in Burma. Author of several books on the campaigns in Burma and the Army Intelligence School. Authority on post-war South-East Asia.

Matsuoka Yōsuke

Graduate of University of Oregon Law School. Foreign Minister who signed the Tripartite Pact with Germany and Italy and the Non-Aggression Pact with the Soviet Union. Headed the Japanese delegation to the League of Nations. President of the South Manchuria Railway Company. Died while on trial as a class A war criminal.

Miki Kiyoshi

Leading philosopher and authority on European intellectual history. Member of the *Shōwa Kenkyūkai*. He urged intellectuals to take an active political role rather than acting as critics from outside.

Minami Jirō

Army General. War Minister, Commander of the Kwantung Army, Governor-General in Korea, member of the Privy Council and House of Peers. Class A war criminal.

Miyazaki Masayoshi

Member of the Research Department of the South Manchuria Railway Company. Graduate of Moscow University. In 1936 drafted a Five-Year Plan for Essential Industries directed toward military preparations against the Soviet Union. His plan was accepted by the War Ministry in 1936. Exponent of East Asia Federation.

Mutaguchi Renya

Lt. General and regimental commander at the Marco Polo Bridge incident. Commander of the 15th Army in Burma and proponent of the disastrous Imphal Campaign. Relieved of his command.

Nishijima Shigetada

Businessman in the Dutch East Indies before the war. During the war under the Office of the Naval Attaché in Java he collected documents on Japanese military administration, now housed in Waseda University's Ōkuma Institute of Social Sciences. Now with the North Sumatra Petroleum Company.

Ōkawa Shūmei

Jurist, politician and Pan-Asian philosopher active in pre-war patriotic societies. Founder of the *Yūzonsha* and *Jimmukai*, patriotic societies. Participated in the May 15 Incident in which Premier Inukai was assassinated. Authority on Indian philosophy and author of many volumes on Asian spiritual and cultural unity.

Named a class A war criminal, his case was dropped when he was found insane.

Shinmei Masamichi

Graduated from Tokyo Imperial University. Taught at Kansai Gakuin University and Tohoku Imperial University, and later at Meiji Gakuen University and Chuo University. Author of several books on sociology and of *A Historical Theory of Nationality*.

Shimada Shigetarō

Navy Admiral and Navy Minister in the Tōjō cabinet. He followed Tojo out of office in July 1944. Tried as a class A war criminal.

Rōyama Masamichi

Professor of political science at Tokyo Imperial University. Member of the Institute of Pacific Relations and founding member of the *Shōwa Kenkyūkai*. During the war he headed a commission of scholars in the Philippines and submitted a report on political growth there. President of Ochanomizu University after the war.

Suzuki Keiji

Army Maj. General. Served as intelligence officer in the Philippines, Dutch East Indies and Burma, where he headed the *Minami Kikan* and organized the Burma Independence Army. Because of his enthusiasm for Burmese independence, he was transferred to Hokkaido.

Suzuki Teiichi

Lt. General. In 1938 headed the Political Department of the East Asia Development Board. Later president of the Planning Board. Class A war criminal.

Takahashi Kamekichi

Free lance critic, leading member of the *Shōwa Kenkyūkai*, and active in the Institute of Pacific Relations. Held positions in the Finance Ministry and Ministry of Commerce and Industry. President of the Takahashi Institute of Economic Research. Awarded Second Order of Merit by the Japanese Government.

Terauchi Masakata

Army Marshal. Born in Yamaguchi and studied in France. Commandant of the Army Staff College. Army Minister.

Governor-General of Korea 1910–16. Premier and Finance Minister on his return to Japan, 1916–18.

Togo Shigenori
Foreign Minister in the Tōjō cabinet. Opposed creation of the Greater East Asia Ministry, fearing it would detract from the Foreign Ministry, antagonize China, and facilitate military control over policy. Foreign Minister in the Suzuki cabinet at the end of the war.

Tōjō Hideki
General. Served in Switzerland, Germany and Manchuria. Army Minister and Premier October 1941-July 1944. Executed in 1948 as a class A war criminal.

Toyotomi Hideyoshi
Peasant boy who rose to general and unified war-torn Japan in the 16th century. Launched expeditions to Korea and hoped to conquer China and the Philippines.

Wachi Takaji
Lt. General. Intelligence officer in China and was a leading China expert in the Army. Chief of staff of the 14th Army and in charge of military administration in the Philippines in 1942.

Yabe Teiji
Professor of political science at Tokyo Imperial University. Member of the *Shōwa Kenkyūkai*. Prepared a position paper on China policy advocating military pressure on Chiang K'ai-shek and establishment of a defence perimeter and autonomy in the occupied zone. Biographer of Konoye and president of Takushoku University after the war.

Yamada Nagamasa
Headed 16th century Japanese Christian immigrants to Siam, fleeing Tokugawa anti-Christian edicts. Commanded the bodyguard of the King of Siam. Became involved in Siamese politics and was poisoned, 1632.

Yamashita Tomoyuki
General known as the 'Tiger of Malaya.' Commander who took Singapore in 1942. Tōjō, fearing his popularity, kept him

away from Tokyo, posted in Manchuria and the Philippines. Sentenced to death for Japanese atrocities in the Philippines.

Yatsugi Kazuo

Director of the *Kokusaku Kenkyūkai*, National Policy Research Institute, serving after the war in the same capacity. Now writing a three-volume work on the Institute.

Others

Agoncillo, Teodoro

Professor of Philippine history at the University of the Philippines, and authority on the development of Philippine nationalism under Spanish, American, and Japanese rule, on which he has written several books.

Aquino, Benigno

Member of the Philippine Nacionalista oligarchy. During Japanese occupation he was Commissioner of the Interior and director of *Kalibapi* (*Kapisanan Sa Paglilingkod Sa Bagong Philipinas*), Association for Service in the New Philippines. Tried for treason after the war but his case was dismissed when he died in December, 1947.

Aziz, Ungku

Nephew of the Sultan of Johore. Holds a Ph.D. in economics from Waseda University, Tokyo. Professor of Economics and Vice-Chancellor of the University of Malaya. Has served in several capacities in UNESCO.

Ba Maw

Lawyer and first Premier of Burma in 1937. Studied at Cambridge and Bordeaux Universities. Formed the Freedom Bloc in 1939 for Burmese independence. Served as wartime Chief Administrator and Premier of independent Burma in 1943. Imprisoned by the British in 1946, arrested by U Nu in 1947 and again by Ne Win in 1966.

Bo Let Ya (Thakin Hla Pe)

Leader of the Rangoon University Student Union, and 1936 student strike. Member of the *Dobama Asiayone* and Freedom Bloc. One of the original 'thirty comrades' trained by the Japanese, he served in the Burma Independence Army, Burma Defence Army, Burma National Army, and Patriotic Burmese Forces. Chief of staff of the Burmese National Army 1943–5. Post-war Deputy Premier and Minister for Home and Defence. Arrested by Ne Win 1963.

Benda, Harry

Professor at the University of Rochester and Yale University, Director South-East Asia Studies Center at Yale and Institute of South-East Asia Studies, University of Singapore. Born in Prague and lived in the Dutch East Indies before and during the war. Pioneered the field of Japanese-occupied South-East Asia with his volume *The Crescent and the Rising Sun* and numerous other studies.

Elsbree, Willard

Professor of Political Science at Ohio University and delegate to the United Nations Economic and Social Council. Author of a classic study, *Japan's Role in South-East Asian Nationalist Movements* (Harvard, 1953, reprinted 1971).

Grajdanzev, Andrew

During wartime a research staff member of the Institute of Pacific Relations. During the occupation of Japan was Chief of the Prefectural Government Section in General Headquarters, Supreme Commander for the Allied Powers, in which capacity he was associated with the land reform programme. Author of books on Japan, Korea and Formosa.

Irikura, James K.

Born in Hawaii. Served as curator of the South-East Asia collection at Yale University and has taught Japanese history at Rutgers University and Kent State University. Has edited bibliographies and documentary studies on South-East Asia and Indonesia in particular.

Lee, Chong-sik

Born in Manchuria. Has worked for the Rand Corporation and taught political science at Dartmouth College and the University of Pennsylvania. An authority on Japanese colonial policies in Korea.

Magistretti, William

Did graduate work in Oriental languages and political science at the University of California. Wrote for *Pacific Affairs* on Japan's pre-war concepts of Pan-Asianism.

Nu, U

Active in student politics at the University of Rangoon in the 1930s, for which he was imprisoned by the British in 1940. Foreign Minister during the Japanese occupation and Premier 1948–58 and 1960–2. Overthrown by Ne Win in 1962 and imprisoned. In exile since 1968.

Silcock, T. H.

Born in China, educated at Oxford. Has taught at Dundee School of Economics, Raffles College and Australian National University. An authority on Malayan economic development and nationalism.

Vargas, Jorge

Lawyer, businessman, and bureaucrat. Pre-war member of President Quezon's office and wartime Secretary of Justice and mayor of Manila. Tried for treason after the war but given amnesty.

Ward, Robert S.

Consular officer in Hong Kong and member of the Far East unit of the U.S. Bureau of Foreign and Domestic Commerce during the Japanese attack on Hong Kong. Interned for six months there. Wrote on Japanese occupation of Asia based on personal experience.

Wang, Ching-wei

Kuomintang leader and intimate political associate of Sun Yat-sen. Rivalled Chiang K'ai-shek for party leadership. During the Sino-Japanese war he headed a Japanese-supported regime, after breaking with Chungking. Died in a Japanese hospital in 1944.

Bibliographical Note

THE appended list of suggested readings in English and Japanese does not purport to be a complete bibliography of literature on the subject. Rather, it is intended to point the way to a so-far neglected area to students and specialists. Most of the sources listed here are published works. For more complete bibliographies on the subject see Irikura, James K., *South-East Asia: Selected Annotated Bibliography of Japanese Publications*, South-East Asia Studies, Yale University, 1956; Ichikawa Kenjirō, comp., *South-East Asia Viewed from Japan*, Data Paper No. 56, Cornell South-East Asia Program, 1965; and Imon Hiroshi, *Taiheiyō senshi bunken kaidai* (Bibliography of the literature on the Pacific War), Tokyo, 1971.

The many unpublished documents and works in private collections will be included in a later bibliography to be prepared by the author in collaboration with Professor Yoji Akashi, in connexion with a projected analytic study of the Greater East Asia Co-Prosperity Sphere.

Suggested Readings

General

ELSBREE, WILLARD H., *Japan's Role in South-East Asian Nationalist Movements* (Cambridge: Harvard University Press, 1953).

GOODMAN, GRANT K., ed., *Imperial Japan and Asia* (New York: East Asian Institute, Columbia University, 1967).
ICHIKAWA, KENJIRŌ, comp., *South-East Asia Viewed from Japan* (Ithaca: Data Paper 56, South-East Asia Program, Cornell, 1965).
IRIKURA, JAMES, *South-East Asia — Selected Annotated Bibliography of Japanese Publications* (New Haven: Yale South-East Asia Studies, 1956).
IRIYE, AKIRA, 'The Failure of Military Expansion', in James Morley, ed., *Dilemmas of Growth in Prewar Japan* (Princeton: Princeton University Press, 1971).
JAMES, DAVID, *The Rise and Fall of the Japanese Empire* (London: Allen & Unwin, 1951).
JONES, F. C., *Japan's New Order in East Asia; its Rise and Fall, 1937–45* (London: Oxford University Press, 1954).
SILVERSTEIN, JOSEF, ed., *South-East Asia in World War II: Four Essays* (New Haven: Yale University South-East Asia Studies, 1966).
TOLAND, JOHN, *The Rising Sun, The Decline and Fall of the Japanese Empire* (New York: Random House, 1970).
WARD, ROBERT S., *Asia for the Asiatics? The Techniques of Japanese Occupation* (Chicago: University of Chicago Press, 1945).
YOUNG, JOHN, *The Research Activities of the South Manchurian Railway Company, 1907–1945; A History and Bibliography* (New York: Columbia University East Asian Institute, 1966).

Burma

BA MAW, *Breakthrough in Burma, Memoirs of a Revolution, 1939–1946* (New Haven: Yale University Press, 1968).
U BA U, *My Burma, the autobiography of a president* (New York: Taplinger, 1959).
Burma Intelligence Bureau, Simla Government of Burma, *Burma during the Japanese Occupation*, 2 vols. (Simla: 1943–44).
CADY, JOHN, *A History of Modern Burma* (Ithaca: Cornell University Press, 1958).
CHRISTIAN, JOHN LEROY, *Burma and the Japanese Invader* (Bombay: Thacker, 1945).
DHAMMIKA U BA THAN, *The Roots of Revolution* (Rangoon: reproduced from *The Guardian*, 1962).

SUGGESTED READINGS 189

GUYOT, DOROTHY, *The Political Impact of the Japanese Occupation of Burma* (Ph.D. dissertation, Yale University, 1966).
U HLA PE, *U Hla Pe's Narrative of the Japanese Occupation of Burma Recorded by U Khin*, (Data Paper no.41, South-East Asia Program, Cornell University, Ithaca, 1961).
MAUNG MAUNG, *Aung San of Burma* (The Hague: Nijhoff, 1962).
———, *Burma in the Family of Nations* (Amsterdam: International Educational Publishing House, 1956).
———, *Burma and General Ne Win* (Bombay: Asia Publishing House, 1969).
U NU, *Burma under the Japanese* (New York: St. Martin's Press, 1954).
OHTA TSUNEZO, 'Japanese Military Occupation of Burma — the dichotomy', *Intisari*, vol. II, no.3, (s.d., Singapore).
SLIM, FIELD-MARSHAL SIR WILLIAM, *Defeat into Victory* (London: Four Square, 1965).
TRAGER, FRANK, ed., *Burma: Japanese Military Administration. Selected Documents, 1941-1945* (Philadelphia: University of Pennsylvania Press, 1971).

India

AYER, S. A., *Unto Him a Witness, The Story of Netaji Subhas Chandra Bose in East Asia* (Bombay, 1951).
BARKER, A. J., *The March on Delhi* (London: Faber and Faber, 1963).
BOSE, Subhas Chandra, *On to Delhi* (Bombay, 1946).
DESAI, Bhulabhai, *I.N.A. Defence* (Bombay, 1946).
DURRANI, Mahmood Khan, *The Sixth Column* (London, 1955).
GIANI, Kesar Singh, *Indian Independence Movement in East Asia, The Most Authoritative Account of the I.N.A. and the Azad Hind Government* (Lahore, 1947).
GHOSH, K. K., *The Indian National Army, Second Front of the Indian Independence Movement* (Meerut: Meenakshi Prakashan, 1969)
KHAN, Shah Nawaz, *My Memories of the I.N.A. and its Netaji* (Delhi, 1946).
———, *The I.N.A. Heroes, Autobiographies of Col. Prem K. Sahgal, Col. Gurbax Singh Dhillon, Maj. Gen. Shahnawaz* (Lahore, 1947).

LEBRA, Joyce C., *Jungle Alliance, Japan and the Indian National Army* (Singapore: Asia Pacific Press, 1971).
RAWAL, R. S., *The I.N.A. Saga* (Allahabad: 1946).
SINGH, Durlab, ed., *Formation and Growth of the Indian National Army* (Lahore, 1946).
SIVARAM, M., *The Road to Delhi* (Tokyo: Charles Tuttle, 1966).
TOYE, Hugh, *Subhash Chandra Bose, the Springing Tiger* (Bombay: Jaico, 1959).
TSUJI, Masanobu, *Singapore, the Japanese Version* (London: Constable, 1962).

Indonesia

ANDERSON, Benedict R. O'G., *Java in a Time of Revolution Occupation and Resistance, 1944–1946* (Ithaca: Cornell University Press, 1971).
———, *Some Aspects of Indonesian Politics under the Japanese Occupation 1944–1945* (Ithaca: Cornell University, 1961).
AZIZ, Muhamed Abdul, *Japan's Colonialism and Indonesia* (The Hague: Nijhoff, 1955).
BENDA, Harry J., *The Crescent and the Rising Sun: Indonesian Islam under the Japanese Occupation, 1942–1945* (The Hague: van Hoeve, 1958).
———, James K. Irikura and Kōichi Kishi eds., *Japanese Military Administration in Indonesia: Selected Documents* (New Haven: Yale South-East Asia Studies Translation Series no. 6, 1965).
DAHM, Bernhard, *Sukarno and the Struggle for Indonesian Independence* (Ithaca: Cornell University Press, 1969).
ECHOLS, John M., *Preliminary Checklist of Indonesian Imprints during the Japanese Period, Mar. 1942–Aug. 1945* (Ithaca: Cornell Modern Indonesia Project Bibliography Series).
FEITH, Herbert, *The Decline of Constitutional Democracy in Indonesia* (Ithaca: Cornell University Press, 1962).
FISCHER, Louis, *The Story of Indonesia* (New York: Harper, 1959)
KAHIN, George Mc. T., *Nationalism and Revolution in Indonesia* (Ithaca: Cornell University Press, 1952).
KANAHELE, George S., *The Japanese Occupation of Indonesia: Prelude to Independence* (Ph. D. dissertation, Cornell University, 1967).

SUGGESTED READINGS 191

MANGKUPRADJA, Raden Gatot, 'The Peta and My Relations with the Japanese: a correction of Sukarno's Autobiography', *Indonesia*, no. 5, 1965 (Cornell University Modern Indonesia Project).

NAKAMURA Mitsuo, 'General Imamura and the Early Period of Japanese Occupation', *Indonesia*, no. 10, 1970 (Cornell University Modern Indonesia Project).

NUGROHO Nototusanto, 'The Revolt of a Peta Battalion in Blitar, February 14, 1945' *Asian Studies*, vol. 7, 1969 (University of the Philippines).

ŌKUMA Memorial Social Sciences Research Institute, *Studies on Japanese Military Administration in Indonesia* (Washington: U.S. Department of Commerce translation, 1965).

PALTHE, Van Wulften, *Psychological Aspects of the Indonesian Problem* (Leiden: Brill, 1949).

PAUKER, Guy, 'The Role of the Military in Indonesia', John Johnson, ed., *The Role of the Military in Underdeveloped Countries* (Princeton: Princeton University Press, 1962).

POPPE, J., *Political Developments in the Netherlands East Indies during and immediately after the Japanese Occupation* (Ph. D. dissertation Georgetown University, 1948).

ROEDER, O. G., *The Smiling General, President Soeharto of Indonesia* (Djakarta: Gunung Agung, 1969).

SJAHRIR, Sutan, *Out of Exile*, transl. Charles Wolfe (New York: John Day, 1949).

Sukarno: an Autobiography as told to Cindy Adams (New York: Bobbs Merrill, 1965).

VAN Mook, H. J., *The Netherlands Indies and Japan, Their Relations 1940-41* (London: Allen & Unwin, 1944).

WEHL, David, *The Birth of Indonesia* (London: Allen & Unwin, 1948).

WERTHEIM, W. F., *Indonesian Society in Transition* (The Hague: van Hoeve, 1964).

WOODMAN, Dorothy, *The Republic of Indonesia* (London: 1955).

Indochina

BRODRICK, Alan, *Beyond the Burma Road* (London: Hutchinson, 1945).

FALL, Bernard B., *The Two Viet-Nams, A Political and Military Analysis* (New York: Praeger, 1963).
HAMMER, Ellen J., *The Struggle for Indochina* (Stanford: Stanford University Press, 1954).
MCALISTER, John T., *Vietnam: The Origins of Revolution* (New York: Doubleday, 1971).
MARR, David G., *Vietnamese Anticolonialism* (Berkeley: University of California, 1971).

Malaya and Singapore

ARDIZONNI, Michael, *A Nation is Born* (London: Flacon Press, 1946).
CHAPMAN, Spencer, *The Jungle is Neutral* (New York: W. W. Norton, 1949).
CHIN, Kee Onn, *Malaya Upside Down* (Singapore: Jitts, 1946).
———, *Silent Army* (New York: Longmans Green, 1953).
COAST, John, *Railroad of Death* (London: Commodore Press, 1946).
DAS, S. K., *Japanese Occupation and Ex Post Facto Legislation in Malaya* (Singapore: G. K. Kiat, 1960).
GILMOUR, O. W., *With Freedom to Singapore* (London: Benn, 1950).
HASTAIN, R., *White Coolie* (London: Hodder & Stoughton, 1947).
KATHIGASU, Sybil, *No Drum of Mercy* (London: Neville Spearman, 1954).
KIN, David George, *Rage in Singapore, The Cauldron of Asia Boils Over* (New York: Wisdom House, 1942).
LOW, N. I., & H. M. Cheng, *This Singapore, Our City of Dreadful Night* (Singapore: City Book Store, 1948).
ROBINSON, J. B. Perry, *Transformation in Malaya* (London: Secker & Warburg, 1956).
ROFF, William, *The Origins of Malay Nationalism* (New Haven: Yale Press, 1967).
TREGONNING, K. G., *A History of Modern Malaya* (Singapore: Eastern Universities Press, 1964).
TSUJI, Masanobu, *Singapore, The Japanese Version* (London: Constable, 1962).
LEASOR, James, *Singapore* (New York: Modern Literary Editions. 1968).

The Philippines

ABAYA, HERNANDO, *Betrayal in the Philippines* (New York: A. A. Wyn, 1946).

AGONCILLO, TEODORO A., *The Fateful Years: Japan's Adventure in the Philippines, 1941–1945* (Quezon City: Garcia, 1965) 2 vols.

GARCIA, MAURO, ed., *Documents on the Japanese Occupation of the Philippines* (Manila: The Philippine Historical Association, 1965).

GOODMAN, GRANT K., *An Experiment in Wartime Intercultural Relations: Philippine Students in Japan, 1943–1945* (Data Paper no. 46, Cornell South-East Asian Studies, 1962).

FRIEND, THEODORE, *Between Two Empires, The Ordeal of the Philippines, 1929–1946* (New Haven: Yale University Press, 1965).

HARTENDORP, A. V. H., *The Japanese Occupation of the Philippines* 2 vols. (Manila: Bookmark, 1967).

ISIDORO, ANTONIO, *Philippine Nationalism in the Schools* (New York: Institute of Pacific Relations, 1950).

LEAR, ELMER, *The Japanese Occupation of the Philippines — Leyte 1941–1945* (Data Paper no. 42, Cornell South-East Asian Studies, 1961).

MCGEE, JOHN H., *Rice and Salt — A History of the Defense and Occupation of Mindanao during World War II.* (San Antonio: Naylor, 1962).

MAHAJANI, USHA, *Philippine Nationalism, External Challenge and Filipino Response, 1565–1946* (Brisbane: University of Queensland Press, 1971).

MALAY, ARMANDO J., *Occupied Philippines: The Role of Jorge B. Vargas during the Japanese Occupation* (Filipiniana Book Guild Series Vol.XII).

PALMA, RAFAEL, *The Pride of the Malay Race, A Biography of Jose Rizal* (New York: Prentice-Hall, 1949).

PHILLIPS, CLAIRE and M. GOLDSMITH, *Manila Espionage* (Portland, Ore.: P Binfords & Mort, 1947).

QUEZON, MANUEL, *The Good Fight* (New York: Appleton-Century 1946).

RECTO, CLARO M., *Three Years of Enemy Occupation: The Issue of Political Collaboration in the Philippines* (Manila: Peoples' Publishers, 1946).

ROMULO, CARLOS, *Crusade in Asia* (New York: John Day, 1955).
——, *United* (New York: Crown, 1951).
——, *I Saw the Fall of the Philippines* (New York: Doubleday, 1942).
——, *I See the Philippines Rise* (New York: Doubleday, 1946).
SANTIAGO, DOMINGO B., 'Philippine Education during the Japanese Occupation,' (M.A. thesis, University of the Philippines, 1951).
SORIANO, RAFAELITA HILARIO, *The Japanese Occupation of the Philippines with Special Reference to Japanese Propaganda, 1941–1945* (Ph.D. dissertation, University of Michigan, 1948).
SPENCER, CORNELIA, *Romulo, Voice of Freedom* (New York: John Day, 1953).
STEINBERG, DAVID JOEL, *Philippine Collaboration in World War II* (Ann Arbor: University of Michigan Press, 1967).
TAKEUCHI TATSUJI, and ROYAMA MASAMICHI, *The Philippine Polity: a Japanese View*, ed. Theodore Friend (Yale South-East Asia Monograph Series no.12, 1967).
TARUC, LOUIS, *Born of a People, an Autobiography* (New York: International Publishers, 1953).
TOLAND, JOHN, *Documents of the Japanese Occupation of the Philippines*.
ZAIDE, GREGORIO, *The Philippine Revolution* (Manila: Modern Book Co., 1954).

Japanese Sources

General

ASAHI SHIMBUNSHA, ed., (Asahi newspaper), *Asahi Tōa nempō* (Asahi East Asia annual report) 1942–43, 3 vols., Tokyo.
AICHI KIICHI, *Nampō kaihatsu kinko kaisetsu* (Explanation of the South-East Asia Development Fund), Tokyo, 1942.
DAI TŌASHŌ, RENRAKU IINKAI (Greater East Asia Ministry, Liaison Committee), *Nampō keizai taisaku* (Economic policies for South-East Asia), Tokyo, 1943.
ENDŌ SHOTEN, ed., *Nampō-sho no kenkyū to kaisetsu* (Studies and commentaries on documents on South-East Asia), Tokyo, 1942.

SUGGESTED READINGS 195

HATTORI TAKUSHIRŌ, *Dai Tōa sensō zenshi* (Complete history of the Greater East Asia War) Tokyo, 1968.

HAYASAKA, YOSHIO, *Nampō kyōeiken to sono seikaku* (The Southern Co-Prosperity Sphere and its characteristics), Tokyo, 1941.

HAYASHI FUSAO, *Dai Tōa sensō kōteiron* (Affirmation of the Greater East Asia war), Tokyo, 1963.

HONJO EIJIRŌ, *Senkakusha no nampō keiei* (Administration of South-East Asia by pioneers), Tokyo, 1942.

IKEDA YŪ, ed., *Hiroku Dai Tōa senshi* (Secret history of the Greater East Asia war), Tokyo, 1953.

IMON HIROSHI, *Taiheiyō sensōshi bunken kaidai* (Bibliography of literature on the Pacific War), Tokyo, 1971.

ITŌ MASANORI, *Teikoku rikugun no saigo* (The end of the Imperial Japanese army) 4 vols., Tokyo, 1959–65.

IYENAGA SABURŌ, *Dai Tōa sensō* (The Greater East Asia war), Tokyo, 1968.

KAMIYAMA SHUMPEI, *Dai Tōa sensō no imi* (The significance of the Greater East Asia war), Tokyo, 1964.

KATAYAMA SHINKICHI, *Nampō minzoku undōshi* (History of South-East Asian nationalist movements), Tokyo, 1942.

KURODA HIDETOSHI, *Gunsei* (Military administration), Tokyo, 1952.

MARUYAMA SHIZUO, *Nakano gakkō tokumu kikan'in no shuki* (Memorandum of a member of the Nakano School Special Agency), Tokyo, 1948.

MINAMI MANSHŪ TETSUDŌ KABUSHIKI KAISHA, Tōa Keizai Chōsakyoku (South Manchuria Railway Company, East Asia Economic Investigation Bureau), *Nampō minzoku undō* (The nationalist movements of South-East Asia), Tokyo, 1943.

MOMBUSHŌ SHIGEN KAGAKU KENKYŪJO (Education Ministry, Natural Resources Research Institute) ed., *Tōa Kyōeiken shigen kagaku bunken mokuroku* (Scientific bibiliography on the literature on resources of Greater East Asia), Tokyo, 1942–43.

MUROBUSE TAKANOBU, *Nanshinron* (The theory of southward advance), Tokyo, 1936.

NAMPŌ KAIHATSU KINKO CHŌSAKA (South-East Asia Development Fund, Research Section), *Nampō minzoku no mondai* (Nationality problems of South-East Asia), Tokyo, 1943.

NAN'YŌ KEIZAI KENKYŪJO (South Seas Economic Research Institute), *Nampō gunsei kensetsu no hōshin* (Policies for establishing military administration in South-East Asia), Tokyo, 1942.

NIHON BŌEKI SHINKŌ KYŌKAI (Japan Association for the Promotion of Trade), *Dai Tōa Kyōeiken bōeki taisaku iinkai hōkokusho* (Report of the Greater East Asia Co-Prosperity Sphere Trade Policy Commission), Tokyo, 1943.

NIHON GAIKŌ GAKKAI (Japan Diplomatic Society), *Taiheiyō sensō gen'inron* (Theories on the origins of the Pacific War), Tokyo 1953.

NIHON KOKUSAI SEIJI GAKKAI (Japan International Politics Society) *Taiheiyō sensō e no michi*, 7 vols. and documentary supplement (The road to the Pacific War), Tokyo, Asahi Shimbunsha, 1963.

NISHIMURA SHINJI, *Dai Tōa Kyōeiken* (The Greater East Asia Co-Prosperity Sphere), Tokyo, 1942.

NOMURA SADAKICHI, *Nampō Kyōeiken o kataru* (The story of the South-East Asia Co-Prosperity Sphere), Tokyo, 1942.

NAMPŌKEN KENKYŪKAI (Southern Sphere Research Association), *Nampō shinkensetsu kōza* (Lectures on the reconstruction of South-East Asia), Tokyo, 1943.

ŌIWA MAKOTO, *Minami Ajiya minzoku seijiron* (The argument for South Asian people's governments), Tokyo, 1942.

ŌKAWA SHŪMEI, *Ajiya kensetsusha* (Builders of Asia), Tokyo, 1941.

———, *Dai Tōa shinchitsujo kensetsu* (Construction of the New Order in Greater East Asia), Tokyo, 1943.

OTAKE MASAO, *Dai niji taisen sekininron* (The theory of responsibility for the second war), Tokyo, 1958.

REKISHIGAKU KENKYŪKAI (Historical studies association), *Taiheiyō sensōshi* (History of the Pacific War), 4 vols., Tokyo, 1953.

RŌYAMA MASAMICHI, *Tōa to sekai* (East Asia and the world), Tokyo, 1941.

———, *Tōa ni kansuru jōyaku to gaikō* (Treaties and diplomacy concerning East Asia), Tokyo, 1942.

SATŌ HIROSHI, *Nampō kyōeiken no zembō* (The panorama of the Southern Co-Prosperity Sphere), Tokyo, 1942.

SATŌ KENRYŌ, *Dai Tōa sensō kaikōroku* (Recollections of the Greater East Asia War), Tokyo, 1966.

SHIGEMITSU MAMORU, *Shōwa no dōran* (The turbulent Shōwa era), 2 vols., Tokyo, 1952.

SUGGESTED READINGS 197

———, *Nihon oyobi Nihonjin no michi* (The way of Japan and the Japanese), Tokyo, 1926.

SAMBŌ HOMBU, (Army General Staff Headquarters), *Haisen no kiroku* (Record of defeat), Tokyo, 1967.

———, (Army General Staff Headquarters), *Sugiyama memo; Dai Hon'ei seifu renraku kaigi nado shuki* (The Sugiyama memo; notes on the Imperial General Headquarters Government Liaison Conferences), 2 vols., Tokyo, 1967.

SUGANUMA TEIFU, *Shin Nippon Tōnan no yume* (New Japan's dreams of the South-East), Tokyo, 1942.

TAKAHASHI KAZUYO, *Nampō keieiron* (Theory of administration of South-East Asia), Tokyo, 1942.

TAKAHASHI SANKICHI, *Nampō kyōeiken o kataru* (On the Southern Co-Prosperity Sphere), Tokyo, 1941.

TAKEDA MITSUJI, *Nampō no gunsei* (Military administration in South-East Asia), Tokyo, 1943.

TAKEI JŪRŌ, *Nampō kensetsu to minzoku mondai* (The establishment of South-East Asia and the nationality problem), Tokyo, 1942.

TAMURA YOSHIO, ed., *Hiroku Dai Tōa senshi; Marē Taiheiyō tosho hen* (Secret history of the Greater East Asia War; volume collected on Malaya and the Pacific), Tokyo, 1953.

TANEMURA SUKETAKA, *Dai Hon'ei kimitsu nisshi* (Secret diary of Imperial General Headquarters), Tokyo, 1952.

TANAKA SUEHIRŌ, *Senkaku shoka, Nampō kensetsuron senshū* (Selected comments on Japanese expansion into the Southern region), Tokyo, 1943.

TANAKADATE HIDEZŌ, *Nampō bunka shisetsu no sesshū* (Administration of cultural institutions in South-East Asia), Tokyo, 1944.

TŌA CHŌSAKAI (East Asia Research Association), *Nampō hōkoku* (Reports on South-East Asia) Mainichi Shimbunsha, Tokyo, 1943.

TŌA KENKYŪJO, *Hōbun zasshi jūyō kiji sakuin* (Bibliography of important articles in Japanese journals), Tokyo, 1942.

TŌA KENKYŪJO, *Nampō chiiki hōbun shiryō mokuroku* (Bibliography of Japanese materials on the South-East Asian region) — Tokyo, 1942.

TSUTSUI CHIHIRŌ, *Nampō gunseiron* (Theory of Military administration in South-East Asia), Tokyo, 1944.

USUI KATSUMI and INABA MASAO, *Gendai shi shiryo* (Documents on modern history), 42 vols., Tokyo, 1964.
YAMADA FUMIO, *Dai Tōa sensō to Nampōken* (The Greater East Asia War and the Southern Sphere), Tokyo, 1942.
──────, *Nampōken no genjitsu to Taiheiyō* (The reality of the Southern Sphere and the Pacific), Tokyo, 1941.

Burma

BŌEICHŌ BŌEI KENSHŪJO SENSHISHITSU (Defence Agency War History Library), ed., *Biruma koryaku sakusen* (Operation for the conquest of Burma), Tokyo, 1967.
DŌMEI TSŪSHINSHA (Domei News Agency), *Biruma sakusen* (Burma military operations), Tokyo, 1942.
IZUMIYA TATSURŌ, *Biruma dokuritsu hishi — sono na wa Minami Bōryaku Kikan* (The secret history of Burmese independence — its name: the Southern Stratagem Agency), Tokyo, 1967.
KOKUBU SHŌZŌ, *Dai Birumashi* (The history of Greater Burma), 2 vols., Tokyo, 1944.
KUMAGAYA KUNIZŌ and ASAMI SENZŌ, *Reimei no Biruma* (Awakening Burma), Tokyo, 1943.
MORI SENDENBU (Mori Propaganda Section), *Biruma kenkoku* (Establishment of the Burmese state), Rangoon?, 1944.
NAKAI GOSHIRŌ, *Junketsu no otakebi — Biruma haisenshi* (War cry of thoroughbreds — history of the lost battle for Burma), Tokyo, 1962.
OGATA TADASHI, *Biruma no genjō* (Present conditions in Burma), Taihoku, 1942.
ŌNO TORU, 'Biruma gunshi', (History of the Burmese Army), pts. 1–3, *Tōnan Ajiya kenkyū* (South-East Asia Studies), vol. 8, nos. 2–4, 1970–71, Kyoto University.
ŌTA TSUNEZŌ, *Biruma ni okeru Nippon gunseishi no kenkyū* (Studies in Japanese military administration in Burma), Tokyo, 1967.
SEKUPANKAI (Sekupan Association), ed., *Sekupan Biruma Nippongo gakkō no kiroku* (Records of the Japanese Language School in Sekupan, Burma) Tokyo, 1970.
BŌEICHŌ BŌEI KENSHŪJO SENSHISHITSU (Defence Agency, Defence Studies Institute, War History Library), *Imparu sakusen:*

SUGGESTED READINGS 199

Biruma no bōei (The Imphal operation; the defence of Burma), Tokyo, 1968.

———, *Irawaji kaisen; Biruma bōei no hatan* (The Irrawaddy engagement; failure of the defence of Burma), Tokyo, 1969.

TAKATA KAZUO, *Biruma minzoku kaihōroku* (The liberation of the Burmese), Tokyo, 1944.

TAKAGI SHIRŌ, *Kōmei* (Insubordination), Tokyo, 1966.

TAKAMI JUN, *Biruma*, Tokyo, 1944.

TSUJI MASANOBU, *Jūgo taiichi — Biruma no shitō* (Fifteen versus one — the death struggle of Burma), Tokyo, 1950.

USHIRO MASARU, *Biruma sensenki* (Burma battle record), Tokyo, 1953.

India

BŌEICHŌ BŌEI KENSHŪJO SENSHISHITSU (Defence Agency, Defence Studies Institute, War History Library), ed., *Biruma kōryaku sakusen* (Operation for the conquest of Burma), Tokyo, 1967.

———, *Marē shinkō sakusen* (Malaya offensive operation), Tokyo, 1966.

FUJIWARA IWAICHI, *F Kikan* (F agency), Tokyo, 1966.

GAIMUSHŌ AJIYAKYOKU (Foreign Ministry, Asia Office), *Subasu Chandora Bosu to Nihon* (Subhas Chandra Bose and Japan), Tokyo, 1956.

HAYASHIDA TATSUO, *Higeki no eiyū — Chandora Bosu no shōgai* (Hero of tragedy — the life of Chandra Bose), Tokyo, 1958.

ISODA SABURŌ, *Isoda Saburō Chūjō kaisōroku* (Recollections of Lt. Gen. Isoda Saburō), Tokyo, 1954.

IWAKURO HIDEO, 'Iwakuro Kikan shimatsuki' (Record of the management of the Iwakuro agency) in *Shūkan Yomiuri* (Weekly Yomiuri), *Nihon no himitsu sen* (Japan's secret war), special no., 8 Dec. 1956, Tokyo.

KUNIZUKA KAZUNORI, *Indōyō ni kakeru niji* (Rainbow over the Indian Ocean), Tokyo 1958.

MURATA HEIJI, *Imparu sakusen — retsu heidan Kohima no shitō* (The Imphal operation — Kohima death struggle of the Retsu group), Tokyo, 1967.

RIBURA, JIOISU, *Chandora Bosu to Nihon* (Chandra Bose and Japan), Tokyo, 1968.

SŌMA KUROHIKO and SŌMA YASUO, *Ajiya no mezame* (The awakening of Asia), Tokyo, 1955.

YOMIURI SHIMBUNSHA, *Shōwashi no Tennō* (The Emperor in Shōwa history), vols. 8, 9, Tokyo, 1969–71.

Indochina

BŌEICHŌ BŌEI KENSHŪJO SENSHISHITSU (Defence Agency, Defence Studies Institute, War History Library), Tokyo, 1970 *Shittan Meigō sakusen* (The Sittang and Operation 'Mei').

KOMATSU KIYOSHI, *Betonamu*, (Vietnam), Tokyo, 1955.

KUSAKA YORINAO, *Hōjin o matsu Futsu-In no hōko* (The wealth awaiting the Japanese in Indochina), Tokyo, 1942.

NAIKAKU, JŌHŌKYOKU (Cabinet, Intelligence Bureau), *Tōa kyōeiken no ikkan to shite no Futsuryō Indoshina* (French Indochina, a link in the Greater East Asia Co-Prosperity Sphere), Tokyo, 1941.

ŌIWA MAKOTO, *Annan minzoku undōshi gaisetsu* (Outline history of the Vietnamese nationalist movement), Tokyo, 1941.

ŌYAMA YUKINOBU, *Indōshina dōran yonjūnen shi* (Forty-year history of Indochinese nationalism).

SEKO MASANORI, *Raosu dokuritsu no shinsō* (The true state of Laos independence), Tokyo, 1964.

TAMURA YOSHIO, ed., *Hiroku Dai Tōa senshi; Marē Taiheiyō tosho hen* (History of the Secret Greater East Asia war; collected volume on Malaya and the Pacific), Tokyo, 1953.

Indonesia

BŌEICHŌ BŌEI KENSHŪJO SENSHISHITSU (Defence Agency, Defence Studies Institute, War History Library), *Ran'in kōryaku sakusen* (Operation for conquest of the Netherlands Indies), Tokyo, 1967.

IKEDA YŪ, ed., *Hiroku Dai Tōa senshi; Hitō Ran'in hen* (Secret history of the Greater East Asia War; Philippines, Netherlands Indies volume), Tokyo, 1954.

IMAMURA HITOSHI, *Imamura Hitoshi taishō kaisōroku* (Recollections of General Imamura Hitoshi), Tokyo, 1960.

KOBAYASHI ICHIZŌ, *Ran'In o kaku mitari* (Looking at the Netherlands Indies), Tokyo, 1941.

SUGGESTED READINGS 201

KURODA HIDETOSHI, *Gunsei* (Military administration), Tokyo, 1952.

MACHIDA KEIJI, *Tatakau bunka butai* (A fighting propaganda unit), Tokyo, 1967.

MASUDA ATAU, *Indoneshiya gendaishi* (Modern Indonesian history), Tokyo, 1971.

MINAMI MANSHŪ TETSUDŌ KABUSHIKI KAISHA, Tōa Keizai Chōsakyoku (South Manchuria Railway Company, East Asia Economic Investigation Bureau), *Waga nanshin seisaku o meguru Ran'In no seiji keizai dōkō* (Political and economic activities in the Netherlands Indies relative to Japan's policy of southward advance), Tokyo, 1941.

MIYOSHI SHINKICHIRŌ, 'Jawa senryō gunsei kaikoroku,' (Recollections of military administration in occupied Java), *Kokusai mondai* (International problems), nos. 61–82, 15 parts, 1965, Tokyo.

NAKAKOJI AKIRA, *Nan'yō minzoku shinryakusen* (Conquest of the peoples of the South Seas), Tokyo, 1941.

NONAKA FUMIO, *Uzumaku Nampō* (Restless South-East Asia), Tokyo, 1937.

ŌKURA MITSUO, *Nichi-Ran kōshō sambyakunenshi* (A three-hundred-year history of Japanese-Netherlands relations), Tokyo, 1943.

SAMBŌ HOMBU (Army General Staff Headquarters), *Indoneshiya tōchi hōsaku yōkō kenkyūan* (Outline of proposed government policy for Indonesia), Tokyo, n.d.

———, *Ran-In jijō* (Conditions in the Netherlands Indies), Tokyo, 1941.

TAKAHASHI KAZUYO, *Shinsei Jawa no tembō* (A view of liberated Java), Tokyo, 1944.

TAKEI JŪRŌ, *Ranryō Indō o kataru* (The story of the Dutch East Indies), Tokyo, 1935.

———, *Tōsa nijūsannen, fugen no Nan'yō* (Natural resources of the South Seas; a twenty-three-year exploration), Tokyo, 1930.

TANAKA MASAAKI, *Fūsetsu yonjūgonen no yume: hikari mata kaeru* (A dream of the vicissitudes of forty-five years; the light returns again), Tokyo, 1959.

TANAKADATE HIDEZŌ, *Nampō bunka shisetsu no sesshu* (Administration of cultural institutions in Indonesia and Malaya), Tokyo, 1944.

WASEDA DAIGAKU SHAKAIKAGAKU KENKYŪJO (Waseda University Social Science Research Institute), *Indoneshiya ni okeru Nihon gunsei no kenkyū* (Studies on Japanese military administration in Indonesia), Tokyo, 1959.

Malaya

BŌEICHŌ BŌEI KENSHŪJO SENSHISHITSU (Defence Agency, Defence Studies Institute, War History Library), *Marē shinkō sakusen* (Malaya offensive operation), Tokyo, 1966.

IKEDA YŪ, ed., *Hiroku Dai Tōa senshi, Biruma, Marē hen* (Secret history of the Greater East Asia War; Burma, Malaya volume). Tokyo, 1954.

KAWADE SHOBŌ (Kawade Bookstore), ed., *Dai Tōa senki; Marē sensen* (History of the Greater East Asia War; the Malayan front), Tokyo, 1942.

KAWAMURA SABURŌ, *Jūsan kaidan o noboru — senpan shokeisha no kiroku* (Climbing thirteen steps — records of those punished [executed] for war crimes), Tokyo, 1952.

The Philippines

DAI HON'EI RIKUGUNBU, *Saikin ni okeru Hitō jijō* (Recent Philippine conditions), Tokyo, 1944.

GAIMUSHŌ ŌBEIKYOKU (Foreign Ministry European and American Affairs Bureau), *Hirippin dokuritsu mondai* (The problem of Philippine independence), Tokyo, 1932.

HINO ASHIHEI, *Nampō yōsai* (The Southern fortress), Tokyo, 1944.

HITŌ HAKENGUN, SENDENHAN (Philippine Expeditionary Force, Propaganda Unit), *Minami jūjisei* (The Southern Cross), Manila, 1942.

IKEDA YŪ, *Hiroku Dai Tōa senshi; Hitō Ran'In hen* (The secret history of the Greater East Asia War; Philippine, Netherlands Indies volume), Tokyo, 1954.

ITOGA ISAO and DEZAKI SEIICHI, *Atarashii Nampō no sugata; Hirippin to Higashi Indō shōtō* (The shape of the new South-East Asia; the Philippines and East Indies), Tokyo, 1943.

JIMBO NOBUHIKO, *Fuirippin no yoake* (The dawn of the Philippines) Tokyo, 1959.

SUGGESTED READINGS 203

MATSUNAMI MICHIRŌ, *Hirippin to Nihon* (The Philippines and Japan), Tokyo, 1921.

MIKI KIYOSHI, *Hitō fūdoki* (Account of the Philippines), Tokyo, 1943.

MINAMI MANSHŪ TETSUDŌ KABUSHIKI KAISHA, TŌA KEIZAI CHŌSAKYOKU (South Manchuria Railway Company, East Asia Economic Investigation Bureau), *Waga nanshin seisaku o meguru Hitō no seiji keizai dōkō* (Political and economic activities in the Philippines relative to Japan's policy of southward advance), Tokyo, 1941.

MIYOSHI TOMOKAZU, *Tōa kyōeiken to Hirippin* (The East Asia Co-Prosperity Sphere and the Philippines), Tokyo, 1941.

MURATA SHŌZŌ, *Hitō nikki*, comp. by Fukushima Shintarō, (Philippine diary), Tokyo, 1969.

NAKAHARA ZENTOKU, *Hirippin dokuritsu seishi* (The true history of Philippine independence), Tokyo, 1944.

ONO TOYOAKI, *Hitō senbu to shukyōhan* (Pacification in the Philippines and the Religious Affairs Unit) Tokyo, 1945.

TAGAMI ŌSAKU, *Atarashiki Firippin* (The new Philippines), Tokyo, 1943.

TAIWAN SŌTOKUFU, GAIJIBU (Formosa Government-General, External Affairs Division), *Hirippin jijō gaiyō* (Outline of Philippine conditions), Taihoku, 1943.

YOMIURI SHIMBUNSHA, *Shōwashi no Tennō* (The Emperor in Shōwa history), vols. 10, 11, Tokyo, 1969–71.

Index

AGONCILLO, Dr. Teodoro, xxi, 132–5, 184.
Agriculture, 29, 64–5, 108, 146.
Aguinaldo, Emilio, xiv.
Akashi Motojirō, Lieut-Gen., 107–8, 178.
All-Java Cultural Movement, 147.
An Ch'ang-ho, 108.
Aquino, Benigno S., 134–5, 184.
Arabia, 35.
Arita Hachirō, xviii-xix, 73–7, 178.
Asia Development Board, 84, 85, 86.
Asia revolution and unity, spiritual basis of, 36–40.
Aung San, 128.
Australia, xii, 34, 46, 78, 80, 89, 95, 97.
Azad Hind Government, 144.
Aziz, Dr. Ungku, 141–5, 184.

BA MAW, Prime Minister of Burma, xx-xxi, 126–31, 157–8, 184.
Bauxite, 34, 35, 95.
Benda, Prof. Harry J., 99, 113–17, 185.
Biruma Kenyūkai (Burma Research Association), xiv, 175.
Black Dragon Society, *see Kokuryūkai*.
Bo Let Ya (Thakin Hla Pe), 184–5.

Bo Mogyo, *see* Suzuki Keiji.
Borneo, 44–5, 65, 95, 100, 116, 137.
Bose, Rash Bihari, xiv.
Bose, Subhas Chandra, 88, 89.
'Brains' trust', *see Shōwa Kenkyūkai*
Brazil, 35.
British Indian Army, 124.
Buddhism, xiii, xvi, 4, 38, 148–9, 177; *see also Mahayana*.
Burma, xii, xv, xix, xxi, xxii, 78, 80, 95, 125, 171, 172, 174, 185–6; Japanese occupation, 126–31, 146, 147, 148; 'independence' granted to (1943), 155, 167, 168; Japanese militarism and, 157–8, nationalism in, 160.
Burma Independence Army (B.I.A.), xxi, 126–31, 175, 179–80, 185.
Burma Research Association, *see Biruma Kenyūkai.*

'CAMPAIGN FIRST' THEORY, 172.
Canada, 34.
Caribbean, 29.
Celebes, 64, 65, 137.
Chiang Kai-shek, 7, 33, 94, 115, 187.
China, Chinese, xi, xvii, xviii, 32, 33, 35, 37, 42, 43, 47, 51, 57, 84, 85, 96, 100, 124, 148, 149, 173; Japa-

INDEX

nese traditional policy towards, xii-xiv; New Order in, xiv, 68–70; proposal for East Asia Federation with, xvii, 3, 4–8; and East Asia Co-operative Body, 9–13, 16, 17; regionalism, 20–3; cultural influence, 38–9, 40; Japanese Navy policy statement (April 1936), 59, 60; and Army HQ's views, 61–2; Co-Prosperity Sphere and, 71–2, 75, 76, 80–1, 84–5, 96; Japanese nationalities policy, 119–21; official statement of 'Aim of Japanese war operation in' (July 1944), 155–6, see also Overseas Chinese; Sino-Japanese wars.

China Incident (1937), 37, 44, 45, 52 64, 68, 71, 72, 165.

Chinese Nationalist Government, 12, 21.

Chōsaka (Navy Research Section), xv.

Christianity, 108, 148, 149, 183.

Chromite, 95.

Chromium, 35.

Chu Hsi philosophy, 38–9.

Coal, 35.

Communism, communists, 9, 111, 144, 146, 150, 166.

Confucius, Confucianism, 38, 108.

Conscription, in Korea, 107, 109 110.

Cooperationism, *see Kyōdōshugi*.

Cooperatives, *see Kyōdō kumiai*.

Copper, 34, 35.

Copra, 95.

Cotton, 34, 35, 95.

Cultural cooperation (in Asia): *Tōa Kyōdōtai* and, 14, 17–18, 19; Ōkawa Shūmei's views, 36–40; Navy administration policy for Southern area, 66, 67.

Dai Ajiya Kyōkai, 16.

Dai Tōa Kyōeiken, see Greater East Asia Co-Prosperity Sphere.

Dai Tōa Kyōzonken, see Greater East Asia Co-Existence Sphere.

Datsua (Depart from Asia policy), xiv.

Dobama Asiayone (Burma), 184.

Dobama Sinyetha League (Burma), 147, 185.

East Asia Cooperative Body (*Tōa Kyōdōtai*), xvii, 9–19, 68, 178.

East Asia Development League, 98.

East Asia Economic Bloc Kenkyū-kai, 100.

East Asian Federation (*Tōa Renmei*), xvii, 3–8, 9, 10, 177.

East Asia League Society, 3.

Economy, Japanese economic imperialism: economic bloc with China and Manchuria, 11–12; trading rights and practices in China, 23; 'Monroe Doctrine's' aims, 28, 29; Greater East Asia Co-Existence Sphere proposal, 31–2, 34–5; importance of Pacific expansion policy, 43–5; emergence of regional world blocs, 46, 76–7; economic leadership in Asia, 48–54 5 Ministers' Conference statement, 62–3; Navy National Policy Research Committee on, 64–5; Sino-Japanese relations, 69–70; Arita Hachirō's defence of Co-Prosperity Sphere, 73–7; exploitation of South-East Asian resources, 95–6, 149–50; Shōwa Research Institute's views on Southern policies, 99–102; Liaison Conference policies for Southern areas, 116–17; Japanese post-war posture, 153.

Elsbree, Willard H., xxi, 159–63,185.

Equal Opportunity principle, 76, 90, 92.

Ethnic affinity theory, 14, 16, 17–19.

Executive Commission (Philippines), 133.

FIVE MINISTERS' CONFERENCE (AUG. 1936), policy statement, 57, 62–4.

Fisheries, Japanese development of, 65.

Foreign Ministry (Japanese), xvi;

limitation of powers, 82, 84–7, 98.
Formosa (Taiwan), 42, 47, 60, 84, 146.
France, French, 7, 42, 65; see also Indo-China.
Free India Provisional Government, 88, 89.
Free trade principle, 74, 75, 76.
Freedom Bloc (Burma), 185.
Friendship of the Japanese and Overseas Catholics, 148.
Fujiwara Iwaiichi, Major, xx, xxi, 122–5, 126, 143, 145, 178–9.
Fujiwara Kikan ('F' Agency), xx, 122–5, 143, 175, 178.
Fukuzawa Yukichi, xiv.
Funayama Shin'ichi, 14.
'Fundamentals of National Policy' statement (Aug. 1936), xiv, xviii.

GENDAI, 43, 44.
Gen'yōsha (Dark Ocean Society), xiv, 175.
Germany, 5, 32, 33, 34, 41, 46, 50, 52, 69, 79.
Grajdanzev, Dr. Andrew, xix, xx, 94–8, 146–50, 185.
Great Britain, xix, 7, 21, 23, 41, 101, 155; Greater East Asia cooperative defence against, 33, 34; economic bolckade of Japan by, 42, 44, 46; Japanese Navy statements on, 60, 65; and Army HQ's views, 61, 62; Co-Prosperity Sphere as economic defence against, 74–7, 78, 79; world hegemony ambitions of, 89–90, 92, 93; and Indian policy, 92, 109; in Malaya, 142, 143, 144; S.E. Asian nationalism and, 159, 160; Japanese reasons for war against, 165, 166, 167.
Greater East Asia Association, 98.
Greater East Asia Autonomous Sphere, see Greater East Asia Co-Existence Sphere.
Greater East Asia Co-Existence Sphere (*Dai Tōa Kyōzonken*), xvii, 31–5, 68, 175.
Greater East Asia Conference (1943), xix, 126, 167; Joint Declaration of, xix, 93, 153–6; Tojo's Address to, 88–92.
Greater East Asia Co-Prosperity Sphere (*Dai Tōa Kyōeiken*), 68, 86, 133, 134, 143; Japanese proclamation of (1940), xv-xvi, xviii, xx, 71–2; spiritual basis of, 36–40; Arita Hachirō on, 73–7; Tōjō on, 78–81, Western view, 94–8; Liaison Conference's policies for, 116; goals and methods, 146–50; postwar implications, 153–6; Iyenaga's critique of, 167–9.
Greater East Asia Ministry: creation (1942), xvi, xix, 48, 88, 94, 97–8, opposed by Togo, 82–7.
Greater East Asia People's Cooperative Body, 119.
Greater East Asia Personnel Training Committee, 96.
Guadalcanal, Allied landing on, 84.
Guam, 34.

HAKKO ICHIŪ, xvii, 4, 10, 119, 150, 168, 172, 175.
Han people, 120.
Harada Kumao, 179.
Hawaii, Hawaiian Islands, xvii, 32.
Hay, John, 76.
Hayashi Fusao, 164.
Hayashi Senjuro, General, 98.
Hideyoshi Toyomoti, 45, 183.
Hikomatsu Kamikawa, 46.
Hiranuma Kiichirō, Premier, 73.
Hiraoka, Colonel, 128.
Hirohito, Emperor of Japan, 86, 87, 127, 143, 148, 165.
Hirota Koki, Premier, 73.
Holland (Netherlands), 42, 51, 60, 165, 172; see also Indonesia; Netherlands Indies.
Hong Kong, 34, 78, 80, 146, 147, 187.
Hoshino Naoki, 84–5, 168.

INDEX

IMPERIAL RULE ASSISTANCE ASSOCIATION, 20, 98, 167.
India, Indians, xii, xiii, xx, 33, 34, 36, 47, 126; Japan's cultural and spiritual ties with, 37, 38, 40; Bose attends Greater East Asia Conference, 88, 89; British and American policies in, 92, 109; and Japanese policy 95, 121; 'F' liaison agency support for independence movement, 122–5; Provisional Government of Free India set up in Singapore, 155; see also Overseas Indians.
Indian Independence League (IIL), 124–5, 142, 144–5, 175.
Indian National Army (INA), xx, xxi, 88, 122, 125, 142, 144, 145, 171, 178.
Indo-China, French, xviii, 33–4 35, 42, 43, 65, 72, 81, 84, 95, 100, 102, 116, 146, 160.
Indonesia, xv; Japanese military administration in, 99, 113–17, 136–40; declaration of independence and 1945 Constitution, 138–40, 174; nationalism in, 160, 162; see also Netherlands Indies.
International Military Tribunal for the Far East, 36.
Inukai Tsuyoshi, assassination of, 36, 182.
Iran, 35.
Irikura, Dr. James K., 99, 113–17, 185.
Iron and steel, 34, 35, 95.
Ishihara Industrial Marine Transportation Co., 43.
Ishihara Kanji, Colonel, xvii, 3, 45, 178, 179.
Ishihara Koichirō, 43–5.
Islam, xvi, 137, 138, 148, 149.
Isolationism, 26, 28.
Itagaki Seishirō, 166.
Italy, 5, 34, 46, 50, 69, 79.
Iyenaga Saburo, Prof., xxi, 164–70, 179.

JAPAN ACADEMY PRIZE, 25.
Japanese Army, xii, xiv, xv, 32, 42, 63, 78, 80, 86, 172; Southern policies, xvi, 99–100, 103; cooperative defence of Greater East Asia by, 31–4; national policy document (June 1936), 57, 61–2; recruitment of Koreans to, 110, 111; 'campaign first' principle, 172; see also Japanese Military Administration.
Japanese Military Administration (in Greater East Asia), xii, xvii, xx, 103; in Indonesia, 99, 113–17, 136–40; nationalities policy, 118–21; 'F' Agency's liaison with independence movements, 122–5; in Burma, 127; in Philippines, 132–5; in Malaya, 141–5; policies and methods of, 146–50; Iyenaga's critique of, 168–9; 'campaign first' theory favours, 172.
Japanese Navy, xii, xvi, 63, 80, 86, 100, 114, 139; South-East Asian research initiated by, xiv-xv; strategic objectives in Pacific, 41–7; 'General Principles of National Policy' (April 1936), 57, 58–60; 'Summary Draft of a Policy towards the South' (Apr. 1939), 57, 64–7; defeated at Midway, 84; number of officials in South-East Asia, 147.
Java, 137–8, 147.
Java Leaders Patriotic Society, 147, 175.
Java Patriotic Service Association, 137.
Jimmukai (Jimmu Society), 36, 176, 181.
Johore, Sultan of, 118, 184.
Jones, F.C., xi.

KALIBAPI ASSOCIATION (PHILIPPINES), 132, 133–5, 147–8, 176, 184.
Kamikawa Hikomatsu, xvii-xviii, 25–30, 179.
Keneko, Mitsuharu, 168.

INDEX

Kan In, Prince, 127.
Kapok, 95.
Katakura Chu, 166.
Katō, Tsukasa, Lieut-Col, 96, 179.
Kawai Eijirō, Prof., 20.
Kawashima Takenobu, 129, 179–80.
Kaya Okinori, 86, 168, 180.
Kazuo Aoki, 95, 98, 178.
Kegon philosophy, 38.
Kempeitai (Japanese military police), 176.
Kesatuan Muda Melayu (Malay Youth League), 176.
Kiai (Muslim religious teachers, Java), 138, 176.
Kigū minzoku (guest peoples), 121.
Kim Ok-siun, xiv.
Kishi Kōichi, vii, xv, xix, 99–103, 113–17, 136–40, 180.
Kita Ikki, 177.
Koiso Kuniaki, 110, 180.
Kokuryūkai (Black Dragon Society or Amur River Association), xiv, 98, 176.
Kokusaku Kenkyūkai (Navy-funded National Policy Research Association), xv, 57, 64–7, 176.
Konoye Fumimarō, Premier, xv, xviii, xix, 3, 10, 21, 31, 71, 73, 165, 166, 180; New Order proclaimed by (Dec. 1938), 68–70, 177.
Korea, Koreans, xi, xiii, xvii, 6, 47, 63, 84, 130, 146, 149, 168; Japanese rule in, xii, xx, 107–12; and nationalities policy, 120.
Korean Army Special Volunteer Troops System, 110.
Kuomintang Government, 21, 68, 144, 186.
Kuriles, xvii, 31.
Kwantung Leased Territory, 84, 97.
Kyōdō kumiai (cooperatives), 16.
Kyōdōshugi (cooperationism), 14–16, 176.

LANGUAGE POLICY, Japanese, 137, 149.

Latin America, 27, 29.
Lao Tsu philosophy, 38.
Lead, 34, 95.
League of Nations, 21, 28.
Lee Chong-sik Professor, xx, 107–12, 185.
Lesser Sundas, 137.
Let Ya, 129.
Liaison Conference, 83, 176; 1941: xx, 113–17; 1942: 168.
Lukouchiao Incident (Sept. 1931), 165.

MAGISTRETTI, William, xviii, 41–7, 186.
magnesium, 35.
manganese, 95.
Mahayana (Northern branch of Buddhism), 4, 176.
Malay Youth Movement (*Kesatuan Muda Melayu*: K.M.M.), 143.
Malaya, Malaysia, xix, 34, 45, 64, 65, 78, 80, 95, 100, 102, 116, 148, 159; Japanese military occupation, 118, 141–5, 146, 147; ILL and INA activities in, 122, 124–5, 142, 144–5.
Manchukuo, xiii, xiv, xvii, xviii, 43, 61, 62, 63, 84, 130, 148, 166, 167, 168; proposed East Asian Federation with, 3, 4, 5; and regionalism, 21; independence of, 28–9; Navy policy statement on, 58–9; New Order in, 68–70; and Co-Prosperity Sphere, 75, 81, 96, *see also* Manchuria.
Manchuria, xiii, xxi, 11, 16, 17, 32, 35, 57, 59, 60, 61, 71, 72, 95, 107, 149, 166; nationalities policies in, 119, 120; *see also* Manchukuo.
Manchuria Affairs Board, 84.
Manchuria Imperial Harmony Society (*Manshū Teikoku Kyōwakai*), 5, 176.
Manchurian Incident (1931–2), xii, xvii, 11, 27, 52, 164, 165.
Mantetsu Chōsakyoku, *see* South Manchurian Railway Company Research.

INDEX

Manila Simbun-sya, 133.
Manshū Teikoku Kyōwakai, see Manchuria Imperial Harmony Society.
March Affair (1931), 36.
Maruyama Shizuo, xxii, 171–4, 180.
Matsuoka Yosuke, Foreign Minister, xv, xviii, 180–1; proclamation of Co-Prosperity Sphere by, 71–2.
May 15 Incident (1932), 36, 181.
Mexico, 35.
Meiji Pan Asianism, xiii-xiv.
Midway, Japanese naval defeat at, 84.
Miki Kiyoshi, 14–15, 19, 181.
Minami Jirō, 110, 181.
Minami Kikan (Japanese Intelligence Agency, Burma), 129, 170, 172–3.
Mindanao, 65.
Miyazaki Masoyoshi, xvii, 3–8, 178, 181.
Mizuno Rentaro, 98.
Moluccas, 137.
Molybdenum, 34.
Mongolia, 120; Inner, 32, 59, 69, 70; Outer, 32.
Monroe Doctrine, analogy between Japanese Pan-Asianism and, xvii-xviii, 25–30.
'Movement for the General Mobilization of the National Spirit', 108.
Murobushi Takanobu, 47.
Muslims, *see* Islam.
Mutaguchi Renya, 181.

NAGAMASA YAMADA, 45, 183.
Nakayama Shozaburō, 168.
Nan'yō Kyōkai (Navy South Seas Agency), 67, 176.
Naoki, Dr. S., 96.
National Policy Research Institute, 53.
Nationalism, nationalist movements, xvi, xxi, 18, 158; Chinese, xvii, 9, 12, 22; industrialism, v, 22; Korean, 107, 109, 110–12; Philippines, 132; Indonesian, 137, 138;

Malayan, 141, 142; Japanese failure to gain support of, 159–63.
Nationality policy, Japanese, 118–21, 123, 173–4.
Natural resources (in occupied territories), Japanese exploitation of, xvi, xx, 34–5, 95–6, 100, 149–50.
Netherlands Indies, xvii, xviii, 32, 35, 43, 45, 64, 65, 67, 72, 80, 95, 100, 102, 103, 116, 146, 147, 148.
New Caledonia, 35, 100.
New Guinea, 65.
Ne Win, General, 126, 184, 186.
New Man Society, *see Shinjinkai*.
New Order in East Asia (*Tōa Shin Chitsujo*), xiv, xviii, 7, 32, 34, 43, 49, 64, 71, 82, 83, 86, 125, 133, 177; proclamation of (1938), xiv, 10, 68–70; cooperative body theory and, 9–11, 12; regionalism as rationale for, 20–4; spiritual basis of, 37–40; basic principles defined by Kamikawa, 46–7; equated with Co-Prosperity Sphere by Matsuoka, 71–2; Maruyama's views on, 171–2.
New Peoples' Association, *see Shinminhoe*.
New Peoples' Society, *see Shinminkai*.
New Structure Movement (*Shin Taisei*), 9, 177.
New Zealand, xii, 34, 46, 95.
Nickel, 34, 35.
Nine-Power Treaty, 24.
Nippon Hyōron, 46.
Nishijima Shigetada, 136–40, 181.
Noguchi Yonejirō, xiii.

OIL, 34, 35, 44–5, 95, 138, 172.
Oka, Admiral, 86.
Okakura Tenshin, xiii.
Ōkawa Shūmei, xviii, 36–40, 177, 181–2.
Okinawa, 67.
Ōkuma Shingenobu, xiii.
Open Door principle, 23, 29, 76, 90, 92.

Ōsaka Mainichi, 133.
Otaku, Capt. 42–3.
Overseas Chinese, 64, 65, 66, 101, 121, 122, 141–2, 144.
Overseas Indians, xx, 121, 122, 142, 144–5.
Ozaki Hotsumi, xvii, 9–13.

PACIFIC, Japan's strategic objectives in, xviii, 41–7.
Pacific War, *see* World War II.
Pahang, Sultan of, 143.
Pan-Asianism, xii, xiii–xiv, xviii, 10, 25, 36, 122, 141, 142, 145.
Patriotic Press Association, 14.
Penang, 125.
Peru, 35.
Philippines, xix, xxi, 34, 42, 43, 64, 65, 78, 80, 95, 100, 116, 160, 184; Japanese occupation, 132–5, 146, 147–8; 'independence' granted to, 155, 167, 168.
'Plan for Leadership of Nationalities in Greater East Asia' (Army Policy Statement, 1940), xx, 118–21.
Poetera (Putera) Movement, 137, 176.
POWs, Indian (in Malaya), 123, 124–5.
Predestined cooperation concept, 16–17, 18.
Priai class (Indonesia), 138, 177.
'Principles Governing the Administration of the Occupied Southern Area' (1941), xx, 113–17.
A Prophecy for Japan, 47.
'Provisional Government of Free India', 155, 158, 167.

REGIONALISM, xviii, 14; *Tōa Kyōdōtai* and, 16–19; as rationale for New Order, 20–4; Monroe Doctrine's policy of, 25–30; emergence of world regional blocs, 46, 76–7.
Religion military administration's policy on, 148–9; *see also* Buddhism; Christianity; Islam; Shintoism.

Rice, 95.
Righteous Army (Korea), 108.
Rinji Chōsaka (Navy Provisional Research Section), xv.
Romania, 35.
Rōyama Masamichi, Prof., xviii, 182; regional theory of, 16–17, 18, 20–4.
Rubber, 34, 35, 95, 172.
Russo-Japanese War, xii, xvi, 39.

SAKHALIN, 84; Northern, 31, 33.
Sakurakai (Cherry Association), 36, 177.
Satō, Premier, 174.
Satō, General Kenryo, 86, 150.
Shakai Shisō, 20.
Shangai, 7.
Shimada Shigetaro, 86–7, 182.
Shina rōnin (Japanese adventurers in China), xiv, 177.
Shinjinkai (New Man Society), 20, 177.
Shinmei Masamichi, xvii, 14–19, 182.
Shinminhoe (New Peoples' Association), 108.
Shinminkai (New Peoples' Society), 5, 177.
Shin Taisei, see New Structure Movement.
Shintoism, 108, 109.
Shōwa Kenkyūkai (Research Association), xv, xix, 9, 20, 31, 99–103, 177, 178, 180, 182.
Shōwa Restoration, xvii, 4, 177.
Shujin minzoku (master peoples), 121.
Siberia, 31, 42.
Silcock, Prof. T. H., 141–5, 186.
Singapore (Shonan), 34, 42, 67, 118, 125, 141, 144, 148, 155, 159, 167, 183.
Singh, Capt. Mohan, 122.
Sino-Japanese Incident, 4, 5, 7.
Sino-Japanese War (1894–5), xii.
Sino-Japanese War (1937), 42, 45, 94, 166.
Sjahrir group (Indonesia), 139.
Sōgō Kenkyūkai (Navy-sponsored

INDEX

General Affairs Research Group) xv, 177.
Sorge Spy Case, 9.
South Manchuria Railway Company, xv, 3; Research Bureau, xv, 36, 176.
South Seas Agency, *see* Nan'yō Kyōkai.
Soviet Union, xiv, 17, 46, 57, 63, 100, 101, 166, 173; Japanese Army's traditional fear of, xvii; East Asia Federation proposals and, 3, 5, 7; and Co-Existence Sphere, 33, 34, 35; Japanese Navy policy statement on, 60; and Army HQ's views, 61-2; Japanese anti-Comintern Agreement against 69; and expansionist aims against, 95; *see also* Russo-Japanese War.
Straits Chinese British Association, 144.
Sugar, 95.
Sumatra, 64, 137, 138.
Sun Yat-sen, xiv, 186.
Sung philosophies, 38-9
Suzuki Keiji, Col. (Bo Mogyo), 86, 126-31, 176, 182.
Suzuki Teiichi, 168, 182.

TAGORE, Rabindranath, xiii, xviii, 37-8.
Taiwan, *see* Formosa.
Taiwan expedition, xii.
Taiwan Governor General's Office, 67.
Takada, Dr., 17-18.
Takagi Yasaka, Prof., 25.
Takahashi Kamekichi, xviii, 48-54, 182.
Takahashi Sokichi, Admiral, 43.
Terauchi Masakata, Gov.-Gen. of Korea, 107, 108, 182-3.
Thailand (Siam), 34, 35, 37, 42, 45, 64, 65, 81, 84, 95, 102, 116, 124, 146, 148, 167.
Tibet, 32.
Tientsin, 7.
Timor, 35, 95, 146.

Tin, 35, 95.
Tōa Kenkūjo (Navy Research organization), xv.
Tōa Kyōdōtai, *see* East Asia Cooperative Body.
Tōa Minzoku-shugi (East Asian nationalism), 18.
Tōa Renmei, *see* East Asian Federation.
Tōa Shin Chitsujo, *see* New Order.
Togo Shingenori, Foreign Minister, xix, 82-7, 183.
Tōjō Hideki, Prime Minister, xix, 3, 183; Address to Diet on Co-Prosperity Sphere (Jan. 1942), 78-81; disagreement with Togo over Greater East Asian Ministry, 82, 83, 84-5, 86, 87; Address to Greater East Asia Conference (Nov. 1943), 88-92; speech in House of Representatives (Feb. 1943), 97.
Tokugawa, Marquis, 118-21, 141.
Tokyo Nichi Nichi, 133.
Tōyō Kenkyū, 99.
Tripartite Axis Pact (Japan, Germany, Italy), 32, 33, 71, 180.
Triple A Movement (Indonesia), 137, 177.
Turkey, 39.

ULAMA (Muslim scholars in Java), 138, 177.
United Nations, 143-4, 154, 159.
United States, xi, xix, 7, 20, 21, 23, 24, 41, 46, 60, 63, 100, 101, 155, 159; Japanese Pan-Asianism compared with Monroe Doctrine, xvii-xviii, 25-30; cooperative defence of Greater East Asia and, 33, 34; economic blockade of Japan by, 34, 35, 51; oriental culture despised by 39; Japanese strategic objectives in the Pacific and, 42, 43, 44, 46; and Navy policy statement on, 60; and Army HQ's views, 61, 62; Co-Prosperity Sphere as economic defence against, 74-7, 78, 79;

world hegemony ambitions of, 89–90, 92, 93; and Indian policy, 92; Japanese nationalities policy, 121; and reasons for war against, 165, 166, 167.
U Nu, 129, 184, 186.
U Ottama, xiv.

VARGAS, Jorge, 135, 186.
Venezuela, 35.
Versailies Treaty, 5.

WACHI TAKAJI, General, 135, 183.
Wang Ching-wei, 21, 33, 150, 166, 167, 178, 186.
Ward, Robert S., xxi, 153–6, 186.
Washington, George, 26.
Wool, 34, 35.
World War II (Pacific War), xi, xii, xiv, xix-xx, 3, 41, 51, 52, 53, 82, 83, 84, 89, 92, 93, 96, 97, 103, 153, 154, 162; Tojo on aims of, 78–81; Japanese liaison with Indian independence movement during, 78–81; Iyenaga's critique of, 164–70.

YABE TEIJI, xvii, 31–5, 183.
Yamashita Tomoyuki, General, 145, 183–4.
Yatsugi Kazuo, 57, 184.
Yi Kap, 108.
Yi Tong-hwi, 108.
Yonai, Premier, 73.
Yuben, Capt. Otaku's article in, 42–3.
Yūjin minzoku (friendly people), 121.
Yunan-Hanoi Railway, 33.
Yūzonsha (ultra-nationalist society), 36, 177, 181.

ZEN BUDDHISM, 38.